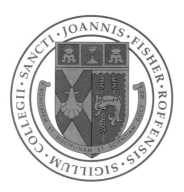

DISCIPLINING THE CHILD VIA THE DISCOURSE OF THE PROFESSIONS

Publication Number 1103
AMERICAN SERIES
IN
BEHAVIORAL SCIENCE AND LAW

Edited by
RALPH SLOVENKO, B.E., LL.B., M.A., Ph.D.
Professor of Law and Psychiatry
Wayne State University
Law School
Detroit, Michigan

DISCIPLINING THE CHILD VIA THE DISCOURSE OF THE PROFESSIONS

Edited by

ROXANNA P. TRANSIT, PH.D.

CHARLES C THOMAS • PUBLISHER, LTD.
Springfield • Illinois • U.S.A.

Published and Distributed Throughout the World by

CHARLES C THOMAS • PUBLISHER, LTD.
2600 South First Street
Springfield, Illinois 62704

©2004 by CHARLES C THOMAS • PUBLISHER, LTD.

ISBN 0-398-07452-6 (hard)
ISBN 0-398-07453-4 (paper)

Library of Congress Catalog Card Number: 2003059640

Printed in the United States of America
SR-R-3

Library of Congress Cataloging-in-Publication Data

Disciplining the child via the discourse of the professions / edited by Roxanna P. Transit.
    p. cm. -- (American series in behavioral science and law)
"Publication number 1103"--Ser. t.p.
Includes bibliographical references and index.
ISBN 0-398-07452-6 (hbk.) -- ISBN 0-398-07453-4 (pbk.)
    1. Discipline of children. 2. Child development. 3. Child psychology. 4. Problem
children. 5. Children's rights. I. Transit, Roxanna P. II. Series.

HQ770.4.D57 2003
649′.64--dc22
                                                                        2003059640

CONTRIBUTORS

Stuart C. Aitken is a Professor of Geography at San Diego State University. His past books include *Geographies of Young People* (2001), *Family Fantasies and Community Space* (1998) and *Putting Children in Their Place* (1994). He is currently an editor of the Routledge journal, *Children's Geographies*.

Adriana S. Benzaquén received her Ph.D. from York University in 1999. After holding a postdoctoral fellowship at the University of British Columbia, she joined the History Department at Mount Saint Vincent University (Halifax) as an assistant professor in 2001. Her research focuses on the history of the scientific study of children and its professional and educational applications. She has published several articles and is completing a book manuscript, *Encounters with Wild Children: Temptation and Disappointment in the History of the Human Sciences*.

Deborah P. Britzman is Professor of Education and currently is serving as the Graduate Program Director of Social and Political Thought at York University (2001-2004). Her research interests are in psychoanalysis and education. She is author of *Lost Subjects, Contested Objects: Toward a Psychoanalytic Inquiry of Learning* (Albany: State University of New York Press, 1998), and the soon to be published book, *After Education: Anna Freud, Melanie Klein and Psychoanalytic Histories* (Albany: State University of New York Press, in press). Britzman also has a book series at SUNY Press titled, *"Second Thoughts: New Theoretical Formations,"* which is an interdisciplinary book series that focus on rethinking persistent social dilemmas, debates, controversies, with new terms.

Janet L. Finn is an associate professor of social work and adjunct professor of anthropology at the University of Montana. Finn earned her M.S.W. from Eastern Washington University in 1982 and Ph.D. in anthropology and social work from the University of Michigan in 1995. Finn has practiced social work in the areas of juvenile justice, child protective services, and foster care. Over the past decade, her work has taken a transnational focus. She is currently documenting the work of grassroots women's organizations in western Montana and Santiago, Chile. She is co-investigator on a pilot study of young people building community in the Americas. Finn teaches courses in social work intervention with individuals, families, groups, and communities; women and social action in the Americas, international social work; community organization; and cultural perspectives on adolescence. Finn is the author of numerous articles on gender, welfare, youth, and community. She is the author of *Tracing the Veins: Of Copper, Culture, and Community from Butte to Chuquicamata* (Berkeley: University of California Press, 1998) and co-author with Maxine Jacobson of *Just Practice: A Social Justice Approach to Social Work* (Peosta, Iowa: Eddie Bowers Publishing, in press).

Joel Jennings is a graduate student at San Diego State University. He has staffed the "living history" program aboard the *Enterpe* for the last four years.

Wayne Martino is a senior lecturer in the School of Education at Murdoch University in Perth, Western Australia. His research has involved exploring the links between masculinities and learning. His work has been published in *Gender and Education, British Journal of the Sociology of Education* in the UK, *Canadian Journal of Education* and the *Journal of Men's Studies*. His latest books are *Boys' stuff: Boys talking about what matters* with Maria Pallotta-Chiarolli (Sydney: Allen & Unwin) and *What about the boys: Issues of masculinity and schooling* with Bob Meyenn (Buckingham: OUP). He has just completed another book, entitled *So what's a boy: Addressing issues of masculinity and schooling* with Maria Pallotta-Chiarolli which will be published in June 2003.

Jeremy Roche is a Senior Lecturer in Law in the School of Health and Social welfare at the Open University. He writes and researches in the field of children's rights and the law and has written and coedited a number of books including *Youth and society* (1997), *Children and society* (2001) and *The law and social work: Contemporary issues for practice* (2001). He is currently working on children, human rights, and professional practice. He is on the Editorial Board of *Social and Legal Studies: An International Journal.*

Roxanna P. Transit, received her Ph.D. in clinical psychology from the University of Detroit-Mercy, Michigan. She is interested in postmodern conceptualizations of the individual that are not derived from modern theories of development. She is active in several professional organizations including the Academy for the Study of the Psychoanalytic Arts. She practices psychoanalysis in Washington, Michigan.

CONTENTS

Page

Introduction 3

Chapter
1. "THE BOY PROBLEM": BOYS, SCHOOLING,
   AND MASCULINITY 19
   Wayne Martino

2. THE ORDERING OF ATTENTION: THE DISCOURSE
   OF DEVELOPMENTAL THEORY AND ADD 34
   Roxanna P. Transit

3. VICTOR'S AFTERLIFE: REINSCRIBING THE
   WILD CHILD IN THE HISTORY OF THE
   SCIENCES OF CHILDHOOD 63
   Adriana Benzaquén

4. TROUBLED IN PARADISE: A CRITICAL REFLECTION
   ON YOUTH, TROUBLE, AND INTERVENTION 90
   Janet L. Finn

5. CLARITY, RITES AND CHILDREN'S SPACES
   OF DISCIPLINE 130
   Stuart Aitken and Joel Jennings

6. MELANIE KLEIN, LITTLE RICHARD AND THE
   PSYCHOANALYTIC QUESTION OF INHIBITION 155
   Deborah Britzman

7. PROFESSIONAL PRACTICE AND THE
   CHALLENGE OF CHILDREN'S RIGHTS 177
   Jeremy Roche

Index 199

DISCIPLINING THE CHILD VIA THE DISCOURSE OF THE PROFESSIONS

INTRODUCTION

This book is a contribution to the increasing interest in the discourse about children, and the role of the professions in creating and maintaining that discourse: a discourse that often disciplines the child in such a way as to primarily advance the interests and voice of the profession while functionally silencing the voice of and restraining the possibilities of children.

Professions

The term profession originally was derived from a religious context and referred to a proclamation of faith, as in one who had professed (*Webster's Dictionary,* 1991). A great professor was one whose religious devotion was unimpeachable based on their special knowledge of religion. By 1675, the term had acquired secular significance, meaning "having claim to due qualifications." At the same time, the laity emerged, referring to all the people not included among the clergy, all of the people not belonging to any given profession and now differentiating between those with such special knowledge and those lacking such knowledge.

In the sovereign state, the professors served under the rule of kings and masters who were thought to represent the power given by god, and whose orders had to be obeyed. With the rise of the modern nation-state and the industrialist society, the form of rule shifted. The power of the king as shown by majestic displays of weapons and of armies was replaced by the verbal power of citizens and individuals. The new forms of power, in part, took the shape of a neutral and abstract symbol system mediated by academically trained specialists that in this egalitarian time helped carve out a new civil space for individuals now understood to be citizens. Professions, beginning with the legal profession, were essential in promulgating and articulating this new secular social and political order, and were accorded great power due to their special knowledges that could be offered to the common man, the citizen: citizens that could now lead the proper sort of life (moral and pious) and have a chance for celestial immortality, something now possible for everyone and no longer reserved solely for royalty.

One of the great analysts of modern society–Emile Durkheim–was the first to believe that professions could be a positive force in society by acting as a bulwark against an authoritarian state. He envisioned professionals establishing moral communities which could act as an alternative source of solidarity in an era where the old ties of the traditional moral order had broken down. His hope was that professionals could be an outpost of independence and autonomy, who would speak the truth, and who with that truth could ensure a better future. It was thought that dire consequences would follow if society failed to appreciate the importance of those with expert knowledge and access to the truth, who were available and had organized to serve the needs and interests of others, not the state (Durkheim, 1957).

This was illustrated during the Progressive Era in the United States. Progressivism represented a secular faith that human intelligence itself was a natural resource as fecund as land or labor when properly exploited and distributed, and offered the hope that the problems facing man could be overcome through the development and exploitation of human knowledge. Human intelligence was enshrined as a new natural resource, and it was believed that scientific and technological advances would allow the mind, through science, to remake the world. Expertise on human being was regarded as critical in realizing that potential and the profession of psychology organized themselves as the professionals with the expertise to know and develop human knowledge and functioning: helping each individual to more effectively use his or her resources for personal and collective good. The profession of psychology constructed intelligence and its standardized assessment as the driving wheel upon which the ideals, methods, and programs of progressivism depended. Psychologists themselves became the engineers of a new machine of efficient democracy, powered by the concept of intelligence and its potential for future world good. A perpetual motion machine was to be implemented wherein technological innovation in psychology–driven by American ingenuity–would produce and discover more ingenuity directly as a result of the expert knowledge of the profession of psychology: at the same time constructing what was to be a welcomed and reassuring narrative of inevitable improvement and advancement with benefits for all.

In contemporary times, the professions have come to mean ". . . a disciplined group of individuals who adhere to ethical standards, are accepted by the public as possessing special knowledge and skills in a widely recognized body of learning derived from research, education, and training at a high level, and who are prepared to exercise this knowledge and these skills in the interest of others" (Professions Australia, www.austprofessions.com.au).

To become a member of a profession is thought to be evidence and testimony of great accomplishment and personal achievement, with the individual answering a higher calling of service to others and placing the welfare of others above their own, as they strive to better the world for mankind one person at a time whilst preserving and deserving the trust and confidence of the public.

Professions still have great power and prestige within society. Part of their prestige in modern times has been derived from the belief that professions offered the truth, expert knowledge derived from scientific rational methodologies that were not compromised by personal, ethnic, or subjective experiences. "Professionals claim authority not as individuals, but as members of a community that has objectively validated their competence" (Starr, 1982). And while celestial immortality may not be the issue it once was, professions are still regarded as the place to go in order to resolve other problems of living that may have emerged, someone to whom one can consult with in private and from whom one can expect a learned opinion in return; an opinion based both on the special knowledges and training of the professional and as well on the particular needs of the individual, and not derived from any other personal or political agenda.

Foucault

The postmodern turn in philosophy has led to a questioning of grand narratives which purport to offer the "truth," and has led to an increasing doubt about the certainties of what we know, who we are, and how we should act, increasingly widening the possibility that things have been and could be different. This revolution has had a phenomenal impact in the social sciences and in the humanities, crossing disciplinary boundaries and making visible and valid very different lines of inquiry. With it has come a questioning of some of the dearly held assumptions about the professions and their role and function in contemporary life as experts having a special connection to "truth." The status and power of professions are no longer unimpeachable and other understandings of what professions offer the people consulting with them have begun to emerge and become more visible, particularly with those known as the helping professions.

Within this critical revolution, we find the work of Michel Foucault, among others, who has brought attention to the relationship between knowledge and power and the role that relationship has played in what he termed governmentality. Foucault defined governmentality, or "mentalities of government," as the complex of notions, calculations, strategies, and tactics through which diverse authorities–political, military, economic, theological, medical, professional, and so forth–have sought to act upon the lives and conduct of each and all in order to avert evils and achieve such desirable states as health, happiness, wealth, and tranquility (Foucault, 1979b).

In his work on governmentality, Foucault described the shift from sovereign power in the medieval times, to disciplinary power and the changes in the way of government necessitated by such a shift. Sovereign power was represented by the king and was signified in the myriad rituals, clothing, and behaviors that represented the special status of royalty. Power was hierarchically arranged with the king reigning superior over his domain. Disciplinary power is a form of power that arose out of the enlightenment impulse to find gentler, more humane ways of meting out justice, and, as well, meet the needs of a government which desired to expand its range of governance inexpensively and effectively. Disciplinary power can be difficult to locate and therefore difficult to resist. A society utilizing disciplinary power controls through an impersonal and invisible gaze, creating a stream of tension which flows through all aspects of society and everyday life, regulating societal institutions, the systems of knowledge, and subjecting everyone to forms of surveillance from others or surveillance imposed by self such that people are ruled, mastered, held in check, administered, steered, and guided by a discourse of discipline . . . one that governs the freedom of possibility–what possibilities can be thought of as a choice and what possibilities cannot be thought of (Foucault, 1979a; Rose, 1988, 1990).

Correlated with the shift to disciplinary power was the development and emergence of "disciplines," professional groups that can demonstrate a learned body of knowledge and expertise from which citizens can consult for direction. Per the mentalities of the new and liberal forms of government, there was a need to create alliances and networks with groups within the state so that the goals and strategies of the government could be implemented. Knowledges came to be regarded as resources to be used in the service of power, driven and shaped by both political and professional interests serving to legitimate and make acceptable the manipulation of human beings for the ends of social order and private benefit. Professions, on the basis of their claims to objectivity, neutrality, effectivity and truth, appeal to and meet the needs of a liberal, democratic government searching to regulate all levels of society whether it be economic, industrial, medical or familial, etc. Professions offer expert knowledges and from these knowledges derive technologies, understandings, methods and practices for human living to justify linking together, and using the forces of individuals and groups in the pursuit of certain objectives. Through their specific techniques, their texts, their language, and the apparatus they have assembled for the delivery of this knowledge, professions inscribe people and offer ways to calculate, judge, diagnose, and manage them collectively and individually.

Government entails the construction of such technologies for acting upon persons in the pursuit of their objectives with the result that many professions have become an essential link within liberal democracies which increasingly depend on their disciplinary power as a mechanism through which the conducts, desires, and decisions of citizens may be aligned with the aspirations and objectives of government (Rose, 1996). Professional expertise weaves loose associations between the programs and objectives of authorities, the values of professionals, and the personal desires of individuals. As the values of the expert are supposed to be grounded in truth, not politics, as their credentials are supposed to come from the academy and the professional organization, not from the civil service or the secret police; as they have promised to serve their clients, not themselves or their own political power in some instances they have offered an ideal illusion and have been an ideal ally through which the government can realize its objectives and whom the state can draw on to legitimate its power.

Over the past century, a complex network of experts with their expert knowledge and practices has taken shape. Professions and the organizations formed to represent them have been fundamentally bound up with and linked to the political apparatus and the sociopolitical aspirations, dreams, hopes, and fears over such matters as the quality of the population, the prevention of criminality, the maximization of adjustment, the minimization of risk, and the promotion of enterprise, all of which have become embodied in a proliferation of social programs and technologies that swarm throughout the texture of everyday life. Professions have served to operate as a relay between government and the individual helping with the management of human beings within schools, reformatories, prisons, asylums, hospitals, factories, courtrooms, business organizations, the military, the domesticated nuclear family, etc., making it possible to govern, construct, and define human beings in ways that are compatible with the contemporary principles of liberalism and democracy. The working arrangement between professionals and the state has been mutually beneficial. The professions provided the means for the implementation of government policy and as a source of expertise which the state could draw on to legitimate its power. In exchange, the state supported the development of professional monopolies and provided professionals with a ready supply of clients, financial security, and a voice in the development of government policy.

The emergence of this alliance between professions and government has not removed the hierarchical structure of governance, but has allowed governmental power to be massively increased, as now the policies and objectives could be in force at all levels, in all directions. No longer was the government the sole application of law and policy in a hierarchical, top-down direction; now there were numerous individuals and groups that would help to implement, apply, and institutionalize the initiatives of the government at all levels and in all sectors. In return, their expertise and power has been endorsed by the government through licensing arrangements and other forms of validation.

Subjectification

The professions, however, do not merely serve the state as de facto "instruments of power" regulating per the goals and objectives of the state. The organizations of the professions very actively work to form, exercise, and advance their own unique discourse, in multiple and diverse ways that will ensure the survival, if not expansion, of their own professional interests, and to those ends they have played a fundamental role in the process of subjectification, helping form and define what people are, the myriad number of ways that people can conceive of themselves, speak about themselves, judge themselves and conduct themselves, regardless of whether they see themselves as men, women, children, or some other.

Ian Hacking (1986) argues that "human kinds emerge and are transformed simultaneously with the languages that describes them." Via their discourse, professions have been fundamental in constituting the being of human. The languages of the professions, the terms within which they construct and define themselves and others, the ways in which they formulate their problems and regulatory strategies; all of the solutions, prohibitions, judgments, and norms through which human beings come to understand and act upon their daily conduct and to be acted upon by others are not merely a technical matter of devising new forms of ideology that advance the discipline. Professions have actually created and brought new sectors of reality into existence, instituting novel and particular ways of understanding the human beings who are the subjects of regulation and governance.

This discourse of the professions, particularly within the helping professions, often functions to problematize, dividing up different kinds of activity and different kinds of people as problematic and in need of professional intervention. This problematizing discourse is often based on the construct of normality and pathology. Discourses of normalization have been elaborated by experts based on their claims of a scientific knowledge of people and their development, even though knowledge of normality has not been derived from the study of normal individuals but has been extrapolated from our attention to those individuals who worry the courts, teachers, doctors, and parents. This valuation of normality contains not only a judgment about what is desirable, but functions as an injunction . . . a goal to be achieved and maintained.

The professions have problematized and categorized the individual we currently know as a child. The discourse of the professions has helped create and maintain a universal picture of the child, and what a child's development through the course of childhood should consist of in order to produce the "normal" child, in contrast to the other ways of being a child. From this discourse, childhood is considered to be a distinctive period of life, detectable across cultures, in which "much the same basic experience was undergone by all young people . . ." (Burman, 1994). In this discourse, we find an individual who is lacking, either in development, in cognitive ability, in physical maturity, in skills, in understanding, etc., and because of these lacks or deficiencies, necessarily needs to be supervised, regulated, and disciplined in order that he or she continues to grow and develop into what is regarded as "normal." Normalization has become one of the great instruments of power—no longer the simple physical coercion used in medieval times, but something more comprehensive and less visible, where the discourse and the application of the discourse via text, procedures, meanings, etc. have become a force of power "working to incite," reinforce, control, monitor, optimize, and organize those under it.

Via this discourse, the soul of the young citizen has become the object of government through expertise and has become the focus of innumerable projects that purport to safeguard it from its own lack, from the physical, sexual, or moral dangers that await the innocent and unknowing, and which would lead to deviations in normal growth and development if left alone, and in a larger sense, deviations from what the government has determined to be appropriate and acceptable being.

A web of legal powers, social agencies, and practices of judgment and normalization have been spread around children designed as abnormal, and has even begun to expand to the normal-but-at-risk child. The medical apparatus of public health has extended its scrutiny to all children, in their homes and in the schools, through registration of births, infant welfare centers, health visitors, school medical officers, education in the domestic sciences, and schools for mothers, using legal powers and statutory institutions to provide a platform for the deployment of medico-hygienic norms and expertise. Around the juvenile court, new powers of judgment and scrutiny have been brought to bear upon the families of troubled and troublesome children, utilizing the legal process as a kind of case conference or diagnostic forum and deploying social workers and probation officers to scrutinize and report upon children and their families so that the reformation could begin. Clinics of mental health have acted as centers for mental hygiene, drawing together the powers of the courts over children who had done wrong and the parents who had wronged them. This web of universal and obligatory scrutiny in the school, of the home, and in the mind has tightened into a powerful network linked by the activities and judgments of doctors, psychologists, analysts, probation officers, social workers, and numerous other professionals.

Disciplined

In this discourse, via the expertise of professionals, the child has been disciplined. Discipline has multiple meanings, both as a segment of formal knowledge and as a treatment that corrects or punishes. The discourse of the professions has come to function as much more than a segment of formal knowledge, and has often come to be used as a method of coercion, a method to discipline those who differ from the norm. Instead of disciplining the body via torture and brutal assault as in earlier centuries, society now seeks to attack the souls of people with the principles of physical, psychological and moral normality in order to control them. The formal knowledge of the professional disciplines has been used not only to shape the way human institutions are organized, but has been used to shape the way the behavior and being of human is conceived, providing justification for interpreting, correcting, and regulating human behaviors which produce "docile bodies" as Foucault would say (Foucault, 1979a, p. 138). In this process, the child has been created as one in need of discipline, and who should be a docile body. The child has been surrounded by and inscribed upon by a discourse that functions to subjugate and correct, control and constrain them to fit into the images and forms already predetermined by the professions with a degree of force, universality, and certainty such that only the normal would be evident and such that other different ways of being a child are regarded as abnormal and in need of correction.

One consequence of this form of discipline by the professions has been to silence the voice of the child, literally per the old saying "children should be seen and not heard" and in myriad other ways where the desires, interests, and communications from children, whether verbal or behavioral, are ignored, denied, or "translated" so as to fit within the discourse already created by others. Kelley et al. (1997) talk about the power and prevalence of these univocal, prejudicial understandings and how they can result in the denial of children's opportunities to speak and be heard. Within the context of this discourse, if children are silent or if their voices are hard to hear, it is often read as a sign of their constitutional incompetence rather than as a result of silencing processes (Cloke & Davies, 1995; Wyness, 1996). And conversely, if their voices are loud or their bodies active, that is often read as a sign of their immaturity, lack of discipline, and the need for regulation. Consequently, the denial and/or "translation" of the desires and communications of those defined as children may very well result in the marginalization of that which is new, and unknown, or different as it perpetually falls outside of the known and the norm.

The "ideological framing" of children's lives as "becoming" . . . developing . . . maturing . . . has served to rationalize and legitimate the administration and regulation of children's lives by others. We would argue that rather than disciplining the "child" in all of its different ways of being, policing, and containing the nascent transformational potential of an emerging being . . . that instead, particular attention should be paid to those bodies which stubbornly resist "belonging." It is perhaps those bodies with their ways of being radically different . . . which resist, which do not and cannot be made to belong within the confines of disciplinary knowledge . . . perhaps those bodies are extraordinarily important for thought, for being, and for life.

And in this discourse, all others have been disciplined such that the voice of the individual professional who may differ or disagree with the professional organizations that had been formed to represent their interests are functionally silenced or marginalized. New ways of thinking and practicing are strictly policed and are not published in the journals for that professional organization, and papers from those professionals who differ are rarely accepted for presentation at conferences when they vary from the accepted bodies of knowledge that the organization is advancing in the political and scientific arenas. The agenda being pursued by the leadership of the professional organization is preserved and protected, regardless of whether it represents the wishes of the membership. The accepted bodies of knowledges are used to discipline that which differs and to prevent or deter change (Trull & Phares, 2001, p. 6).

Conclusion

The discourse of the professions has constructed the modern child as a being in need of discipline and regulation, muting the voices of the individual child with a univocal and universal schema for scientifically knowing and growing the (desired) normal child . . . to be like all other children . . . and to have the sort of proper and necessary childhood that will produce such normality, in accordance with the profession's version of truth and reality and in a way compatible with the demands of social order, political governance, harmony, and well-being.

There is a growing awareness and resistance to this discourse of the professions that has formed and dominated the modern picture of the child. There are powerful arguments against the existence of a universal experience for every child, given the tremendous historical and cultural variability of the experience of the young (Aries, 1962; Hendrick, 1990). Because it has been realized that the individual we know as a child is not a preexisting body of knowledge waiting to be discovered and known through scientific empirical methods, but has been constructed and created, there is a clear trend away from such universal theoretical statements about children. Further, studies of children using techniques such as ethnography and participant observation now predominate over general theoretical statements within the social study of childhood (Burman, 1994; Morss, 1996; Stainton Rogers, 1992). The empirical scientific methods that have been the conceptual foundation of many professions are no longer accepted as the sole arbiter of truth and reality, or as the sole creator of the child.

And there are emerging alternative understandings of the professions. Optimally, and optimistically, the professions, per the wishes of Durkheim (1957), were to be empowering and to serve as an independent opposition to government, and an independent source of "truth" and power newly available for the individual citizen. Instead the discourse of the professions has too often, instead represented the economic and institutional interests of the profession primarily. Investigations of professionals have shown that they are not "always motivated purely and simply by the ideal of service and their behavior does not always match their publicly stated codes of practice." Professionals are alleged to have engaged in monopolistic practices and are themselves an intrinsic part of bureaucratic mechanisms (Wilding, 1982, p. 109). In recent years, it has become clear that efforts to serve children's best interests are themselves capable of harming children, particularly when the child's experience and desires are not given voice in the decisions to be made (Butler-Sloss, 1988; Illich, 1977; Plotnikoff & Wolfson, 1995; Butler-Sloss, 1988).

Professionals can no longer claim that their knowledge is an unbiased objective source of expertise. Their involvement with power has inevitably compromised their claims to truth. Formal knowledges have become resources used in the service of power, driven and shaped by political interests that serve to legitimate and mask the manipulation of human beings for the ends of social order and private profit. To that end, the human being and the being of human have been constructed as containing and/or lacking certain attributes, elements, or conditions that reflect and advance the particular body of knowledge produced by the profession and which only that certain professional is deemed best qualified to restore, treat, or regulate, in effect guaranteeing them, the profession, an ongoing target and object of practice and guaranteeing the survival of the profession (Rose, 1985a).

This use of formal knowledge to order human affairs can be understood as an act of domination over those who are the object. It is not about the "truth" of the knowledge base of the profession, but about the power-knowledge relationship wherein professions have become an agent of the state and through that alliance have implemented practices and knowledges that advance the goals of the state and the profession, and can be least about serving the interests and needs of the individual. Too often, the professions have very actively functioned as a form of disciplinization over the object, rather than as an agent of empowerment for the subject.

Discourse and the languages it appropriates does not refer to some tranquil and consensual universe of meaning, but to a domain of struggles and conflicts over what is or is not truth, who has the power to pronounce the truth, who is authorized to speak the truth and to whom. Importantly it is being recognized what language does, that language enables human beings to imagine and to do, whether it be spoken, written, or otherwise. And that this power of language to create meaning, reality, and truth also resides within the individual, whether they be a "child" or adult, female or male, professional or layman: through language they too speak their truth, with authority and power.

If so, this book and each chapter within it can be regarded as a contribution by the authors to the discourse; a contribution that may allow for different perspectives on the disciplines we call professions and on professional discipline and its relationship to the child, and how that individual child can be understood.

In Chapter 1, Wayne Martino applies a Foucauldian analytic which draws attention to the impact and effects of certain modes of subjectification and normalization within the context of "truth games" and draws attention to the emergence of "the boy" as a specific kind of gendered subject in need of a particular form of heternormative surveillance and monitoring. He discusses the normalizing regimes of practice and how the "boy problem" gets inscribed through the proliferation of various gendered discourses in the popular media, and by therapists and teachers in school that are in the business of reinstating a hegemonic heterosexual and monolithic masculinity.

In Chapter 2, Roxanna Transit offers an examination of the discourse of developmental theory that has been created and promulgated by professionals and which orders the very being of the child as necessarily following certain developmental lines and experiences with any deviations being pre-determined to be abnormal and in need of interventions, so as to restore order. This theory of development has been widely disbursed throughout educational settings with the classroom serving as a template for behavioral and temporal order, resulting in any differences receiving attention and discipline. From within this context, a child exhibiting certain behaviors or ways of thinking and interacting with the world may be regarded as outside the norm and ab-normal and may receive the diagnosis of Attention Deficit Disorder (ADD) or Attention Deficit/Hyperactive Disorder (ADHD), requiring professional intervention and professional discipline that will order the beings of these children.

In Chapter 3, Adriana Benzaquén, through the story of Victor, the "wild child," raises questions about both the story and its enduring evocative power on schools of thought about the care, education, and treatment of children. She raises the visibility of the "unimpeachable scientific credentials of the authors" and creators, Francois Truffaut, Pierre-Joseph Bonnaterre, Philippe Pinel, and Jean-Marc-Gaspard Itard, and questions their authenticity in creating the medico-pedagogical legend encircling Victor and his afterlife. The many ways in which the story was appropriated, interpreted, and reinterpreted within the disciplines and professions dealing with childhood and children during the past two hundred years is presented for consideration along with the idea that the story of Victor's afterlife exposes unresolved anxieties surrounding the disciplinary configuration of childhood in modern sciences and professions.

In Chapter 4, Janet Finn talks of troubled youth being sent to off-shore "specialty schools" as a drastic form of intervention, to be contained and pathologized as a demonstration of the ways in which the discourses and practices regarding youth, trouble, and intervention have been both mutually constituting and mutually amplifying. In this chapter, she critically examines and offers a historical, political, and cultural analysis of the making of adolescence, trouble, and professional intervention by examining the history of interlocking discourses and practices regarding youth in the context of capitalist development and class formation in the U.S. She traces the invention and elaboration of the concept of adolescence in relationship to a range of practices that have served to both pathologize adolescence and discipline adolescents. She pays particular attention to the proliferation of private, for-profit youth containment and treatment facilities in recent years and reflects on the discursive power at work in the construction of youth as so troubled and troubling that such drastic disciplinary measures are not only deemed warranted, but framed as a measure of good parenting.

In Chapter 5, Stuart Aitken and Joel Jennings talk about the everyday spaces of a child and the disciplinary rules that are encoded in those spaces illustrated via a highly successful educational program aboard the ship *Euterpe* that effectively "bootcamps" children into the context of late nineteenth century maritime rules. They argue that discipline in a child's world—in the home, the classroom, and neighborhood is often hidden or unfairly meted out, without explanation or contingency and that the *Euterpe* program reflects and refracts contemporary social and spatial constructions of childhood organized around disciplining young minds and bodies.

In Chapter 6, Deborah Britzman drawing from her work in psychoanalysis, presents us with a discussion of the work of Melanie Klein from the context of her radical understanding of what children were capable of and how the imposition of the others' knowledge actually serves to murder curiosity in the child. Melanie Klein saw the nature of psychoanalytic work with children as an occasion of thinking with children, not as a prescription or a modeling of the roles of living, thinking, or being and if anything settled on the insistence that it was only through exploring the forbidden that personal knowledge could even be made. From this perspective, normality cannot be stated in terms of objective criteria, but in terms of liberty, fluidity, and variety in the creation of fantasies and anything else can become a fatal discipline.

In Chapter 7, Jeremy Roche explores the issues raised for professional practice by the modern children's rights movement. He reviews the problematizing discourses surrounding children today, particularly the way in which public discourse positions children as either victims or threats. They are seen as objects of concern, in need of rescue or control, and as fundamentally incomplete . . . in a deeply disturbing sense they are denied any authority over the meaning of their own lives and situations. One of the consequences of this positioning of children has been a neglect of children's social agency such that children are subjected to new disciplinary regimes in order to be saved from the imminent chaos of their lives. There has been little space for a more honest conversation about children and the complexity of the lives they lead. The demand for the right to be an active participant in one's own story is central and integral to the project of imagining different kinds of adult child relations and thus different encounters between children and professionals.

REFERENCES

Ariès, P. (1962). *Centuries of childhood.* London: Cape.

Butler-Sloss, E. (1987). *Report of the inquiry into child abuse in Cleveland,* HMSO.

Burman, E. (1994). *Deconstructing developmental psychology.* London: Routledge.

Cloke, C., & Davies, M. (Eds.). (1995). *Participation and empowerment in child protection.* London: Pitman.

Durkheim, E. (1957). *Professional ethics and civic morals.* Translated by Cornelia Brookfield. London: Routledge and Kegan Paul.

Foucault, M. (1979a). On Governmentality. *I & C, 6:* 5–21, 1979a.

Foucault, M. (1979b). *The history of sexuality: Vol. 1: An introduction.* London: Allen Lane.

Hacking, I. (1986). Making up people. In T.C. Heller, M. Sosna, & D.E. Wellberg (Eds.), *Reconstructing individualism* (p. 222–236). Stanford, CA: Stanford University Press.

Hendrick, H. (1990). Constructions and reconstructions of British childhood: An interpretive survey, 1800 to the present. In A. James and A. Prout (eds.), *Constructing and reconstructing childhood: Contemporary issues in the sociological study of childhood.* London: Falmer Press.

Illich, I. (1977). The myth of meeting needs in adult education and community development. *Critical Social Policy, 2:* 24–37.

Kelley, P., Mayall, B., & Hood, S. (1997). Children's accounts of risk. *Childhood, 4*(3):305–4.

Morss, J.R. (1996). *Growing critical: Alternatives to developmental psychology.* London: Routledge.

Neufeldt, V., & Guralnik, D.B. (Eds.). (1991). *Webster's new world dictionary, Third College Edition.* Cleveland: Simon & Schuster.

Professions Australia, *Definition of a profession.* www.austprofessions.com.au.

Rose, N. (1985a). *The psychological complex: Psychology, politics and society in England, 1869–1939.* London: Routledge and Kegan Paul.

Rose, N. (1988). Calculable minds and manageable individuals. *History of the Human Sciences, 1:*179–2000, 1988.

Rose, N. (1990). *Governing the soul: The shaping of the private self.* London: Routledge.

Rose, N. (1996). *Inventing our selves psychology, power and personhood.* New York: Cambridge University Press.

Rose, N. (1999). *Governing the soul The shaping of the private self* (2nd ed.). London: Free Association Books.

Stainton Rogers, W., & Stainton Rogers, R. (1992). *Stories of childhood: Shifting agendas of child concern.* Hemel Hempstead: Harvester Wheatsheaf.

Starr, P. (1982). *The social transformation of American medicine.* New York: Basic Books.

Trull, T., & Phares, E. J. (2001). *Clinical psychology* (6th ed.). Belmont, CA: Wadsworth.

Wilding, P. (1982). *Professional power and social welfare.* London: Routledge & Kegan Paul.

Wyness, M.G. (1996). Policy, protectionism and the competent child. *Childhood, 3*(4): 431–48.

Chapter 1

"THE BOY PROBLEM": BOYS, SCHOOLING, AND MASCULINITY

Wayne Martino

Introduction

In recent times, boys have emerged as a particular kind of problem or object of surveillance specifically in the field of education and within the context of postindustrialized economies and backlashes against feminism (Lingard & Douglas, 1999; Martino & Meyenn, 2001; Delamont, 2001). The public media, educational policy, official ministerial inquires into boys' education, teacher and popular discourse about the problem of boys at school and in the broader society constitute, I argue, "surfaces of emergence" for the appearance of boys in recent times as particular kinds problems and objects of concern (see Cohen, 1998; Lingard, 2003; House of Representatives Standing Committee on Education and Training, 2002; Epsetin et al., 1998). In fact, in the United States, there has been a proliferation of books by therapists "who alternate between psychological analyses of boys" development and handy guides for raising good boys' (Foster, Kimmel, & Skelton, 2001; see also Gurian, 1998; Polack, 1998; Polce-Lynch, 2002). Similar work by Steve Biddulph, a psychologist in the Australian context, has also fuelled a populist discourse about boys and their problems which are related to obstacles that prevent them growing into *healthy* men.

This kind of thinking which casts boys as gendered psychologized subjects in need of therapeutic intervention has infiltrated discourses about the social and educational needs of boys in schools. For instance, Biddulph (1995) claims that:

Boys with no fathers , or with fathers who are not around much, are much more likely to be violent, to get into trouble, to do poorly in schools, and be a member of a teenage gang in adolescence' (132).

Hoff-Sommers also reiterates the need for fathers to help boys become apparently *proper* or *normal* men and stresses the "misery" that is caused for boys by those in schools who deny what is *natural* or in boys' nature:

It is obvious that a boy wants his father to help him become a man, and belonging to the culture of manhood is important to almost every boy. To impugn his desire to become "one of the boys" is to deny that a boy's biology determines much of what of what he prefers and is attracted to. Unfortunately, by denying the nature of boys, education theorists can cause them much misery. (Hoff Sommers, 2000)

Such appeals to "common sense" are appropriated by the Right as a normalizing strategy and, as Apple (2001) illustrates, are driven by a neoconservative and neoliberal politics which, I argue here, is in the business of reasserting and retraditionalizing hegemonic masculinities (see Lingard & Douglas, 1999; Lingard, 2003).

These concerns about *the absent father* and its effect on boys' developing masculinity have also fuelled the call for more male teachers in schools who are needed, it is implied, to address boys' social problems and learning difficulties (Mills, 2000; King, 2000). Implicit in such calls for more male role models is the assumption that the feminizing influences of schools and, more specifically, female teachers are having a detrimental impact on boys' learning and social development. In fact, schoolboys have emerged in public discourses and debates, proliferated by the media and men's movement advocates, as homogenous, heterosexualized, white subjects invested with *natural* predispositions for learning or behaving simply on the basis of their sexed bodies (Harding, 1998; Fausto-Stering, 2000; Petersen, 1998).

Much of the public debate and backlash discourse about schoolboys and their problems, it has been argued, are misguided and, as Foster et al. (2001) point out, "misdiagnosed":

The real boy crisis usually goes by another name known as "teen violence," "youth violence," "gang violence," "suburban violence," "violence in the schools." And girls are certainly not perpetuating such acts of violence . . . that these school killers were all middle-class white boys seems to have escaped most people's attention. The real boy crisis is a crisis of violence, about cultural inscriptions that equate masculinity with the capacity for violence. (p. 16)

This denial or erasure of the specific gendered nature of violence in schools, it is suggested here, is to protect the interests of privileged white middle-class boys. This also appears to be the case in a recent Parliamentary Inquiry into the Education of Boys in Australia, where there is a call for a *recasting* of the current national gender equity policy—which includes a discussion of the gendered dimensions of violence and harassment—to incorporate more "positive values and goals" in relation to addressing the educational needs of boys (House of Representatives Standing Committee on Education and Training, 2002).

What often emerges in the way that boys get constructed as particular kinds of subjects in the popular media, educational reports, and by therapists and many teachers in schools is a sense of the need to recuperate and reinstate what is understood to be a *natural* masculinity that has been thwarted in its development by a number of detrimental feminizing influences in boys' lives. In fact, as Flood (2000) points out, while feminist gender reform in schools involved a commitment to expanding behavioral boundaries and repertoires for girls, this has not been the case for boys:

> On the other hand, the behavioural boundaries for boys remain rigid. Boys are still universally encouraged to purge themselves of any hint of softness or femininity. In contrast to the new situation that prevails for girls, many male role models in the world of athletics and the media continue to support stereotypes of masculinity. It is no wonder, then that males grow up attuned to and comfortable expressing themselves with violence. (p. 4)

In this chapter, hence, I am concerned to apply a particular Foucauldian analytics which draws attention to the impact and effects of certain modes of subjectification and normalization within the context of notions of "truth games" to draw attention to the emergence of "the boy" as a specific kind of gendered subject in need of a particular form of heteronormative surveillance and monitoring that is in the business of the reinstating white hegemonic heterosexual masculinities (Frank, 1987; Epstein & Johnson, 1998; Martino & Pallott-Chiarolli, 2003). In short, the notions of boyhood and the categories of masculinity that are embedded in various public discourses about boys are illuminated in a discussion which draws attention to the emergence of the male child as a mono-cultural gendered subject prescribed within the heteronormative limits of *normal* masculinity.

I draw on media reports about boys in Australia as well as an interview with one male elementary school teacher to illustrate the effects of normalizing regimes of practice in relation to how the "boy problem" gets inscribed through the proliferation of various gendered discourses that are in the business of reinstating a hegemonic heterosexual and monolithic masculinity (Frank, 1987).

Games of Truth and Regimes of Normalizing Practices

Foucault (1984) proposes a critical inquiry that is committed to an analysis of the historically contingent regimes of normalizing practices within which the limits of particular modes of subjectification are circumscribed. This interpretive analytics is particularly useful when thinking about the ways in which certain *truths* about boys and their natures emerge within the public domain through the proliferation of various discourses about boys as the "new disadvantaged" that are perpetuated by the public media. In fact, Lingard (2003) has argued that the media has played a significant role in setting the policy agenda about boys' education in Australia and the UK. Given the policy vacuum or lack of government commitment until recently, he claims that media reports have functioned "almost as defacto policies for schools' with regards to setting the boys" educational agenda. This is pertinent given the role of the media as a powerful technology for inserting the notion of boys as "victims" into a particular regime of normalizing practices or "game of truth." Within such a regime, boys acquire the status of "competing victims" who have been apparently neglected as a result of the reverse sexism of feminist educators (see Epstein et al., 1998; Foster, 1996; Francis, 2000; Skelton, 2001).

This relates to the issues Foucault raises about how the subject gets inserted or enters "a certain game of truth" and the role that the media plays in the circulation and production of certain truths about boys and their subjectivities:

> My problem has always been . . . the problem of the relationship between subject and truth. How does the subject enter into a certain game of truth? My first problem was, how is it, for example, that beginning at a certain point in time, madness was considered a problem and the result of a certain number of processes—an illness dependent upon a certain medicine? How has the mad subject been placed in this game of truth defined by knowledge or a medical model? . . . In fact, there were practices—essentially the major practice of confinement which had been developed at the beginning of the seventeenth century and which had been the condition for the insertion of the mad subject in this game of truth—which sent me back to the problem of institutions of power,

much more than to the problem of ideology. So it was that I was led to pose the problem knowledge/power, which is not for me the problem of relationships between subject and games of truth. (1987: 120–21)

What Foucault writes here about madness could equally be applied to boys who emerge as a particular kind of subject in postindustrial times and within a context of backlash against feminism involving certain knowledge power/relations proliferated within certain disciplinary regimens (Falaudi, 1991). For instance, psychological discourse and knowledge produced about brain sex differences has been used to establish the truth that boys and girls essentially have different learning and behavioral orientations, despite the medical research which refutes such claims (see Gilbert & Gilbert, 1998 for a discussion of this medical research). Psychologized discourses drawing on spurious medical research about the impact of testosterone on boys' behavior, for example, have been accorded a particular truth by the media which functions as an apparatus for the proliferation of a right wing and neoconservative agenda in the promotion and legitimation of certain notions of boyhood (see Mills, 2002; Apple, 2001).

These kinds of discourses circulate within the culture and permeate the consciousness of those working in schools and education bureaucracies. For example, Lingard (2003) claims that many schools have "bought into the recuperative masculinist stance, utilising much of the work of Biddulph and Pollack (*Real Boys*) as a justification for particular policies and programs." He further reiterates:

> The "boys as the new disadvantaged" rhetoric by contrast feeds into many of teachers' taken for granted assumptions, that is, boys require more time in class, require more discipline, are behaviour problems, are poor at expressing their emotions etc. There is a way then in which the current backlash politics demands a return to the *status quo ante*: many teachers would be happy with that situation.

Various media reports both in Australia and in the United Kingdom and United States function as "surfaces of emergence" upon which the boy problem is inscribed within the context of "moral panic" and a backlash against feminism (see Foster et al., 2001). Moreover, appeals to a fundamental or essential notion of boyhood and what constitutes *natural* behavior for schoolboys also emerge in how boys get constituted as particular kinds of *normal* subjects. For example, Bettina Arndt, a journalist for *The Sydney Morning Herald,* in an article entitled "A Better Deal for Boys" (Tuesday 29 May, 2001), claims "that schools are far from boy friendly." She quotes extensively from a book written by a headmaster of a boys' school, Dr Tim Hawkes, to assert "the importance of providing more action-based learning rather than docile, literary-based tasks." Hawkes is quoted to support this assertion: "Most boys like to be physically involved, they like to do, they like to touch," says Hawkes, who also mentions the research which shows boys are more likely to respond to short "closed" tasks rather than long open-ended tasks.

This appeal to selective research to establish the *truth* that boys are essentially different from girls through invoking gendered binary classificatory systems is significant and endemic in the media and in the way that many teachers in schools construct boys. This leads Arndt and many others to construct the problem around the need for schools to *defeminize* and *remasculinize* the curriculum and pedagogy. In short, the feminization of emasculating influences of schooling emerge as the source of the problem for boys and accounts for their failure. For instance, Hawkes is quoted by Arndt as posing the following question: "When at least 80 percent of primary teachers are female, is it surprising that boys equate school and learning with femininity?"

Michael Duffy (June 2, 2001), from another Australian newspaper, *The Daily Telegraph*, refers to an Australian member of parliament, Rodney Sawlford, who chaired the Federal Parliament's National Inquiry into Boys' Education. He is of the view that "boys' marks can be brought up the level of girls . . . through strong principals, active learning methods, and more structured classes with clearly identifiable steps and measurement techniques." In this article *failing boys* emerge as victims of a feminist agenda in education which is in the business of denying the reality of the problems that boys are experiencing. For example, Duffy quotes from a submission by the New South Wales Department of Education and Training to the parliamentary inquiry which states that there is no "clear evidence that there are any particular approaches and emphases in school and classroom practice that are of more or less benefit to either boys or girls." Sawlford is quoted as disagreeing: ". . . Sawlford in disagreeing with this . . . believes 'the research is leaning towards the idea that boys and girls are different in the main' and therefore require different teaching approaches."

In most media accounts, research is selectively drawn on within a backlash context of anti-feminism and "moral panic" to constitute a specific deployment of knowledge/power relations which are in the business of constituting boys as gendered subjects who are essentially different from girls in their behavioral and learning orientations. This becomes particularly evident when Duffy writes:

> The curious thing, of course, is that when girls had problems 20 years ago, teachers and bureaucrats were only too enthusiastic to publicise [the idea that boys and girls are different in the main] and take successful action to address [these differences].

Another element of this discourse, which is consistent with that emerging in other media reports about the boys elsewhere, is the powerful way in which "common sense" is invoked in the assertion that boys and girls are essentially different (see Apple, 2001). Moreover, what is even more significant is the homogenizing tendency to normalize all boys. There is no sense that not all boys are alike. Diversity amongst boys in relation to class, sexuality, race, ethnicity, geographical location, disability, and how these influences might impact differently on individual boys has been erased from these "poor boy" discourses (see Collins et al., 2000; Thorne, 1997; Epstein et al., 1998; Martino & Pallotta-Chiarolli, 2003; Lingard, Martino, Mills & Bahr, 2002). These reports about boys draw attention to the role that the media plays in its capacity to insert boys into a certain "game of truth" and normalizing regime in which their difference from girls is established and legitimated. It is within a complex field of social institutional practices and disciplinary regimens involving the deployment of quite specific knowledge/power relations that the media functions as an apparatus for the proliferation of certain truths about boys.

Boys Need More Male Role Models?

This analysis is further informed by Foucault's notions of subjectification and the whole question of knowing and how we come to know boys and what they need. What is rejected is an a priori theory of the subject, which presupposes, for example, that there is a knowledge about masculinity waiting to be freed from repressive or ideological mechanisms of power at play within the social field:

> What I wanted to know was **how the subject constituted himself**, in such and such a determined form, as a mad subject or as a normal subject, through a certain number of practices which were games of truth, applications of power, etc. I had to reject a certain *a priori* theory of the subject in order to make this analysis of the relationships which can exist between the constitution of the subject or

different forms of the subject and games of truth, practices of power and so forth. (Foucault, 1987: 121) (my emphasis)

Foucault is careful to situate this focus on the constitution of the subject within a field or game of truth/power relations. Hence, different forms of the subject cannot be separated from a regime of practices through which power is channeled and particular truths established. In short, the formation of subjectivity is not understood in terms which rely on the explanatory category of ideology. Rather, attention is drawn to the technologies, administrative apparatuses, disciplinary regimes of knowledge production, and deployment of knowledge/power relations within specific institutional sites to produce certain truth claims about the *normal* subject.

This represents a set of cultural techniques for working on and fashioning the gendered self, which are made available within existing regimes of practice to constitute the subject, or boys in this case, as endowed with particular traits or as having a particular *nature* (Hoff-Sommers, 2000; Biddulph, 1995). Such an interpretive analytics leads to an investigation of what Foucault (1978) terms "polymorphous techniques of power" in relation to examining the constitution of boys and their masculinity as requiring a particular form of problematization in relation to their contamination as a result of feminizing, feminized, and feminist influences at school or within the context of the single-parent family (see Epstein et al., 1998; Flood, 2000; Thorne, 1997; Martino & Berrill, forthcoming).

The ways in which modalities of power are channeled through normalizing regimes of practice and disciplinary regimens of knowledge production to elaborate certain truth claims about the nature of boys and their ways of knowing, relating, and behaving is what is of concern in this chapter. How such power relations permeate individual modes of behavior and incite particular forms of desire cannot be separated from the technologies of the self within which such relations to the self and to others are established:

> . . . my main concern will be to locate the forms of power, the channels, and the discourses it permeates in order to reach the most tenuous and individual modes of behaviour, the paths that give it access to the rare or scarcely perceivable forms of desire, how it penetrates and controls everyday pleasure—all this entailing effects that may be those of refusal, blockage, and invalidation, but also incitement and intensification: in short the "polymorphous" techniques of power. (Foucault, 1978: 11)

Such technologies of the self are implicated in the desire to normalize boys and to produce them as heterosexualized subjects in schools whose problems are somehow connected or attributed to a contaminated masculinity. There is always a sense in the public debates about the boy problem that heteronormative masculinity needs to be restored to boys. This becomes particularly pertinent when discussing or rather tracing the proliferation of certain discourses informing teachers' talk about boys in schools.

Due to the apparent *fact* or "truth claim" that boys are essentially different from girls, the former emerge though the public media and through discourses informing many teachers' discussions about the "boy problem" as *at risk* in the feminized and feminizing context of the school (see Lingard & Douglas, 1999). The school, in fact, often gets constructed as a site which disconfirms boys' *natural* masculinity and, hence, approach to learning. In one media report in Western Australia, "Schools fail boys: report" by Ben Ruse (*The West Australian*, October 22, 2002)–which comments on the findings of the Parliamentary Inquiry into Boys' Education in Australia–these discourses are invoked through the links or associations that are made between boys' failure at school and the need for more male role models, as a means of addressing the problems they face at school. Ruse understands the need for widespread reform from his reading of the parliamentary report as necessarily involving: "More male teachers, recognition of the fact that boys learn differently and programs aimed specifically at boys were three of the measures the committee recommended to reverse the [widening gap in performance between boys and girls at school]." He quotes the chairman of the House of Representatives committee on education: "He said boys tended to learn visually, required stronger discipline and needed male role models in schools" (p. 3). The implication is that female teachers are unable to deal with boys and that boys need men to confirm their masculinity. Such claims are grounded in problematic role theories about the scripting of masculinity and are driven by a degree of misogyny in terms of how female teachers and their labor in school are constituted.

One male teacher in an elementary school in Australia invoked similar discourses in his interview as part of a larger research project (see Lingard, Martino, Mills, & Bahr, 2002). He talked about the need to "connect with kids" and how this appeared to matter more for boys in order to engage them in learning. What emerges is a view that boys require a particular kind of relationship with teachers that is essentially different from the one that girls need. This relates to the view propagated in the inquiry report on boys' education in Australia which states that: "Girls respond more readily to content while boys respond more to their relationships with teachers" (p. 78). However, there is a sense in this teacher's interview that such a relationship for boys involves a particular form of male bonding (see Roulsten & Mills, 2000). He stresses the value of being a particular male role model for boys which involves teaching boys to "connect with their emotions." He indicates that his own recognition of emotional literacy for boys and the need to be emotionally supported by men is tied to his own experiences of not "having a dad at home":

> So really I've only got one word for it now and that's connect, connect with kids and they will work for you. So I've read Steve Biddulph and listened to Steve Biddulph. . . . He's done some good work, take your face off, that you don't have to have facades. Steve Biddulph tells a great story about how his little boy puts his armour on when he gets closer to school. Five hundred meters from school he turns out from being this loving honest caring kid to this tough straight strong child who goes and walks into the corridor like this. One of the things with boys education I think you need (is) to teach boys how to connect with their emotions, So we talk about you don't just feel good, how was your weekend, good. How was your weekend, well I was a bit anxious on Saturday because I had a footy grand final on Sunday and I was a little bit apprehensive. So we teach the boys the emotive language.

Interestingly, this teacher draws on a particular knowledge about boys espoused by Steve Biddulph, a popular psychologist in Australia, who draws on mythopoetic and biological determinist views about boys' behavior, to establish certain truth claims about the need for a relational pedagogy for boys. This is related to the need to get behind the mask that all boys supposedly wear to hide their true selves! The underlying reasons why some boys might feel the need to wear such masks are not considered. There is a sense that this is just a *natural* behavior for all boys, a consequence of simply being boys–that boys just don't learn or are not required to express what they feel because they are simply boys.

This teacher also draws on his own experiences as a boy with male teachers at his school who appeared to function as surrogate fathers in the kinds of support they provided him. He suggests that the kind of capacity to form such connections with boys is limited nowadays, however, due to the surveillance of male teachers' sexuality, which constructs the desire in men to form close relationships with students as potentially a deviant rather than a nurturing and caring association:

> I, of course, refer back to the teachers who meant significant things to me, they were prepared to give a little bit of themselves. So that's where I learnt the connectiveness. My rule was, I was in remedial maths for a long time and I got this guy, Mr. X in Year 8, 9 and 10 and he invited me over to his house. This is before paedophilia and all those sort of things used to be a concern for teachers. And he would invite me over to the Ag school where he was a house master and say what do you need to know for this test tomorrow. And I'd say well I know this and he'd sit down and he'd spend 10 minutes with me, and sometimes it would be an hour. One time he said do you know any geometry, do you know what geometry is, do you know how to play pool. I'd never had a pool table, I didn't know what a pool table was and he said come over to my house at 4 o'clock. And he showed me, and he talked about angles so he taught me how to play pool with these numbers. This is the angle, you've got to get the black into that pocket over there, now if you hit it here what angle will it be. I thought this is fantastic.

However, informing his own construction of the teacher as male role model is the discourse of the "absent father" in his own life as a boy and which he talks about in relation to the increasing number of boys at his school who are in single parent families:

> I didn't have a dad because he died when I was very young. . . . So all my life was made up with these, not all males but lots of them and that was really important to me to have a male because I didn't have a dad at home. My rule was that I had to pay these guys back for their good service by doing the same thing they did for me back to someone else.

This teacher kept reiterating the role of the teacher as crucial, but the way he constructs such a role is suffused with mythopoetic discourses about rites of passage informed by the work of Steve Biddulph:

> Teacher: If you can learn through your teacher not from your teacher you've got it sussed . . . it's just a matter of being empathetic. This job is worth two, there's two parts to it. Number one, you are an actor, you're a regularly paid actor. You're not a highly paid actor but you're a regularly paid actor. Two, you've got to show your soft underbelly. Me telling stories about my brother-in-law dying and having a few tears in my eyes when I tell it, and blasting some kid for calling out and then going look mate I'm really dreadfully sorry, I can't believe I did that. I just feel really crappy inside, I just feel like I've just been smashed. But now you know, when you call out and you hurt someone like that, that's like being kicked in the stomach. Showing both sides, the tough masculine side versus, well not versus, that's wrong I've fallen into a trap of what people expect. Showing the soft side, showing the hard masculine side and talking about how difficult it is being a boy, being a man. For girls it's easy, one

moment you're a girl, when you're 13 you menstruate you're a woman. That's it. Celebrate like billyo that day, go out for dinner, don't go to school that day, whatever, make a big deal about becoming a woman. But for boys it's so damn hard, you don't know where you are. There are times as a 40-year-old you're wondering if you're a boy or a man.

There is a sense that the splitting of male subjectivity, which is a result of maintaining a tough masculine side and which prevents boys/men from showing their soft underbelly, is at the heart of the tensions and crises which afflict the male psyche. This leads to the construction of men/boys as *victims*–it is difficult being a man in times of great uncertainty brought about, it is implied, by feminist interrogations of traditional masculinity. He draws on simplistic gender comparisons in his explanation that becoming a woman is a straightforward matter signified through menstruation in a way that becoming a man is not. What is left out of such a version of what it means to be a woman is a whole history and politics of gender around enforcing women's inferior positioning and delegitimation on the basis of their biological and sexed bodies (see Petersen, 1998). This idea of invoking a crisis masculinity is reiterated below in this teacher's emphasis on the ambiguity that has been brought to bear on what now constitutes acceptable male role behaviors. Implicit in his discourse is a feminist backlash politics (Falaudi, 1991; Lingard & Douglas, 1999).

> There are boundaries, what are you supposed to do. In the old days and this is probably well past our parents' days but the rules were that you were a disciplinarian, you were the breadwinner and that's it. Now boys don't know whether they're supposed to be the soft, sensitive new age guy or they're supposed to be the tough macho guy who goes around breaking heads. We really don't know what we're doing. I mean for you, you're lucky you're well educated. For me I'm lucky I'm well educated but for people who don't have that. For kids in our little area here they don't have role models like that. It's tough just to work here. I mean if we're sitting in here and we're having a few beers it's not a bad thing to let go with the "f" every so often but it wouldn't be appropriate when my wife's sitting here next to us. How do you learn those things, well probably from your parents and if your parents don't know then how do you know?

What emerges here also is this teacher's perception of the rules governing what it means to do masculinity in acceptable ways . Homosocial contexts afford acceptable sexist modes of relating and forms of male bonding, the limits of which need to be taught to boys by other men. But the problem is that there are few male role models in school to teach boys these social scripts: And we have a big problem in that there are not many boys, male teachers in education, and certainly not male teachers who are prepared to give of themselves.

This male teacher's talk about boys and their needs is another example of how a gender politics around the constitution of hegemonic and normative masculinity informs the emergence of certain discourses of boyhood. These are driven by certain knowledge/power relations which are themselves produced within normalizing and disciplinary regimens that are in the business of enforcing a monocultural and heteronormative masculinity for boys. In short, adult men, in the absence of the father, must establish or model for boys a culturally validated heterosexual masculinity to ensure that the latter's health is maintained or restored.

Conclusion

The focus of this chapter has been on examining the "boy problem" within a Foucauldian framework for interrogating specific "surfaces of emergence" upon which an essentialized and, by implication, heteronormative masculinity gets inscribed and problematized. Through an analysis of the role that the public media plays in how schoolboys are constituted as particular kinds of subjects in need of specific interventions in schools involving male teachers as role models, attention has been drawn to the normalizing tendencies that can be traced in both public and private spaces where the topic of boys is raised for discussion. My aim has been to draw attention to the gender politics that inform the articulation of a masculinity crisis in boys' education where the schoolboy is not so much pathologized, but rather emerges as a victim of reverse sexism and the emasculating and contaminating influences of female teachers and schools which are constituted as feminized learning sites that are contributing to the failure of boys.

REFERENCES

Apple, M. (2001). *Educating the "right" way: Markets, standards, God and inequality.* New York & London: Routledge Falmer.

Biddulph, S. (1995) *Manhood.* Sydney: Finch.

Cohen, M. (1998). "A habit of healthy idleness": Boys underachievement in historical perspective. In Epstein et al. (Eds.), *Failing boys?: Issues in gender and achievement.* Buckingham: Open University Press.

Collins, C., Kenway, J., & McLeod, J. (2000). *Factors influencing the educational performance of males and females in school and their initial destinations after leaving school.* Geelong: Deakin University.

Delamont, S. (2001). *Changing women, unchanged Men? Sociological perspectives on gender in a post-industrial society.* Buckingham: Open University Press.

Epstein, D., & Johnson, R. (1998). *Schooling sexualities.* Buckingham: Open University Press.

Epstein, D. Elwood, J. Hey, V., & Maw, J. (Eds.) (1998). *Failing boys?: Issues in gender and achievement.* Buckingham: Open University Press.

Faludi, S. (1991). *Backlash: The undeclared war against women.* London: Vintage.

Fausto-Stering, A. (2000). *Sexing the body: Gender politics and the construction of sexuality.* New York: Basic Books.

Flood, C. (2000). Safe boys, safe schools. *WEEA Digest,* November, 4–7.

Foster, V. (1996). Space invaders: Desire and threat in the schooling of girls. *Discourse: Studies in the Cultural Politics of Education, 17*(1), 43–63.

Foucault, M. (1978). *The history of sexuality: Volume 1.* Trans. R. Hurley. New York: Vintage.

Foucault, M. (1984) What is enlightenment? Trans. Catherine Porter. In P. Rabinow (Ed.), *The Foucault reader.* London: Penguin.

Foucault, M. (1987). The ethic of care for the self as a practice of freedom. *Philosophy and Social Criticism, 12,* 113–131.

Foster, V., Kimmell, M., & Skelton, C. (2001). "What about the boys?": An overview of the debates. In W. Martino & B. Meyenn (Eds.), *What about the boys?: Issues of masculinity and schooling.* Buckingham: Open University Press.

Francis, B. (2000). *Boys, girls and achievement: Addressing the classroom issues.* London and New York: Routledge, Falmer.

Frank, B. (1987). Hegemonic heterosexual masculinity. *Studies in Political Economy, 24,* Autumn, 159–170.

Gilbert, R., & Gilbert, P. (1998). *Masculinity goes to school.* Sydney: Allen & Unwin.

Gurian, M. (1998). *A fine young man.* New York: Tarcher/Putnam.

Harding, J. (1998). *Sex acts: Practices of femininity and masculinity.* London, Thousand Oaks, New Delhi: Sage.

Hoff Sommers, C. (2000). The war against boys. *The Atlantic Monthly, 285* (5), 59–74.

House of Representatives Standing Committee on Education and Training (2002). *Boys' education: Getting it right.* Canberra: Commonwealth Government.

King, J. (2000). The problem(s) of men in early education. In N. Lesko (Ed.), *Masculinities at school.* Thousand Oaks, London, New Delhi: Sage.

Lingard, B. (2003). Where to in gender theorising and policy after recuperative masculinity politics? *International Journal of Inclusive Education, 7* (1), Jan–March, 33–56.

Lingard, B., Martino, W., Mills, M., & Bahr, M. (2002). *Addressing the educational needs of boys.* Canberra: Department of Education, Science and Training. http://www.dest.gov.au/schools/publications/2002/boyseducation/index.htm.

Lingard, B., & Douglas, P. (1999). *Men engaging feminisms: Profeminism, backlashes and schooling.* Buckingham: Open University Press.

Martino, W., & Berrill, D. (Forthcoming). Boys, schooling and masculinities: Interrogating the 'right' way to educate boys. *Education Review.*

Martino, W., & Pallotta-Chiarolli, M. (2003). *So what's a boy?: Addressing issues of masculinity and schooling.* Buckingham: Open University Press.

Martino, W., & Meyenn, B. (Eds.). (2001). *What about the boys?: Issues of masculinity and schooling.* Buckingham: Open University Press.

Mills, M. (2002). Educating the right way: Markets, standards, God and inequality (Review). *British Journal of the Sociology of Education, 23* (3), 489–494.

Mills, M. (2000). Issues in implementing boys' programmes in schools: Male teachers and empowerment. *Gender and Education, 12* (2): 221–238.

Petersen, A. (1998). *Unmasking the masculine: Men and identity in a sceptical age.* London, Thousand Oaks & New Dehli: Sage.

Pollack, W. (1998). *Real boys: Rescuing our sons from the myths of boyhood.* New York: Henry Holt. Oakland: New Harbinger.

Roulston, K., & Mills, M. (2000). Male teachers in feminised teaching areas: Marching to the men's movement drums. *Oxford Review of Education, 26*(1): 221–237.

Skelton, C. (2001). *Schooling the boys: Masculinities and primary education.* Buckingham: Open University Press.

Thorne, B. (1997). Children and gender: Constructions of difference. In M. Baca Zinn, P. Hondagneu-Sotelo, & M. Messner (Eds.), *Through the prism of difference: Readings on sex and gender.* Boston: Allyn & Bacon.

Chapter 2

THE ORDERING OF ATTENTION: THE DISCOURSE OF DEVELOPMENTAL THEORY AND ADD

ROXANNA P. TRANSIT, PH.D.

Attention Deficit (ADD), as part of the Attention Deficit Hyperactive Disorder, is one of the most frequently given psychiatric diagnoses of children in the United States today, according to the National Institute of Mental Health (NIMH, 1998). It is estimated to affect between 3 and 5 percent of school-age children, and to occur three to four times more often in boys than in girls and depending on the definition being used, the population being studied and the geographic locale, estimates can go as high as 20 percent (Barkley, 1998). The prevalence of the ADD/ADHD diagnosis has grown from 500 thousand in 1985 to between 5 and 7 million today, and is being viewed by some as an epidemic (Baughman, F. www.adhdfraud.org). According to the Drug Enforcement Agency, the production of Ritalin, the most common medication used to treat ADD, increased 450 percent in the early 1990s (Armstrong, 1996). According to the International Narcotics Control Board, an agency of the World Health Organization, "10–12 % of all boys between the ages of 6 to 14 in the United States have been diagnosed as having ADD and are being treated [with Ritalin]," with the United States using approximately 90 percent of the world's Ritalin supply (Breggin, 2000). This dramatic increase in the frequency of the diagnosis followed by the popular treatment utilizing the medication Ritalin, has made the disorder of ADD the object of great controversy and the focus of increased attention and scrutiny.

Note: This paper was originally presented at the 2001 Fall Conference of the Michigan Society for Psychoanalytic Psychology, entitled Meeting (with) the "Child": Different Perspectives within Psychoanalysis.

In this chapter, I will consider the diagnosis of ADD as being a product of the discourse of developmental theory. Discourse, as defined by Foucault (1972), refers to ways of constituting knowledge, together with the social practices, forms of subjectivity, and power relations which can be found in such knowledges and the relations between them. Discourses are more than ways of thinking and producing meaning. They can constitute the words and language, text and talk, which help constitute knowledge, and the ways of knowing and seeing the world which emerge in practices that represent and objectify the ideas and meanings of the discourse.

Developmental theory, referring to a normal core of development unfolding according to biological principles, has become a powerful discourse that has been foundational in constituting the individual we know as a child, what the childhood of that child should consist of in terms of their environment and education, and different forms that child can take if their development through childhood does not proceed optimally, as thought to be in the case of the ADD child. This discourse of developmental theory reverberates far beyond the theory or the lab and has informed a number of professional practices in psychology, psychoanalysis, education, and pediatric medicine. In this chapter, the term developmental theory rather than developmental psychology has been purposefully chosen in order to speak to its broad impact and incorporation into many different professions and locations.

Developmental Theory

Modern developmental theory arose in the late nineteenth century as a response to such questions as "What is life?" that had arisen from evolutionary theory, physiology, anthropology, and philosophy. In the 1700s, the perspectives of vitalism and mechanism were offered as answers. In mechanistic thought, all the activities of a body could be explained in terms of its material composition and the interaction of its parts at the physical-chemical level. Vitalism described a variety of beliefs united in opposition to mechanism, and contended that living processes could not be entirely explained by reference to their material composition and physio-chemical activity (Benton, 1974–1975). Its fundamental axiom was "the idea of becoming, the restlessness of nature, ever self-renewing and hereby life-constructing processes . . ." (Jacyna, 1984).

Knowledge from physiology and biology in the area of cell theory focused attention inward, to the interior of the smallest known unit of life. The cell theory of physiology attempted to explain the fundamental laws governing organic life (Forster, 1885) believing that within the very nature of a cell was a pattern of mechanical progressive development that would be revealed as time went by and growth took place (Jacyna, 1984). It was thought that the "essential inwardness and interiority" of the cell body contained the nature of things, which will figure itself forth, from inside to outside, even though [that nature] "was always beyond the reach of visibility or total comprehension" (Figlio, 1976).

In the late eighteenth century, two different approaches to the study of life forms were prominent: idealistic and functional morphology (Allen, 1978). Functional morphology focused on physiological and embryological processes, with the structure of an organism providing the key to comprehending its function (Coleman, 1968). The idealist searched out similarity among different animals and plants, hoping to delineate the ideal-type from which one would know the laws of growth for all others (Lenoir, 1982).

Other explanations of life came from Darwin's evolutionary biology which conceived of growth as purposeful, orderly, and goal directed. The individual in his or her lifetime was understood to reproduce the patterns and stages of development exhibited by the development of the species. The smallest of the species was positioned as the beginning, the primitive, the to-be-developed, containing the entire history of the species within their biological body. Time passing was now seen as a causal agent of change, and the "real" events taking place over time were connected in a linear fashion to the future. Evolutionary theory introduced the prospect that entire species could die and never exist again, becoming extinct. The social upheaval and unrest in the world in the late 19th century was seen in a new light and within this context of survival of the fittest vs. extinction, questions developed about the quality of certain classes of people, and how those qualitative differences threatened the strength of others and civilized society.

Psychology responded to these concerns over population quality and began to classify, measure and regulate those populations deemed a social threat to the prevailing order. Characteristics of living things came to be used as visible signs of an underlying order, a "buried depth" within. Psychology created the "individual" by relying upon physical characteristics and by developing methods of measurement that transform the [in-(the)-visible signs of the] individual into numbers and categories making visible that which was thought to be within. Such practices as craniology, phrenology, and physiognomy posited that measurements of physical attributes such as head size, brain weight, jaw angle, and limb length could indicate human character and potential. Population groups became constructed, giving qualities to groups of individuals. The individual became defined and produced in a new way, as part of a class and as classifiable categorically, and the science of the individual as a member possessing shared and universal characteristics began.

Psychometrics, the theory and practice of measuring mental processes, used in conjunction with the laws of statistics and empiricism, became a widely used means of visualizing, disciplining, and inscribing differences and was the first venture into the interiority of the soul. The psychological test is a simple technical device that can be used to realize almost any schema for differentiating individuals in a brief time span, in a manageable space, at the will of the expert, rendering the object knowable in a very limited way, via numbers, scores, and profiles. The test became a new way of visualizing and constituting the idea of normality and difference with its meaning predefined and predetermined.

Numerous measurements and data were gathered on childrens' bodies and their growth, with the information being compartmentalized into sequential phases of development and giving what appeared to be an itemized account of the way a child grows up; an account of orderly, progressive, almost law-like growth through stages to ever greater competence and maturity. These growth studies provided a detailed understanding of the processes that produce the adult body. The growth of the body was equated to growth within and attention shifted quickly to what was thought to be within, the mind. From an evolutionary perspective the child and the "savage" were equated; seen as intellectually immature "primitives," allowing for a study of the mind in its simplest form, the dim foreshadowing of our selves when mature and developed.

Various theories of the developing biological mind were created and remain popular, including the stages of moral development theorized by Kohut, the stages of cognitive development formulated by Piaget, and others from Erikson, Klein, Fairbairn, and Mahler, etc. In psycho-analysis, the intellectual history of our discipline is intricately bound up with a particularly detailed and vivid developmental model which became a framing edifice (Schwartz, 1999). Freud's vision of libidinal development, the theory of drive development based on different bod-ily zones and processes, the psychosexual stages, the facts of a patient's childhood, the sort of fixations encountered, which in turn will identi-fy the body parts and body functions that are likely to be thematic, form the foundation of classical psychoanalysis.

Each of these theories of development reflects the belief in the sys-tematic influence of the past on the present and make the claim that universally, as a feature of being human, very particular and special things must happen in the course of human life in order for its more valued features to be achieved, and further that the structure of human beings reflect their prewired predispositions to move toward these developmental goals. And per evolutionary theory, these develop-mental structures are seen as having contributed to the survival of the species in some significant way. The span of human life is thus seen as the universal unfolding, of certain highly compelling and far-reaching biological, organismic processes linked in a smooth, comprehensible line that transcend culture and individual experience.

The "Child"

Today, the individual we know of as a "child" (in quotes) is a rela-tively recent addition to the family of man. Philippe Aries, in his book the *History of the Child,* presents art, literature, and other texts docu-menting the changing view and understandings of the individual we currently know of as a "child" (Aries, 1962). In the past, children were viewed as miniature adults and participated fully in adult life, dressing like and participating in the same activities as adults. (Aries, 1962; Hoyles & Evans, 1989). According to Aries (1962), the modern Western conception of childhood began to develop during the sixteenth centu-ry with the rise of the middle class and its demand for formalized edu-cation for its sons. Compulsory elementary schooling was established as a way to care for and protect citizens, particularly those newly defined as morally vulnerable, dependent, and in need of education while at the same time keeping order across the land (Hendrick, 1990; Meyer, 1983; Rose, 1990; Walkerdine, 1984).

The psychology of the individual has been a central aspect of the education system and its schools. Schools enabled the observation of numbers of children of the same age and of children of different ages under controlled, almost laboratory-like conditions, transforming the child into a visible, observable, and analyzable specimen-like object whose recorded differences became the basis for disciplinization, normalization, and standardization. Standardization is the collection of comparable information on a large number of subjects analyzed in such a way as to construct norms. A developmental norm was based upon the average abilities of children of a certain age on a particular task. These data, in the form of records, photographs, measurements, and tests were accumulated, correlated, and consolidated into age norms along an axis of time. Norms not only presented a picture of what was normal for children of each age, but also enabled the normality and abnormality of any child to be assessed by comparison with this norm (Rose, 1990).

This child study movement, inspired partly by Darwin's theories of biological evolution applied to the social realm (social Darwinism), focused initially on questions of heredity and the body. It posited that children develop in ways that parallel the evolution of the "human race." "Child development" was newly posited as "racial evolution." That is, over the centuries, a higher form of humans was thought to have evolved from "savagery" to "civilization" through the biological imperatives of genetics and "natural selection." The child, in its growth toward adulthood, developed in stages marked by this history of evolution (Darwin, 1977):

> "The parallelism was known as the 'law of recapitulation'. This law declares that the individual in his development passes through stages similar to those through which the race has passed and in the same order, . . . In the brief period from the earliest moment of life to maturity the individual passes through or represents all the stages of life, through which the race has passed from that of a singled celled animal to that of present adult civilized man" (Partridge, 1912). Ontogeny recapitulates phylogeny.

From early on, the body and the meanings attached to the body have been critical in forming the understandings of the child. Observation of children and attention to the child's body was encouraged and a semiology of infancy was created that could be used to detect ill-health in children. It was thought scrutiny of the body and its outward manifestations (cries, movements, head size and shape, and other body features) would guide watchful parents to another level of observation, to that within, the circulatory, respiratory, digestive (Cory, 1834), and in later years, to the emotional and cognitive systems.

The (modern) self was located spatially within the physical body of the child, formed within the time of their childhood, the result of the laying down and accretion of childhood experiences, the bits and pieces of a personal history in a place inside. Knowledge was acquired through conditioning, through selective reinforcement based on environmental contingencies. Based on the philosophical framework of empiricism, the mind was conceived of as a blank slate or as "blooming buzzing confusion" (James, 1890) where critical periods existed during which certain knowledges or developments would be permanently lost if the proper environment or interventions did not take place. Per developmental theory, the self of the child is incomplete and lacking, and by some accounts defined as primitive. Due to this lack of full development, the child is regarded as not knowing, and as having no voice, no agency, being the passive recipient of real events taking place in their environment and lacking the development needed to organize experience and make meaning.

Attention also turned to that which surrounded the child, and the time we know as childhood came to be regarded as crucial to the development of the child. Carolyn Steedman (1995) suggests that the idea of childhood emerged at the same time as the modern idea of history as a way to express history within individuals. "History" in its conventional meaning assumes a linearized cause and effect relationship between the past, present, and future, and suggests that a painstaking dredging through the detritus left behind—the memories, events, documents, and other traces—retrieving and reviewing what was allows us to conjure the past before our very eyes (Ashplant & Wilson, 1988), even reviving and reliving it.

The work of Freud and classical psychoanalytic theory reflected the belief in this causal relationship between the time of childhood as historical past forming the future of the childadult (one word). In his work with the individuals on which psychoanalytic theory was formulated, he deconstructed their present being and "symptomatology" by reconstructing their historical past and the "real" events that took place in the time of childhood which he believed were directly and causally connected to their present functioning. Though he subsequently acknowledged the existence of fantasies, multiple realities, and the self experience of the person, he continued to believe the events of childhood were causal and formative for adulthood, and that the functioning and intrapsychic structure of the future adult was contingent on the child's progression and successful mastery of the tasks specific to each stage of development. Key to Freud's model was the concept of biological evolution where the psychic structures represent the growth and maturity of the species and of the individual.

The significance given to childhood has grown profoundly in the past century. While the "young" have always been identifiable by their physical size and body, the meanings given to these differences and that time have changed. A central meaning of childhood has been the ideology of rescue—that children were intrinsically innocent but vulnerable and needed to be rescued (Schnell, 1979). Another meaning of childhood defines it as a time for the child's needs to be met if "development" is to proceed at a smooth and orderly pace, so the child does not get "stuck" or deviate at some point along the journey, remaining a child in the guise of an adult (Walkerdine, 1984).

Childhood today has come to be defined as a surround that needs to be filled with certain types of parents, certain experiences and exposures, stimulations, milestones, medical care, proper foods, education, and much more, to be made available in a linear synchrony of events, at the right amount and duration if the child is to develop normally. These knowledges and concepts appear routinely in the familiar landscape of the present and have served as the organizing basis for the educational system, and for a proliferation of new services solely for children, such as orphanages, corrective institutions for delinquents, children's hospitals, and multiple other programs formed to aid and protect the vulnerable and dependent child. These knowledges form the backdrop to the practices of therapists and their clients, readers and writers of "self-help" manuals, policy makers, welfare workers, police officers, court personnel, teachers, historians, biographers, and many others (Urwin, 1984) and have served to legitimize the segregation, protection, discipline and regulation of those younger individuals we know as "children" (Canella, 1997; Foucault, 1977, 1978, 1980).

The "child" in western liberal democratic societies today is positioned as a special category of person who lacks, for a long time, the complete range of capacities necessary for full functioning as a citizen

(Minson, 1985) and who is defined as the other of the adult through reference to a lack of these and other adult attributes. This lack is not based in any deficiency as would be the case for an "irresponsible adult." Instead, it exists in the nature of the child as being a product of his or her biological inheritance and environmental influences, passively being buffeted by the forces in his or her life, without any individual self agency to act on his or her own behalf (Hogg & Brown, 1985). The "child" is understood to acquire those capacities by progressing steadily along a universal path of development to emerge as a self-regulating, autonomous individual, the possessor of a range of attributes, including the ability to recognize one's own best interests and to be responsible for oneself (Tyler, 1993).

Schools and Education

Mutual Relationships

Developmental theory and the field of education have been intimately involved with forming each other and simultaneously forming the object of their gaze, the "child." It was within schools, with their large numbers of children available, that developmental theory found its first objects of study, and it was these objects which became the source of data for a variety of developmental theories by such folks as Anna Freud (1965), Melanie Klein (1921–1945), Piaget (1920, 1953), Bowlby (1951), Winnicot (1958a, 1965), Mahler (1965), and Spitz (1945), to name a few.

Concomitantly, education in the Western cultures has been virtually constructed using the assumptions of the psychological and medical sciences (Pinar et al., 1995; Burman, 1994) in a context of learning, in the space concretized by schools and classrooms and within the relationship of teacher-and-student. From these assumptions a discourse of education has emerged that legitimizes the belief that science(s) has revealed what younger and older human beings are like, what we can expect from them at various ages, and how we should differentiate our treatment of them in educational settings. In this discourse, the child is constituted as lacking, as growth in motion, relative to an adult, and in need of rescue, protection, knowledge, socialization, and a space organized around his or her needs as discovered by science and developmental theory. In contrast, the older being, the adult, which in schools is often the teacher, is constituted as the one who knows, who has attained rationality, who is a living, breathing body of knowledge, with the credentials and certificates to vouch for it. There was a time when one could legitimately expect that a person who was educated had, literally, read all of the books in the world and had a foundation based on the great knowledges of the past. The teacher's job was to transmit that knowledge to students, constituting him—the teacher—as an authority and one who knows, who will determine what is knowledge, and who is to apply that knowledge to the student bodies before him. And if knowledge is the stuff of power, the teacher as holder of the knowledge also holds the power (Gore, 1998).

Communication

In pedagogical practice, communication is narrowly defined and tightly regulated; who can speak, when they can speak, what they are to speak about, and how they are to speak are all enforced as part of the order of the classroom. The teacher speaks as the powerful voice of knowledge and authority and the entire classroom, including the student bodies, is organized to facilitate hearing the teacher's voice . . . even to the degree of giving the teacher a microphone and installing speakers around the classroom.

Pedagogy has traditionally been based on the transmission model of communication which relies primarily on text, written and spoken (Lakoff & Johnson, 1980) and assumes that meaning is to be found only within the text (Carey, 1989). This model fixes and separates the roles of "sender and receiver" and is a mechanistic, linear, one-way model of communication that ascribes a secondary role to the "receiver" who is seen as passively taking in the information that has been transmitted and who is expected to communicate back in a similar linear fashion, relying on written and spoken text. The transmission model does not allow for the possibility of multiple meanings in a communication, nor does it allow for the dynamics of emotions, the irrational, desire, fantasy, sensuality, the body, the play of the unconscious and other aspects of the individual. And it does not allow for the idea that listeners actively organize and make meaning outside of the text, based on their interpretations, understandings, and experiences of what was communicated. This model strictly regulates communication and does not recognize other modes, such as those that include the body and actions of the body with the result that children who may communicate via mindbody (one word) would not be heard and these different forms of communication would be defined as something other, i.e., ranging from inappropriate behavior, to deficiencies of development and/or character pathologies and warranting intervention of some sort—discipline or treatment. If accepted at all, communications that involve the body might be relegated to classes in the performing arts.

Classification & Regulation

According to the Boston School Committee in the 1860's, a teacher's job was defined as:

> . . . taking children at random . . . undisciplined, uninstructed, often with inveterate forwardness and obstinacy, and with the inherited stupidity of centuries of ignorant ancestors, forming them from animals into intellectual beings and . . . from intellectual beings into spiritual beings, giving to many their first appreciate of what is wise, what is true, what is lovely. (Katz, 1968, p. 120)

In today's schools, this job takes place in a hierarchical class system. During the agrarian age, education was organized as the one-room schoolhouse, and in the industrial age, schooling began to conform to an assembly-line model. The processes of mental measurement, a belief in a linear stage model of development, and the assumptions and classifications of mental age worked together to produce and legitimate different forms of school provision for different ages and groups of children, informed by particular understandings of the work of Piaget. Individual students were organized into classrooms based on their chronological age and their physical bodily development, with their bodies signifying what would be found within and serving to structure the information and knowledge they were to be taught. Curriculums were predetermined and increasingly regulate what teachers are to teach. The developmental stages that had been hypothesized became regulatory and normalizing pedagogic practices (Walkerdine, 1984).

The Visible

One form of popular pedagogy, which has continued to this day, was the monitorial school based on a model of constant surveillance and ceaseless activity which would allow for regulation of the population, its moral habits, and its behavior (Jones & Williamson, 1979). The monitorial model allowed for the observation and recording of naturalized development, relying on what can be seen. The schools and schoolroom were organized so as to establish a regime of visibility in which the observed is distributed within a single common plane of sight. This plane of sight produces an organization of time and space, a spatial grid of perception where the architecture, the content and materials within, the toys and furniture . . . every object was organized to optimize the development of the existing "nature" of children (Rose, 1996). The classroom space itself came to function as a living, dynamic measurement device for the monitoring and facilitation of child development.

In this modern classroom, the teacher is positioned at the front of the classroom in full view of the seated children, illustrating the hierarchical superiority accorded his or her position and facilitating the transmission of knowledge that is supposed to take place. From this position of knowledge, authority, power, and visibility, the teacher can survey and monitor the activities taking place within the classroom space, and be seen by every child as they attend to the lessons being taught. If necessary, the teacher can intervene with the child who is behaving outside the norm, notifying the family and recommending the appropriate experts who can restore the child to the universal developmental track all children are to go down. Quoting Foucault (1977): "A relation of surveillance, defined and regulated, is inscribed at the heart of the practice of teaching, not as an additional or adjacent part, but as a mechanism that is inherent to it, and which increases its efficiency" (p. 176).

Childhood

Education was not just an apparatus to confer intellectual abilities and qualifications, but became a vital apparatus of citizenship whose purpose was to discipline the child; eliminate certain habits, and morals; compensate for the deficiencies of heredity (Riley, 1983), and the environment; and inculcate other morals deemed more desirable (Hendrick, 1990; Meyer, 1983; Rose, 1990; Walkerdine, 1984).

If the development of the child was to be found in his or her environment, in the surround that was his or her childhood, then the idea of the normal child simultaneously defined the idea of the normal family, and "normal" child-rearing practices. From this perspective, it seemed an obvious conclusion that some families were not qualified to raise the sort of healthy, well-adjusted, normal children that developmental psychology deemed possible. The education of parents and families became a goal, and the aspirations, values, and techniques of the school were to be infiltrated into the home. Mothers and families were encouraged to participate in preschool schemes, enabling them to be subtly instructed in the attitudes and responses deemed important to the development of their child. Psychological theories of cognitive development, and the designation of the "the early years" as important produced an explosion of literature which has made up some of the cult of childcare that has transformed the everyday life of the family into a complex of educational opportunities. Every aspect of the daily routine, from breakfast to bedtime, is visualized as a learning experience, promoting thought, language, perception, and creativity, optimally ordering the entire environment of the child so as to produce the normal if not exceptional child (Rose, 1996).

It has been argued that education itself has been transformed into a therapeutic enterprise and behaviors once interpreted through the lens of older codes of moral understanding, i.e., interpretations of behavior as good/bad, right/wrong have been replaced with therapeutic interpretations of behavior in terms of pathologies, disorders, dysfunctions, disabilities, and addictions (Chriss, 1999) such as that found in the DSM. And though educators are not allowed by law to practice medicine, the adjudication of a child with disorders is often done by a team which includes the parent, a teacher, a social worker, a special education teacher and the principal, raising concerns about the medicalization of educational issues (Johnson, 2000).

Attention Deficit Disorder (ADD)

The field of medicine is derived from a matrix of thought and practice which conceptualizes individual life on a continuum of health and illness, where specificable processes and attributes can be diagnosed, treated, and cured within the biological body of the person, founded on an ethic of what is rational, healthy, and normal. Psychiatry is the branch of medicine concerned with the study, treatment, and prevention of disorders of the mind, believing that the mind is a product of the development and functioning of the physical body and its organs, particularly the brain.

In the nineteenth century, a heterogeneous network of agents, sites, practices, texts, and techniques were created as part of medicine's efforts to disseminate their truth and knowledge and way of thinking about individuals. As part of this network, psychiatry has devoted much effort to legitimate itself as both a scientific enterprise and as a medical authority, given the difficulties of scientific research in linking "mental illness" to any brain lesion or dysfunction and the charges made that categories of mental illness actually represent socially devalued behaviors and ways of being (Kirk & Kutchins, 1997; Szasz, 1970; Laing, 1967). Psychiatry has created mutually beneficial relationships and associations between other fields of study such as biology, chemistry, neurology, psychology, psychoanalysis, and pedagogy and has formed numerous alliances with different societal institutions such as the judicial system, the health care industry, the pharmaceutical industry, the government and the military, as well as the educational system. In the connections between these diverse elements, practices, and surfaces that make up the field of medicine, space is made for medical truth and practice, as well as for the human beings that medicine concerns itself with. The objects of medicine, the patient, do not merely exist, sickly and mutely awaiting its attention, they are formed by differentiation, and produced within the elements that make up this network.

The primary text of psychiatry is the *Diagnostic and Statistical Manual* (DSM) (APA, 1998), which represents the current scientific knowledge and understanding of mental illness, defined as a manifestation of a behavioral, psychological, or biological dysfunction in the individual. In 1952, the first *Diagnostic and Statistical Manual of Mental Disorders* (APA, 1952) was published and contained some 50 to 60 different psychogenic disturbances in 106 categories. DSM II witnessed the addition of 76 additional new diagnostic categories. DSM III, in response to challenges and criticisms that its classifications lacked validity, broke with the tradition of using psychoanalytically based diagnoses and adopted a scientifically based system of diagnosis which included "explicit diagnostic criteria, a multiaxial system, and a descriptive approach that attempted to be neutral with respect to theories of etiology" hoping to shift attention away from the concerns of validity. The DSM continues to scrutinize its diagnoses, dropping those considered no longer relevant, and adding others. In its most recent version, the DSM IV–R contains over 300 diagnostic categories and classifications, and in the first year, brought in over 18 million dollars in revenue for the American Psychiatric Association (Kirk & Kutchins, 1997).

The Past–Attention Deficit Disorder (ADD)

Attention Deficit Disorder was originally offered as a diagnosis with the publication of DSM III in 1980. In the 1940s, brain disease or damage came to be associated with behavioral pathology, an idea that later evolved into the concept of minimal brain damage (MBD) in the 1950s and 1960s. Though there was no documentation or evidence, it became fashionable to consider most children hospitalized in psychiatric facilities who were active or inattentive, to have suffered from some type of brain damage. At this time, hyperactivity was considered to be a behavioral syndrome recognized chiefly by greater than normal levels of activity, was not necessarily associated with demonstrable brain pathology or mental retardation, and was considered to be relatively common and benign. The concept of a hyperactive child syndrome (Laufer & Denhoff, 1957; Chess, 1960) was first defined in the DSM II published in 1968 (American Psychiatric Association, 1968).

In the 1970s, Virginia Douglas (1972) at McGill University argued that hyperactive children had some of their greatest difficulties on tasks assessing sustained attention such as the Continuous Performance Task (CPT). Dr. Douglas and the research published by her team at McGill University (Douglas, 1980a, 1980b, 1983; Douglas & Peters, 1979) were very influential in the disorder being renamed Attention Deficit Disorder when the third version of DSM was published in 1980 (American Psychiatric Association, 1980).

In the 1980s, a great deal of research was conducted on the etiology of ADD. Brain damage as an etiological explanation was reduced to a minor role, although the development or lack of development of other brain mechanisms such as underarousal, neurotransmitter deficiencies (Wender, 1971), and neurological immaturity (Kinsbourne, 1977) were being explored. Several studies on cerebral blood flow revealed patterns of underactivity in the prefrontal areas of the CNS and the limbic system (Lou et al., 1984; Lou et al., 1989). Others looked for deficiencies in dopamine, and norepinephrine as explanations for patterns of brain underactivity (Hunt, Cohen, Anderson & Minderaa, 1988; Rapoport & Zametkin, 1988; Shaywitz, Shaywitz, Cohen & Young, 1983; Shekim, Glaser, Horwitz, Javaid & Dylund, 1987).

In the 1990s, neuroimaging research proposed that ADHD children suffered from frontal lobe or executive dysfunction (Barkley, 1997b; Barkley et al., 1992; Goodyear & Hynd, 1992). One study used Positron Emission Tests (PET) to detect states of brain activity and its localization within the cerebral hemispheres. Results indicated significantly reduced brain metabolic activity in adults diagnosed with ADHD (Zametkin, 1990), though it has never been possible to replicate these results. Another study used Magnetic Resonance Imaging (MRI) to evaluate brain structures in children given the diagnosis of ADHD and found that those children, at that time, had abnormally smaller anterior cortical regions and they lacked "normal" right-left frontal asymmetry (Hynd, Semrud-Clikeman, Lorys, Novey & Eliopulis, 1990). It was thought that these studies were evidence of the structural differences in the brain that underlie this disorder.

The Present—Attention Deficit Hyperactivity Disorder (ADHD)

The DSM III was revised to reflect the emphasis on empirical validation of its diagnostic criteria, and ADD was renamed Attention Deficit Hyperactivity Disorder. According to Russell Barkley, a leading expert, these diagnostic categories with somewhat different terms and criteria refer to children sufficiently similar such that clinical generalities can be drawn about them even though the research may have involved any one of the related diagnoses over the years. The current definition of this disorder is: ". . . a persistent pattern of inattention and/or hyperactivity-impulsivity that is more frequent and severe than is typically observed in individuals at a comparable level of development. . ." (1994). Additionally, the child must present with a sufficient number of symptoms in two areas of behavior: inattention and hyperactivity. The symptoms of inattention and/or hyperactivity must have persisted for at least six months to a degree that is maladaptive and inconsistent with developmental level. And these symptoms that have caused impairment must be present before the age of seven years. Impairment occurs when there is clear evidence of interference with developmentally appropriate social, academic, or occupational functioning.

These diagnostic criteria have been primarily derived from empirical research and are some of the most rigorous in the history of this disorder. It was estimated that by 1979, more than 2000 studies existed on this disorder (Weiss & Hechtman, 1979) and this figure has likely doubled if not tripled in the past 20 years. The research, looking into all aspects and variants of ADD and ADHD has been largely unable to substantiate the diagnosis, its symptoms, and/or its proposed etiologies.

The defining and essential feature, inattention, has required some imagination to operationally define, with there being no agreed upon definition (Douglas & Peters, 1979). An increasing number of studies have failed to find consistent evidence of problems with attention (Douglas, 1983, 1988; Barkley, 1984; Draeger et al., 1986; Rosenthal & Allen, 1978; Sergeant, 1988; Sergeant & van der Meere, 1989; van der Meere & Sergeant, 1988a, 1988b) and in general find these children to be no more distractible than normal children of the same age and gender (Campbell, Douglas & Morgenstern, 1971; Cohen, Weiss & Minde, 1972). Moreover, if attention was conceptualized as involving the perception, filtering, and processing of information, no substantial evidence has been found for any such deficits. Summarizing, attentional deficits as a criteria and symptom do not distinguish children receiving the diagnosis from other children.

The second defining area of symptomatology, per the DSM, is hyperactivity-impulsivity, where the child demonstrates excessive or developmentally inappropriate levels of activity including restlessness, fidgeting, and other unnecessary gross bodily movements (Luk, 1985; Still, 1902; Porrino et al., 1983; Teicher, Ito, Glod & Barber, 1996). Studies using objective measures and/or behavior ratings have not been able to substantiate hyperactivity as a separate factor or dimension. Problems of impulsivity have sometimes been scientifically defined as a pattern of rapid, inaccurate responding to tasks (Brown & Quay, 1977), or poor sustained inhibition of responding (Barkley, 1997a; Gordon, 1979), poor delay of gratification (Campbell, 1987; Rapport, Tucker, DuPaul, Merlo & Stoner, 1986), or difficulties regulating or inhibiting behavior in social contexts (Barkley, 1985; Kindlon et al., 1995). Studies that have factor analyzed ratings of impulsive behavior mixed in with ratings of inattention and overactivity (Achenbach & Edelbrock, 1983; DuPaul, 1991; DuPaul, Anastopoulos et al., 1997) have failed to differentiate a separate impulsivity dimension.

Typically for a disorder to be viewed as a syndrome, its major features should be related. Objective measures of ADD symptoms do not correlate well with each (Barkely, 1991; Barkley & Ullman, 1975; Routh & Roberts, 1972; Ullman et al., 1978). And the defining features of ADD do not discriminate ADD from other types of psychiatric disturbance in children. Additionally the primary symptoms of ADD show significant fluctuations across various settings and caregivers (Barkley, 1981b; Zentall, 1985), varying by the environmental demands, the particular parent involved, the repetition of instructions, the degree of novelty and task stimulation, the magnitude of consequences, the time of day, etc. The disorder is more likely to be diagnosed in North America and treated with medication, than in Europe where it is viewed as uncommon. And the individual symptoms of ADD can be found in a large percentage of normal children (Lapouse & Monk, 1958).

Thousands of studies have failed to substantiate the deficit of attention and hyperactivity that comprise the symptomatology of the ADD/ADHD diagnosis (Reeves, Werry, Elkind & Zametkin, 1987; Werry, Elkind & Reeves, 1987) and there are efforts underway to redefine and reconceptualize the disorder to explain the lack of findings. Russell Barkley (1997), in his most recent book, argues for a new model of ADD/ADHD defined as a behavioral disorder with a deficiency in response inhibition, derived from an understanding of normal child development. Using the "normal" curve, 14 percent of the population would meet this new definition of hyperactivity (DuPaul, 1991). Others feel the criteria should be rewritten, lowering the age of onset to younger than age seven years, and including different items as a criterion (Glow & Glow, 1979; Rosenthal & Allen, 1978; Sroufe, 1975).

Summary

Developmental theories can be understood as a modern, Western construction, which have been pushed from their intended status as descriptions into normalizing prescriptions, providing a powerful discourse that has played a fundamental role in the creation of the kind of present in which we in the Western cultures have come to live, ordering our attention such as to create a regime of visibility where certain aspects of the world have been made visible and amenable to thought and action per the systems of knowledge and truth that have become part of that discourse. In the view of developmental theory, if one looks where directed, one will find order (a certain world order, and a certain ordering of the world) and one will participate in that order by looking at and only seeing what one has been told is there.

In this discourse, the "child" (in quotes) has been formed by development theory as a certain category of individual who is a product of his or her biological stage, defined by features of his or her physical body, representing a historical accretion of the "real" events and people of his or her past and present environment which have directly determined his or her shape in the present and in the future, and whose growth will proceed in a mechanistic fashion along a universal path of development. In this discourse, the environment is of critical importance in producing a child who is developing properly and the very idea of childhood developed as one way to represent the environmental surround of the child, and the complex elements and dynamics that are to take place—including but not limited to the family (Tyler, 1993), the home, education, health/medical care, etc., and the synchrony of these elements so as to create the milieu thought necessary for proper development.

In theory, the properly developing child would achieve control over his or her passions through the steady acquisition of language as the appropriate vehicle for the expression of wishes and the resolution of conflicts. Along-side rationality, the properly developing child would move steadily toward total independence by taking every opportunity to exercise greater control and autonomy without the need for coercion. The child's continued growth and accomplishments would be evidenced in their compliance and obedience to the rules imposed by adults, whether involving the body and its actions from raising one's hand, to remaining in one's seat, or whether it involves the mind and its control over such things as thoughts, feelings, or attention.

Education has become a major component of the childhood environment, becoming the mandated, legally required space that children will spend up to 70 percent of the calendar year attending and over 50 percent of their waking hours participating in, displacing the family as the primary architect of the surround of the child. In the environmental space of the schoolroom, developmental theory has created a regime of visibility where attention is directed to and focused on certain differences that, in the order of things, have come to mean disorder and abnormality. Per this view, in a dynamic complex of events taking place in a schoolroom with the children and the adult, the teacher, the behaviors of some children can become classified as symptomatic of a psychiatric disorder such as ADD.

As the child is first a biological being, per developmental theory, ADD represents bio-physiological development that is abnormal, and deviant, a disorder, signifying that the child has not mastered control of him or herself, and his or her body or mind and its ability to attend where ordered to, for the duration. Quick interventions are imperative so as to restore the child to the normal, universal developmental track, and it seems that biochemical treatments such as Ritalin, have become so popular, in part, due to the promise by pharmaceutical companies of a simple and quick treatment intervention that will restore the biochemical deficiencies the symptomatic behavior is thought to represent.

Yet, as reviewed and presented earlier, thousands of empirical studies attempting to substantiate scientifically the clinical profile of ADD/ADHD from its etiology, to its prevalence, to its presentation, to effective treatments, have been unsuccessful. To quote from the National Institutes of Health recent Consensus Development Conference Statement on the Diagnosis and Treatment of Attention Deficit Hyperactivity Disorder:

> "Finally, after years of clinical research and experience with ADHD, our knowledge about the cause or causes remains largely speculative . . . as of yet there is no independent valid test. . . ." And they go on to say that it has yet to be firmly established as a brain disorder.

Different Perspectives

A discourse and its truths are continually contested as competing discourses make visible and focus attention on what had been separated and marginalized by the dominant views, that which disturbs the nicely ordered present as we know it. In recent years, as attention has shifted outside of modernistic philosophies and understandings of the world, there has been a critical rethinking of the regime of truth imposed by developmental theory, including the sort of individual it makes visible and identifies as a child, as well as certain ways of knowing, being, living, communicating, and learning as a child that have been privileged as desirable within the space called normal, marginalizing other ways as abnormal and often inferior in the hierarchy of developmental progress. A regime of truth that has gone so far as to impose an ordering of a child's thoughts and attention such that the focus and duration of his or her attention is to be regulated, measured, and like others. Even within psychoanalysis with its particularly detailed and vivid developmental model (Schwartz, 1999), there has begun a rethinking of theory, philosophy, and practice which does not rely on a hierarchical, linear development that would be universal to everyone (Academy for the Study of the Psychoanalytic Arts website).

The answers to such epistemological questions as "What constitutes knowledge? What does the body symbolize? What is language? What is communication? are no longer being answered solely by traditional theories of development based on modernist beliefs that assume predetermined truth and progress (Canella, 1997). Previously, relying upon the visible, physical body as a signifier of an interior knowledge and rationality, some individuals (those with larger, older bodies) were defined as having knowledge based on the belief that time inevitably brings with it change, growth, and other desired attributes such as wisdom. Per developmental theory, those defined by their bodies as adult were granted a privileged status of having a voice, knowledge, wisdom, and rationality. Others, in this case, the child (often defined by their smaller, younger bodies), were defined as having no voice (though often making loud sounds), no knowledge, and being irrational, primitive, and immature. In the educational systems of the Western cultures, what constitutes Knowledge has often been narrowed to what can be demonstrated in a recitation, and what can be communicated verbally and textually with a worded language. Knowledge communicated in other ways has been ignored or perceived as a lack, representing a failure of education, of development, and of parenting.

There has been a growing recognition of the validity as well as the complexity of other forms of human communication, the many and diverse modes of communication that do not rely on words, for example, sound, movement, silence, rhythm, the body, the gaze, attention, where symbolic representation and communication take place in such a way as to not privilege the word over the action, the mind over the body, the sound over silence. The complexities and integrity of the language and myriad other forms of communication that "children" do use, that may not be expressed through the dominant/adult form of language, are being recognized, including the idea that the body and the body as language can be a powerful mode of communication, in size, in activity, in motion, in timespace. The body and its activities can also be an instrument of learning rather than simply being marginalized as a failure of communication, of regression, evidence of a developmental delay, or a deficiency. It is being understood that bodies are more than a biophysiological object, traditionally important for housing the center of rationality, the brain, and to be trained, managed, controlled, disciplined, and dominated.

There has been much public debate over the past two decades about the myth or reality behind the label "ADD" and now "ADHD." Those who dispute the validity of the diagnosis often do so on the grounds that it represents nothing but a Procrustean means of controlling authentic, if troublesome expressions of individuality (West Australian, June 22, 1996, p. 9). Some believe the diagnosis is no more than a political artifact of social control a "de facto agent of the status quo" (Conrad, 1975; McGinnis, 1997; Schrag & Divoky, 1975). And others believe that ADD and the raft of medications being marketed as a biochemical treatment of the disorder represent the success of the medical network in inserting and privileging its perspectives in the Western cultures, in particular within the institution of education.

Given that truth is always contested it may be that the growing dissatisfaction with developmental theory may allow these different perspectives to become more visible and available in the discourse at large, reducing the dominance of developmental theory in constituting the child along the continuum of normal and abnormal, ordered and disordered. And though the research on Attention Deficit Hyperactivity Disorder will likely continue to expand, representing the advancement of the discourse of science and medicine, perhaps there can be a different ordering of attention so that the multiple and diverse ways in which the individual lives, signifies, and organizes his or her world and truths can be heard and responded to as something other than a disorder warranting treatment and regulation.

As a closing note, it is important to realize that the professions, particularly the helping professions, have been a driving force in advancing the discourse of developmental theory, both as part of their professional identity and in part to create the object and focus of their professional practice. The teaching professions in alliance with the psych disciplines have worked closely together in organizing the understanding of the "child" and in organizing the classroom space within which the child is to learn per developmental theory and the discipline it imposes on the being of a child. The discourse of the professions spoken through this theory has functionally disciplined the child to fit within the space of the normal and otherwise risk the force of discipline when found within the space of the abnormal, such as with those children who have been diagnosed with ADD.

REFERENCES

Academy for the Study of the Psychoanalytic Arts, www.academyanalyticarts.org.

Achenbach, T., & Edelbrock, C. (1983). Empirically based assessment of the behavioral/emotional problems of 2- and 3-year-old children. *Journal of Abnormal Child Psychology, 15.*629–650.

Allen, G. (1978). *Life sciences in the twentieth century.* Cambridge: Cambridge University Press, 1978.

American Psychiatric Association. (1952). *Diagnostic and statistical manual for mental disorders* (1st ed.). Washington, DC: American Psychiatric Association.

American Psychiatric Association. (1968). *Diagnostic and statistical manual of mental disorders* (2nd ed.) (DSM-II). author: Washington, DC.

American Psychiatric Association. (1980). *Diagnostic and statistical manual of mental disorders* (3rd ed.) (DSM-III). author: Washington, DC.

American Psychiatric Association. (1994). *Diagnostic and statistical manual of mental disorders* (4th ed.) (DSM-IV). author: Washington, DC.

Aries, P. (1962). *Centuries of childhood.* Harmondsworth: Penguin.

Armstrong, T. (1996). ADD: Does it really exist? *Phi Delta Kappan,* February.

Ashplant, T., & Wilson, A. (1988). Present-centred history and the problem of historical knowledge. *The Historical Journal, 31*(2): 253–274.

Barkley, R., Grodzinsky, G., & DuPaul, G. (1992). Frontal lobe functions in attention deficit disorder with and without hyperactivity: A review and research report. *Journal of Abnormal Child Psychology, 20,* 163–188.

Barkley, R., & Ullman, D. (1975). A comparison of objective measures of activity level and distractibility in hyperactive and nonhyperactive children. *Journal of Abnormal Child Psychology,* 213–244.

Barkley, R. (1981b). Hyperactivity. In E.J. Mash & L.G. Terdal (Eds.), *Behavioral assessment of childhood disorders.* New York: Guilford Press.

Barkley, R. (1984). *Do as we say, not as we do: The problem of stimulus control and rule-governed behavior in attention deficit disorder with hyperactivity.* Paper presented at the Highpoint Hospital Conference on Attention Deficit and Conduct Disorders, Toronto, Canada.

Barkley, R. (1985). The social interactions of hyperactive children: Developmental changes, drug effects, and situational variation. In R. McMahon & R. Peters (Eds.), *Childhood disorders: Behavioral-developmental approaches*, New York: Brunner/Mazel.

Barkley, R. (1991). The ecological validity of laboratory and analogue assessments of ADHD symptoms. *Journal of Abnormal Child Psychology, 19,* 149–178.

Barkley, R. (1997a). Inhibition, sustained attention, and executive functions: Constructing a unifying theory of ADHD. *Psychological Bulletin, 121,* 65–94.

Barkley, R. (1997b). *ADHD and the nature of self-control.* New York: Guildford Press.

Barkley, R. (1998). *Attention-deficit hyperactivity disorder: A handbook for diagnosis and treatment* (2nd ed.). New York: Guilford Press.

Baughman, F. Essays, articles and other information pertaining to the fraud of attention deficit hyperactivity disorder (ADHD). http://www.adhdfraud.org/about-fred.htm.

Benton, E. (1974–1975). Vitalism in nineteenth century scientific thought. A typology and reassessment. *Studies in the History and Philosophy of Science, 5*(1), 17–28.

Bowlby, J. (1951). *Maternal care and mental health.* Geneva: World Health Organization.

Breggin, P.R. (2000). Testimony before the U.S. House of Representatives Subcommittee on Oversight and Investigations hearing entitled "Behavioral Drugs in Schools: Questions and Concerns" September 29, 2000, www.house.gov/ed_workforce/hearings/106th/oi/ritalin92900/breggin.htm.

Brown R.T., & Quay, H.C. (1977). Reflection-impulsivity of normal and behavior-disordered children. *Journal of Abnormal Child Psychology, 5,* 457–462.

Burman, E. (1994). *Deconstructing developmental psychology.* London: Routledge.

Canella, G.S. (1997). The scientific discourse of education: Predetermining the lives of others–Foucault, education, and children. *Contemporary Issues in Early Childhood, 1*(1), 36–44.

Carey, J.: *Communication as culture.* New York: Routledge.

Campbell, S. (1987). Parent-referred problem three-year-olds: Developmental changes in symptoms. *Journal of Child Psychology and Psychiatry, 28,* 835–846.

Campbell, S., Douglas, V., & Morgenstern, G. (1971). Cognitive styles in hyperactive children and the effect of methylphenidate. *Journal of Child Psychology and Psychiatry, 12,* 55–67.

Chess, S. (1960). Diagnosis and treatment of the hyperactive child. *New York State Journal of Medicine, 60,* 2379–2385.

Chriss, J.L. (1999). *Counseling and the therapeutic state.* New York: Aldine de Gruyter.

Cohen, N., Weiss, G., & Minde, K. (1972). Cognitive styles in adolescents previously diagnosed as hyperactive. *Journal of Child Psychology and Psychiatry, 12,* 203–209.

Coleman, W. (1977). *Biology in the nineteenth century. problems of form, function and transformation.* Cambridge: Cambridge University Press.

Cory, E.A. (1834). *The physical and medical management of children, adapted for general perusal.*

Darwin, C. (1877). A biographical sketch of an infant. *Mind, 2,* 285–294.

Department of Health and Human Services. (2001). *Attention-deficit/hyperactivity disorder in children and adolescents.* Fact Sheet. Washington, DC: Department of Health and Human Services.

Diagnosis and treatment of attention deficit hyperactivity disorder. NIH consensus Statement, Nov 16–18; 16 (2): 1–37, 1998.

Douglas, V. (1972). Stop, look, and listen: The problem of sustained attention and impulse control in hyperactive and normal children. *Canadian Journal of Behavioral Science, 4,* 259–282.

Douglas, V. (1980a). Higher mental processes in hyperactive children: Implications for training. In R. Knights & D. Bakker (Eds.), *Treatment of hyperactive and learning disordered children.* Baltimore: University Park Press.

Douglas, V. (1980b). Treatment and training approaches to hyperactivity: Establishing internal or external control. In C. Whalen & B. Henker (Eds.), *Hyperactive children: The social ecology of identification and treatment,* New York: Academic Press.

Douglas, V. (1983). Attention and cognitive problems. In M. Rutter (Ed.), *Developmental neuro-psychiatry.* New York: Guilford Press.

Douglas, V. (1988). Cognitive deficits in children with attention deficit disorder with hyperactivity. In L.M. Bloomingdale & J.A. Sergeant (Eds.), *Attention deficit disorder: Criterian, cognition, intervention.* London: Pergamon Press.

Douglas, V., & Peters, K. (1979). Toward a clearer definition of the attentional deficit of hyperactive children. In G.A. Hale & M. Lewis (Eds.), *Attention and the developments of cognitive skills.* New York: Plenum.

Draeger, S., Prior, M., & Sanson, A. (1998). Visual and auditory attention performance in hyperactive children: Competence or compliance. *Journal of Abnormal Child Psychology, 14*(3), 411–424.

DuPaul, G. (1991).Parent and teacher ratings of ADHD symptoms: Psychometric properties in a community-based sample. *Journal of Clinical Child Psychology, 20,* 242–253.

DuPaul, G., Anastopoulos, A., Power, T., Reid, R., Ikeda, M., & McGoey, K. (1997). Parent ratings of attention-deficit/hyperactivity disorder symptoms: Factor structure, normative data, and psychometric properties. *Psychological Assessment, 9,* 436–444.

Ferrari, L. (1999). Psychoanalytic considerations regarding attention deficit syndrome. *Journal for the Psychoanalysis of Culture & Society, 4*(2).

Figlio, K.M. (1967). The metaphor of organisation. An historical perspective on the bio-medical sciences of the early nineteenth century. *History of Science, 14,* 17–53.

Forster, M. (1885). *Encyclopaedia Britannica* (9th ed.). Edinburgh: Adam & Charles Black, 19, p. 12.

Foucault, M. (1972). *The archaeology of knowledge* (translated by A.M. Sheridan Smith). New York: Pantheon Books.

Foucault, M. (1977). *Discipline and punishment.* London: Allen Lane.

Foucault, M. (1978). *The history of sexuality* (Vols I–III). New York: Pantheon

Foucault, M. (1980). The politics of health in the eighteenth century. In M. Foucault, *Power/knowledge: Selected interviews and other writings, 1972–1977.* Brighton: Harvester.

Freud, A. (1965). *The writings of Anna Freud: Vol. 6. Normality and psychopathology in childhood: Assessments of development.* New York: International Universities Press.

Glow, P., & Glow, R. (1979). Hyperkinetic impulse disorder: A developmental defect of motivation. *Genetic Psychological Monographs, 100*, 159–231.

Goodyear, P., & Hynd, G. (1992). Attention deficit disorder with (ADD/H) and without (ADD/WO) hyperactivity: Behavioral and neuropsychological differentiation. *Journal of Clinical Child Psychology, 21*, 273–304.

Gordon, M. (1979). The assessment of impulsivity and mediating behaviors in hyperactive and non-hyperactive children. *Journal of Abnormal Child Psychology, 7*, 317–326.

Gore, J. (1998). Disciplining bodies: On the continuity of power relations in pedagogy. In T.S. Popkewitz & M. Brennan (Eds.), *Foucault's challenge discourse, knowledge, and power in education.*

Hendrick, H. (1990). Constructions and reconstructions of British childhood: An interpretive survey, 1800 to present. In A. James & A. Prout (Eds.), *Constructing and reconstructing childhood: Contemporary issues in the sociological study of childhood.* Basingstoke: Hants: Falmer.

Hogg, R., & Brown, D. (1985). Reforming juvenile justice: Issues and prospects. In J. Murray & A. Borowski (Eds.), *Juvenile delinquency in Australia.* London.

Hoyles, M., & Evans, P. (1989). *The politics of childhood.* London: Journeyman Press.

Hunt, R.D., Cohen, D.J., Anderson, G., & Minderaa, R.B. (1988). Noradrengergic mechanisms in ADDH. In L. Bloomingdale (Ed.), *Attention deficit disorder. Vol. 3: New research in attention, treatment and psychopharmacology.* New York: Pergamon Press.

Hynd, G., Semrud-Clikeman, M., Lorys, A., Novey, E., & Eliopulis, D. (1990). Brain morphology in developmental dyslexia and attention deficit disorder/hyperactivity. *Archives of Neurology, 47* 919–926.

Jacyna, L.S (1984). The romantic programme and the reception of cell theory in Britain. *Journal of the History of Biology, 17*(1), 13–48. Quoting G. Valentin, Handbuch der Entwickelungsgeschichte des Menchen (Guide to the History of the Development of Human Beings), Berlin: Rucker, 1835.

James, W. (1981). *The principles of psychology.* Cambridge, MA: Harvard University Press (originally published 1890).

Johnson, P. (2000). Testimony before the U.S. House of Representatives Subcommittee on Oversight and Investigations hearing entitled *"Behavioral Drugs in Schools: Questions and Concerns"* September 29, 2000, www.house.gov/ed_workforce/hearings/106th/oi/ritalin92900/johnson.htm.

Jones, K., & Williamson, J. (1979). Birth of the schoolroom. *Ideology and Consciousness, 6*, 59–110.

Katz, B. (1968). *The irony of early school reform: Educational innovation in mid-nineteenth century Massachusetts.* Cambridge, MA: Harvard University Press.

Kindlon, D., Mezzacappa, E., & Earls, F. (1995). Psychometric properties of impulsivity measures: Temporal stability, validity and factor structure. *Journal of Child Psychology and Psychiatry, 35*, 645–661.

Kinsbourne, M. (1977). The mechanism of hyperactivity. In M. Blau, I. Rapin, & M. Kinsbourne (Eds.), *Topics in child neurology.* New York: Spectrum.

Kirk S.A., & Kutchins, H. (1997). *Making us crazy: The psychiatric bible and the creation of mental disorders.* New York: Free Press.

Klein, M. (1921–1945). (1948). *Contributions to psychoanalysis.* London: Hogarth.

Laing, R.D. (1967). *The politics of experience.* New York: Ballantine Books.

Lakoff, G., & Johnson, M. (1980). *Metaphors we live by.* Chicago: University of Chicago Press.

Lapouse, R., & Monk, M. (1958). An epidemiological study of behavior characteristics in children. *American Journal of Public Health, 48,* 1134–1144.

Laufer, M., & Denhoff, E. (1957). Hyperkinetic impulse disorder in children's behavior problems. *Psychosomatic Medicine, 19,* 38–49.

Laurence, J., & McCallum, D. (1998). The myth-or-reality of attention-deficit disorder: A genealogical approach. *Discourse: Studies in the Cultural Politics of Education, 19*(2).

Lenoir, T. (1982). The strategy of life, teleology and mechanism in nineteenth century German biology. Dordrecht: Reidel.

Lou, H.C., Henrisksen, L., & Bruhn, P. (1984). Focal cerebral hypoperfusion in children with dysphasia and/or attention deficit disorder. *Archives of Neurology, 41,* 825–829.

Lou, H.C., Henriksen, L., Bruhn, P., Borner, H., & Nielsen, J.B. (1989). Striatal dysfunction in attention deficit and hyperkinetic disorder. *Archives of Neurology, 46,* 48–52.

Luk, S. (1985). Direct observations, studies of hyperactive behaviors. *Journal of the American Academy of Child and Adolescent Psychiatry, 24,* 338–344.

Mahler, M. (1965). On the significance of the normal separation-individuation phase. In M. Schur, *Drives, Affects, and Behavior,* (2nd ed.). New York: International Universities Press.

Meyer, P. (1983). *The child and the state: The intervention of the state in the family.* Cambridge: Cambridge University Press.

Minson, J. (1985). *Genealogies of morals, Nietzsche, Foucault, Donzelot and the eccentricity of ethics.* London.

Diagnosis and treatment of attention deficit hyperactivity disorder. National Institutes of Health, Consensus Statement Online 1998, November 16-18; 16(2): 1–37. (http://odp.od.nih.gov/consensus/cons/110/110_statement.htm).

Partridge, G. (1912). *Genetic philosophy of education: An epitome of the published educational writings of President G. Stanley Hall of Clark University.* New York: Sturgis & Walton.

Piaget, J. (1920). (1977). Psychoanalysis and its relations with child psychology. In H. Gruber & J.J. Voneche (Eds.), *The Essential Piaget.* London: Routledge & Kegan Paul.

Piaget, J. (1953). *The origin of intelligence in the child.* London: Routledge & Kegan Paul.

Pinar, W., Reynolds, W., Slattery, P., & Taubman, P. (1995). *Understanding curriculum: An introduction to the study of historical and contemporary curriculum discourses.* New York: Peter Lang.

Porrino, L.J., Rapoport, J.L., Behar, D., Sceery, W., Ismond, D., & Bunney, Jr., W. (1983). A naturalistic assessment of the motor activity of hyperactive boys. *Archives of General Psychiatry, 40,* 681–687.

Rapoport, J.L., & Zametkin, A. (1988). Drug treatment of attention deficit disorder. In L. Bloomingdale & J. Sergeant (Eds.), *Attention deficit disorder: Criteria, cognition, and intervention.* New York: Pergamon Press.

Rapport, M., Tucker, S., DuPaul, G., Merlo M., & Stoner, G. (1986). Hyperactivity and frustration: The influence of control over and size of rewards in delaying gratification. *Journal of Abnormal Child Psychology, 14,* 181–204.

Reeves, J., Werry, J., Elkind, G., & Zametkin, A. (1987). Attention deficit, conduct, oppositional, and anxiety disorders in children: II. Clinical characteristics. *Journal of the American Academy of Child and Adolescent Psychiatry, 26,* 133–143.

Riley, D. (1983). *War in the nursery: Theories of the child and the mother.* London: Virago.

Routh, D., & Roberts, R. (1972). Minimal brain dysfunction in children: Failure to find evidence for a behavioral syndrome. *Psychological Reports, 31,* 307–314.

Rose, N. (1996). *Inventing our selves psychology, power and personhood.* New York: Cambridge University Press.

Rose, N. (1999). *Governing the soul: The shaping of the private self* (2nd ed.). London: Free Association Books.

Rosenthal, R., & Allen, T. (1978). An examination of attention, arousal, and learning dysfunctions of hyperkinetic children. *Psychological Bulletin, 85,* 689–715.

Schrag, P., & Divoky, D. (1975). *The myth of the hyperactive child and other means of child control.* New York: Pantheon Books.

Schnell, R.L. (1979). Childhood as ideology: A reinterpretation of the common school. *British Journal of Educational Studies, 27.*

Schwartz, D. (1999). The temptations of normality: Reappraising psychoanalytic theories of sexual development. *Psychoanalytic Psychology, 16* (4), 554–564.

Sergeant, J. (1988). From DSM-III attentional deficit disorder to functional defects. In L. Bloomingdale & J. Sergeant (Eds.), *Attention deficit disorder: Criteria, cognition, and intervention.* New York: Pergamon Press.

Sergeant, J., & van der Meere, J. (1989). Toward an empirical child psychopathology. In D.K. Routh (Ed.), *Disruptive behavior disorders in children.* New York: Plenum.

Shaywitz, S.E., Shaywitz, B.A., Cohen D.J., & Young, J.G. (1983). Monoaminergic mechanisms in hyperactivity. In M. Rutter (Ed.), *Developmental neuropsychiatry.* New York: Guilford Press.

Shekim, W.O., Glaser, E., Horwitz, E., Javaid, J., & Dylund, D.B. (1987). Psychoeducational correlates of catecholamine metabolites in hyperactive children. In L. Bloomingdale (Ed.), *Attention deficit disorder: New research in attention, treatment, and osychopharmacology,* 3. New York: Pergamon Press.

Spitz, R. (1945). Hospitalism: An inquiry into the genesis of psychiatric conditions in early childhood. *Psychoanalytic Study of the Child, 1,* 53–72.

Sroufe, L. (1975). Drug treatment of children with behavior problems. In F. Horowitz (Ed.), *Review of child development research.* Chicago: University of Chicago Press.

Steedman, C. (1995). *Strange dislocations, childhood and the idea of human interiority 1780–1930.* Cambridge, MA: Harvard University Press.

Still, G. (1902). Some abnormal psychical conditions in children', *Lancet*, 1008–1012, 1163–1168.

Szasz, T. (1970). *The manufacture of madness*. New York: Harper & Row.

Teicher, M., Ito, Y., Glod, C., & Barker, N. (1996). Objective measurement of hyperactivity and additional problems in ADHD. *Journal of the American Academy of Child and Adolescent Psychiatry, 35,* 334–342.

Tyler, D. (1993). Making better children. In D. Meredyth & D. Tyler (Eds.), *Child and citizen genealogies of schooling and subjectivity*. Institute for Cultural Policy Studies, Faculty of Humanities, Griffith University;.

Ullman, D., Barkley, R., & Brown, H. (1978). The behavioral symptoms of hyperkinetic Children who successfully responded to stimulant drug treatment. *American journal of Orthopsychiatry, 48,* 425–437.

Urwin, C. (1988). Power relations and the emergence of language. In J. Henriques, W. Hollway, C. Urwin, C. Venn, & V. Walkerdine (Eds.), *Changing the subject psychology, social regulation and subjectivity*. London: Routledge, Reissue.

van der Meere, J., & Sergeant, J. (1988). Focused attention in pervasively hyperactive children. *Journal of Abnormal Child Psychology, 16,* 627–640.

van der Meere, J., & Sergeant, J. (1988b). Controlled processing and vigilance in hyperactivity: time will tell. *Journal of Abnormal Child Psychology, 16,* 641–656.

Walkerdine, V. (1984). Some day my prince will come. In M. Nava & A. McRobbie (Eds.), *Gender and generation*. London: Macmillan.

Walkerdine, V. (1998). Developmental psychology and the child-centred pedagogy: The insertion of Piaget into early education. In J. Henriques, W. Hollway, C. Urwin, C. Venn, & V. Walkerdine (Eds.), *Changing the subject psychology, social regulation and subjectivity*. London: Routledge, Reissue.

Weiss, G., & Hechtman, L. (1979). The hyperactive child syndrome. *Science, 205,* 1348–1354.

Wender, P. (1971). *Minimal brain dysfunction*. New York: Wiley.

Werry, J., Elkind, G., & Reeves, J. (1987). Attention deficit, conduct, oppositional, and anxiety disorders in children: III. Laboratory differences. *Journal of Abnormal Child Psychology, 15,* 409–428.

Winnicott, D. (1958a). *Collected papers*. New York: Basic Books.

Winnicott, D. (1965). *The maturational processes and the facilitating environment*. New York: International Universities Press.

Zametkin, A., Nordahl, T., Gross, M., King, A., Semple, W., Rumsey, J., Hamburger, S., & Cohen, R. (1990). Cerebral glucose metabolism in adults with hyperactivity of childhood onset. *New England Journal of Medicine, 323,* 1361–1366.

Zentall, S.S. (1985). A context for hyperactivity. In K.D. Gadow & I. Bialer (Eds.), *Advances in learning and behavioral disabilities*. Greenwich, CT: JAI Press.

Chapter 3

VICTOR'S AFTERLIFE: REINSCRIBING THE WILD CHILD IN THE HISTORY OF THE SCIENCES OF CHILDHOOD

ADRIANA S. BENZAQUÉN

> Given the time in history, an almost nonexistent knowledge base with regard to educational practice, and total ignorance of "Victor's" origins, Itard's work is nothing short of remarkable and profound. In its entirety it is a statement for all special educators for all time. Its timelessness removes it from the realm of historical curiosity and will forever project it toward contemporary brilliance.
>
> L.M. Lieberman, *Itard: The Great Problem Solver.*[1]

The story of the strange and speechless boy captured in the vicinity of the town of Saint-Sernin, department of Aveyron, in southern France in early January 1800 has fascinated writers and readers for more than two centuries and occasioned a beautiful cinematic rendering, François Truffaut's *L'Enfant sauvage* (1970). The "wild child" was studied for several months by the naturalist Pierre-Joseph Bonnaterre in Rodez (the capital of Aveyron) and later transferred to Paris, where he was admitted at the Institution for Deaf-Mutes, examined by one of the foremost medical authorities of the day, Philippe Pinel (who declared him a hopeless idiot), and experimentally trained by the young resident doctor of the Institution, Jean-Marc-Gaspard Itard, with

---

[1] Lawrence M. Lieberman, "Itard: The Great Problem Solver," *Journal of Learning Disabilities 15,* no. 9 (November 1982): 566.

63

the assistance of Mme Guérin, who looked after the boy's everyday needs. After Itard discontinued the experiment, the boy, whom Itard had named Victor, remained with Mme Guérin, first at the Institution, and then in a nearby apartment, his expenses covered by a government pension, until his death in early 1828.[2]

The purpose of this chapter is not to examine the wild boy's life but to explore his *afterlife,* that is, the many ways in which the story was appropriated, interpreted and reinterpreted within the disciplines and professions dealing with childhood and children during the past two hundred years. That Victor has become the most famous of the known "wild children" is due to the enormous significance attributed to the training he received from Itard. In conjunction with the rise of a body of knowledge about human beings and the invention of a set of techniques to extract knowledge from human beings, Itard designed the training of the wild child as a medical and pedagogical experiment. By tracing the later uses and interpretations of Victor's life and of Itard's account of his education in the fields of special education, child psychiatry, progressive pedagogy, and social work, I show how the findings and procedures Itard derived from Victor's training were in time to affect the treatment and care of increasingly larger groups of children. Moreover, by considering how these disciplines and professions inscribed the story of the wild child as a founding moment or turning point in their attempts to construct and validate a history for themselves, I hope to unsettle reductive and unilateral readings which "discipline" not only the wild child but also the "normal" child. The chapter thus interrogates the tensions between historical understanding and current theory and practice, and between the extraordinary and normal child. Yet as it follows the thread of scientific and professional

---

2. On Victor's life, see Harlan Lane, *The Wild Boy of Aveyron* (Cambridge: Harvard University Press, 1976) and Roger Shattuck, *The Forbidden Experiment: The Story of the Wild Boy of Aveyron* (New York: Kodansha, 1994; first published in 1980 by Farrar, Straus and Giroux). The standard English translations of Itard's reports are *The Wild Boy of Aveyron,* ed. and trans. G. and M. Humphrey (Englewood Cliffs: Prentice-Hall, 1962) and *Wolf Children and the Problem of Human Nature,* ed. L. Malson, trans. E. Fawcett, P. Ayrton and J. White (New York: Monthly Review Press, 1972), but the editors' introductions are unreliable. Most of the documents relevant to the case are in Thierry Gineste, *Victor de l'Aveyron: Dernier enfant sauvage, premier enfant fou,* 2nd ed. (Paris: Hachette/Pluriel, 1993). For a critical reconstruction of Victor's life in relation to earlier and later stories of wild children, see my forthcoming book, *Encounters with Wild Children: Temptation and Disappointment in the History of the Human Sciences.*

engagement with Victor, the chapter also seeks to make visible, as a counterpart to the progress of scientific knowledge and the educational feats of intelligent adults, the fact that what motivated the interminable barrage of descriptions and prescriptions was the puzzling presence and haunting memory of a silent child who came out of the forest.

* * * *

Whereas in his first report, composed less than a year after he took charge of the wild boy, Itard had expressed his conviction that Victor's future progress would amply satisfy his expectations and reward his patience and ingenuity, the ambivalent tone of his second report, written in 1806 at the request of the minister of the interior, fed later suspicions that the doctor-teacher had come to view his work as a failure and his pupil as an incurable idiot. In fact, Itard himself included in the report hints as to how he wanted it to be read and judged. He insisted that Victor, "to be judged soundly, must be compared only with himself," and enhanced the comparison by depreciating Victor's earlier state (drawing on Pinel's description of the boy's behavior and obliterating the more complex, and sympathetic, accounts produced before his arrival in Paris): "I will not retrace for you, Sir, the hideous picture of this man-animal as he was when he came out of his forests." Itard was not present when the boy came out of "his forests," and the people who were did not describe him in those terms; still, by denigrating the boy's condition before the medico-pedagogical experiment, Itard magnified the transformation he effected in him and his own scientific and pedagogical contribution.

Regardless of his personal feelings in connection with the outcome of his work, Itard must have been very pleased with the evaluation of his report by the French National Institute, which officially underwrote the interpretation he had suggested. First, Victor must be compared only to himself: the evaluators marvelled at "the distance that separates the point of departure from that which he has reached, and by how many new and ingenious methods this immense interval has been filled." Second, Victor's remarkable changes were due to Itard's skill and his unremitting deficiencies to his own inferiority: "it would have been impossible for the teacher to conduct his lessons, his exercises and his experiments with more intelligence, wisdom, patience and courage, and if he has not obtained a greater success, this must be attributed not to a defect in zeal or talent, but to the imperfection of the organs of the subject on whom he worked." Third, the observations, techniques, and conclusions Itard arrived at during his work with Victor were crucial for the education of children in general: the evaluators recommended that the report be published because it would prove extremely useful "to everyone involved in the education of young people." The minister who had ordered the evaluation had the report printed at government expense because in it "men engaged in the education of childhood will be able to find new and useful views." The scientific and political authorities agreed that Itard's experiment, originally conceived as the observation and training of a *wild child,* had revealed general (medico-pedagogical) methods and principles concerning the education of both extraordinary and ordinary *children.*[3]

In his article "Idiotisme" (1818), the prominent Parisian aliéniste Jean-Etienne-Dominique Esquirol thus epitomized Victor's story:

> A guilty mother, a hapless family abandon their idiot or imbecile son; an imbecile escapes from the paternal home and gets lost in the woods, not knowing how to find his way back; favourable circumstances protect his existence; he becomes light-footed to avoid danger; he climbs trees to save himself from peril; pressed by hunger, he eats whatever he finds; he is fearful because he has been frightened; he is stubborn because his intelligence is weak. This miserable child is encountered by some hunters, taken to a village, led to a capital, placed in a national school, entrusted to the most celebrated instructors; the court, the city are interested in his fate and his education; scholars write books to prove that he is a savage, that he will become a Leibniz, a Buffon. The observant and modest doctor claims that he is an idiot. This judgment is appealed; new accounts are written; everyone wants to take advantage of this event; the best methods, the most enlightened care are implemented for the education of the so-called savage. But of all these promises, of all these hopes, what is the result? That the observant doctor had judged rightly. The savage was nothing but an idiot.

---

3. Itard, *De l'éducation d'un homme sauvage, ou des premiers développemens physiques et moraux du jeune sauvage de l'Aveyron* (Paris: Goujon fils, 1801) and *Rapport fait à son excellence le ministre de l'intérieur, sur les nouveaux développemens et l'état actuel du sauvage de l'Aveyron* (Paris: de l'Imprimerie impériale, 1807), 13; letter from Dacier, permanent secretary of the class of History and Ancient Literature of the Institut national, to Minister of the Interior Champagny (November 19, 1806) and letter from Champagny to Itard (November 26, 1806), both reproduced in Itard, *Rapport,* 7–9, 5–6. Unless otherwise noted, all translations are mine. On the accounts of the boy's behavior following his capture and before his arrival in Paris, see *Encounters with Wild Children.*

It would seem that Esquirol was siding with Pinel, the "observant and modest doctor," against Itard, who had undertaken the treatment in defiance of his eminent teacher's judgment that the boy's condition would never improve and he should therefore be confined in a hospice; but when in 1838, the year of Itard's death, Esquirol–Itard's friend and like him a student of Pinel's–incorporated the article on idiocy into his *Traité des maladies mentales,* he added this note: "It is impossible to read anything more interesting than Dr. Itard's two reports on the admirable care our colleague lavished on this idiot to develop his intelligence."[4] Likewise, in his eulogy for Itard, J.B.E. Bousquet, secretary of the Academy of Medicine, proclaimed that "to turn a disgusting antisocial creature into a bearable obedient boy" had been "a victory over nature, . . . almost a new creation."[5] This is then the first appropriation of Victor's story, insinuated by Itard himself in his second report: the outcome of Itard's rash experiment demonstrated that the boy was not a savage but an idiot or imbecile (as Pinel had claimed), but *precisely for that reason* it was remarkable that the young doctor had been able to effect such an extraordinary transformation in him. The more the wild boy was believed to have been an idiot–and the more his initial condition was disparaged–the more Itard's accomplishment stood out as both admirable and exemplary.

This rendering of the story received a more positive and practical turn in the writings of Édouard Seguin, widely recognized as the founder of what is now known as special education. In 1837, Itard was asked to give language instruction to a young "idiot." His poor health prevented him from accepting the commission, but he agreed to supervise Seguin, one of his and Esquirol's medical students. Seguin later asserted that this brief treatment, based on the medico-pedagogical principles Itard had discovered in his training of the wild boy of Aveyron, constituted the starting point of his own pioneering work in the education of idiots, to which he devoted the rest of his life, first in Paris and then in the United States (a Saint-Simonian socialist, Seguin left France after the failed 1848 revolution). According to Seguin, while

---

4. Esquirol, "Idiotisme," in *Dictionnaire des Sciences médicales,* vol. 23 (1818), 507 and *Traité des maladies mentales,* vol. 2 (1838), 333, cited in Gineste, *Victor,* 98–9, 111n. 45.

5. J.B.E. Bousquet, "Eloge historique de J.M.G. Itard," *Mémoires de l'Académie royale de médecine* 8 (1840), cited in Shattuck, *Forbidden Experiment,* 164–5. See also Louis-Jean-François Delasiauve, "Le sauvage de l'Aveyron," *Journal de médecine mentale* 5 (1865): 197–211.

Itard had failed to cure or fully rehabilitate Victor–and even if his diagnosis had been wrong and Pinel's right–he succeeded in proving what until then was unthinkable, the *educability of idiots,* and laid down the bases upon which their education should be conducted.[6] Through Seguin's widespread influence, the wild boy's memory was kept alive at the same time as the reduced interpretation of his condition (based exclusively on Pinel's and Itard's accounts) was entrenched. Late nineteenth- and early twentieth-century textbooks and overviews of idiocy, mental retardation, or mental deficiency routinely inserted references to Itard and Victor. In these texts, the history of mental retardation is construed as the move from mistreatment and neglect to enlightened concern, treatment, and education, a battle between obscurantism and progress in which doctors and philanthropists play the starring roles while the "idiots," like Victor, are filthy and disgusting examples of flawed humanity that must be reformed or hidden away. Just as praise of Itard is invariably accompanied by certainty about and depreciation of Victor, in the triumphalist history of mental retardation, the objects of study and treatment are devalued and the (medical and philanthropic) transformation imposed on them–always in the direction of closeness to us–is stressed.[7]

Here are some examples of how Itard and Victor were represented in these works. For William Ireland, while Itard's pamphlet was "plainly the work of a superior mind," he "overestimated the mental capabilities of his pupil" and the result of his venture "proved the correctness of Pinel's diagnosis"; still, Itard's method of education "has

---

6. See Seguin, "Origin of the Treatment and Training of Idiots," *American Journal of Education* 2 (1856): 145–52 and Lane, *Wild Boy,* 261–78.

7. As part of the context within which the entrenchment of the story of Victor and Itard took place, we must note: the growth, diversification and institutionalization of the human sciences; the rise of statistics and professional expertise grounded on the organizing concept of normalcy; the anthropological preoccupation with race and its relation to the medical and psychiatric attention to degeneracy, and the gradual expansion of schooling; see Ian Hacking, *The Taming of Chance* (Cambridge: Cambridge University Press, 1990); Roger Smith, *The Fontana History of the Human Sciences* (London: Fontana, 1997) and Nikolas Rose, *The Psychological Complex: Psychology, Politics and Society in England, 1869–1939* (London: Routledge & Kegan Paul, 1985). As regards "idiocy," the nineteenth century witnessed two tendencies: from the 1840s on, the medico-philanthropic movement to educate idiots (led by Seguin) as an attempt to recuperate them for humanity; a little later, the institutionalization of the mentally defective as a means to protect society from the danger they were believed to pose. By the end of the century, the rising intolerance and fear found an outlet in eugenic ideas and policies; see Leo Kanner, *A History of the Care and Study of the Mentally Retarded* (Springfield: Charles C. Thomas, 1964).

been of use in the training of idiots." Martin Barr specified that Itard's work was "the first successful demonstration of the possibility of educating an idiot by physiologic means with a philosophic aim." Even if "unwittingly," Itard was "the discoverer of a reflective power in idiots that once awakened might be trained." Likewise, Pierre Pichot first pointed out that Itard's "starting point was not quite correct" since the boy was feeble-minded "and no educational method could make up for that." Yet Itard must be commended both for his courageous attempt to educate "a subject who was looked upon by all as a mere curiosity" and for the "educational technique" he invented.[8] Although the overblown exaltation of his work was tinged with slight condescension (his discovery of the educability of idiots was momentous but unintentional; he adhered to outdated and inadequate theories which misled or blinded him), from the late nineteenth century until roughly the 1960s, Itard was approached mainly as a predecessor or precursor, a groundbreaking historical figure who had to be given due credit in the brief historical reviews which introduced textbooks and handbooks of mental retardation and deficiency. In this vein, the tenth edition of *Tredgold's*

---

8. Ireland, *The Mental Affections of Children, Idiocy, Imbecility and Insanity* (London: J. & A. Churchill, 1898), 419–20; Barr, *Mental Defectives: Their History, Treatment and Training* (Philadelphia: P. Blakiston's Son & Co., 1904), 28 and Pichot, "French Pioneers in the Field of Mental Deficiency," *American Journal of Mental Deficiency* 53, no. 1 (July 1948): 130. Ireland was medical superintendent of the Scottish Institution for the Education of Imbecile Children and medical officer of Miss Mary Murray's Institution for Girls at Preston. Barr, chief physician of the Pennsylvania Training School for Feeble-Minded Children, elaborately inscribed Victor into the history of idiocy: "the savage of Aveyron might be likened to a guide-post reading two ways. Standing at the beginning of the nineteenth century, a literal symbol of the parting of ways for his caste, in this uncouth figure is represented all the cruelty of the past and the beneficent influences of a new era. The last of those of whom history or tradition speaks as, either through neglect or through wilful desertion, driven from the haunts of men; he is also the first example recorded of an idiot reclaimed from the life of a mere animal to be trained to a human existence" (*Mental Defectives,* 30–1). Similar appraisals may be found in texts by special educators. For Eugene E. Doll (who taught special education at the University of Tennessee) "[t]he combination of scientific sagacity, affectionate humanism, and practical resourcefulness with which Itard labored over his *'sauvage'* for five years makes epic reading." Although mistaken ("Victor was, indeed, an imbecile, quite incapable of anything beyond the most elementary stages of learning"), Itard had "proved the educability of imbeciles" and devised a training program "in terms of the child's organic needs—mental, moral, social, and esthetic"; "A Historical Survey of Research and Management of Mental Retardation in the United States," in *Readings on the Exceptional Child: Research and Theory,* ed. E.P. Trapp and P. Himelstein (New York: Appleton-Century-Crofts, 1962), 24–5. For Paul F. Cranefield, Itard's failure was "a victory in disguise, if looked at correctly," because it showed the world "that a rather seriously retarded boy could be enormously improved and could be brought to a very much higher level of function than anyone would have supposed"; "Historical Perspectives," in *Prevention and Treatment of Mental Retardation,* ed. I. Philips (New York: Basic, 1966), 9.

Textbook of Mental Deficiency (Subnormality) (1963) stated that it was Itard who "first described attempts to train a subnormal child," anticipating "by a century and a half some part of modern theory and practice in connection with the teaching of young or slow learning children."[9]

By the 1960s, professionals in the field of mental retardation had no doubts concerning Victor's diagnosis. But as the field grew and broke down into subfields, researchers and practitioners started to perceive Itard differently, as not just a revered forerunner but also a model or inspiration for present theory and practice. They claimed his legacy (his medico-pedagogical principles and instructional techniques) for particular methods and approaches within the field and interpreted his goals and strategies in light of their own. More detailed analyses of Itard's reports led to reevaluations of Victor's condition and progress. For instance, John F. Gaynor reinstated Itard's view that the cause of Victor's retardation was the long period he had spent in isolation in the wild while rejecting Itard's estimate of the boy's progress: "He is in danger of being remembered as the man who considered his efforts to educate Victor a failure, rather than as the author of specialized training for the mentally retarded."[10] Itard's technique was reevaluated as well. While certainly innovative for its time, had it been good enough to elicit the best possible outcome? Would Victor have made further progress had Itard employed a more sophisticated technique—such as the one propounded by the author(s) of the article or book in question? Many modern professionals manifest a strong personal identification with Itard, that is, they see *themselves* in him. As they appropriate Itard and profess to recognize their own commitments and methods in his, professionals consistently position Victor as the consummate object of knowledge and intervention—or *child*.

In Thomas S. Ball's *Itard, Seguin and Kephart* (1971), we find one of the most conspicuous cases of massive identification with and appropriation of Itard. Ball's aim was to develop an approach to sensory edu-

---

9. Roger F. Tredgold and Kenneth Soddy, eds., *Tredgold's Textbook of Mental Deficiency (Subnormality)*, 10th ed. (Baltimore: Williams and Wilkins, 1963), 350. See also G.E. Shuttleworth, *Mentally-Deficient Children: Their Treatment and Training* (London: H.K. Lewis, 1895), 1; Alfred Binet and Th. Simon, *Mentally Defective Children,* trans. W.B. Drummond (London: Edward Arnold, c.1914), 3; J.E. Wallace Wallin, *Children with Mental and Physical Handicaps* (New York: Prentice Hall, 1949), 134 and Leo Kanner, "Itard, Seguin, Howe–Three Pioneers in the Education of Retarded Children," *American Journal of Mental Deficiency* 65 (July 1960): 2–10.

10. Gaynor, "The 'Failure' of J.M.G. Itard," *The Journal of Special Education* 7, no. 4 (1973): 440–3.

cation that would integrate the Skinnerians' behaviourism and Kephart's cognitivism. Itard and Seguin must be included in this discussion, he explained, because they were the "true pioneers and innovators of sensory education" and because "the assumptions upon which the whole field was based might best be understood by returning to their original sources." The book opens with a lyrical account of Ball's own relation to Itard. Ball (of Pacific State Hospital) first read Itard's "classic" reports on the wild boy of Aveyron some years after completing his doctorate:

> It was a beautiful, deeply moving experience, timed at precisely the right moment in my life and career. . . . As I have read and reread Itard, the hiatus of years that separates our lives has slowly disappeared. Each time, he becomes more of the teacher-physician-scientist-humanitarian and sensitively responsive human being. Although I do not view this in a mystical sense, my mind has become the scene of a dialogue involving three parties: great men of my contemporary experience, Itard, and myself. As I know these contemporaries better, I know Itard better. With enhanced understanding of Itard, I understand more deeply my own reactions to what I have personally experienced. Out of the chemistry of these interactions I begin to come in contact with what I would like to call *wisdom*. It is with whatever wisdom I can bring to bear upon this topic that is so close to my heart that I proceed with the dialogue.

The subjective and emotional tone of this passage starkly contrasts with the behaviourist terminology and unmitigated scientism that pervade the rest of the book. Ball got carried away again when depicting the link he sensed between (his) Itard and his contemporary hero, Kephart:

> In many respects I understand Kephart better through Itard than I do through Kephart himself. This is because I see in Itard's work with Victor a brilliant and penetrating, yet exhaustive, clinical documentation of sensory education carried from its most rudimentary level on to the development of abstract functioning. In part, the limitations of this material lie in the fact that it is based on a single case. But what it lacks in this respect is more than compensated by the breadth and scope of what can be truly described as a monumental effort–a work of genius. And it turns out that Itard's presentation does, in fact, have great generality. I can find in many of his experiences and observations exact counterparts to my own and those of others.

Since Itard was "the point of departure, the fountainhead of the field of sensory education," it was imperative that his work be understood "as clearly as possible within a modern framework." And this is what Ball did: he recast Itard's work with Victor in terms of "the theoretical framework of operant conditioning" and "the concepts and methodology stemming from Pavlov's original formulation of the orientation reaction." Ball maintained that Victor's progress was greater than many, including Itard, we're inclined to admit, but he also believed that the boy would have benefited from a better technique. As to Victor, Ball (predictably) equated him with a rat: "Like a rat pushing a lever which leads to the presentation of a food pellet, for Victor, presenting the word cards led to the presentation of a reinforcing object."[11]

Even as the behaviourists saw Itard as a proto-Skinnerian, professionals of a different bent, who focused on other elements of his work and described and labeled it differently, saw in it an anticipation or reflection of their own concerns and practices. In the final chapter on "Psychotherapy" of *Psychological Problems in Mental Deficiency* (1949), Seymour B. Sarason, professor of psychology at Yale, emphasized, as the central factors of Itard's success with Victor, the individualized attention Itard bestowed on his pupil-patient, his open attitude towards Victor's prospects, and the intersubjective relation established between them. Itard's experiment illustrated "the degree of behavioral change which can be effected by efforts which are planned, intensive, personalized, and therapeutically oriented." In Sarason's opinion, Itard's (psychotherapeutic) feat showed the validity of psychotherapy as a method to treat defective children:

> Had the boy been treated in accord with the diagnosis made by the authorities of the day there probably would have been no change in his behavior, a finding which then would have been utilized as proof of the validity of the diagnosis of incurable idiocy. The hopeless attitude which is expressed today regarding the defective individual's amenability to psychotherapy seems also to be a result of diagnostic labels.

---

11. Ball, *Itard, Seguin and Kephart: Sensory Education—A Learning Interpretation* (Columbus: Charles E. Merrill, 1971), ix, 3–4, 5, 9, 35. According to Ball, Itard "anticipated the modern concept of imitation training" and discovered "what Kephart calls *training in generalization rather than specificity*"; the "practical techniques" he worked out are "almost identical to those employed 160 years later" (5). Itard and Seguin "evolved treatment applications of escape-avoidance conditioning many years before the *births* of Watson, Thorndike, or Pavlov" (83). Ball outlined the "fading" technique *he* would have used, and which, in his view, would have allowed Victor to achieve vocal speech, in "Training Generalized Imitation: Variations on an Historical Theme," *American Journal of Mental Deficiency* 75, no. 2 (1970): 140. Lane, who followed Ball in seeing Itard as the inventor of behaviour modification, also affirmed that Victor "could have learned to speak with the proper conditioning technique" and gave his version of it (based on Lovaas's work) in *Wild Boy,* 153–4. For yet another behaviourist appropriation of Itard, see Steven R. Forness and Donald L. MacMillan, "The Origins of Behavior Modification with Exceptional Children," *Exceptional Children* 37, no. 2 (October 1970): 93–100.

A decade later, Sarason and Tomas Gladwin indicated that the "most important conclusion" to be drawn from Itard's work was that "even in severely defective individuals the quantity and quality of interpersonal relationships is an important variable in determining the level of complexity and efficiency of psychological functioning." Victor was still grasped as "severely defective," but the accent shifted from intelligence and language to personality structure and emotional expression. Sarason and Gladwin measured the "phenomenal" progress Victor made under Itard's care not in words uttered or read but in "the development of various ego functions, the capacity to delay responsiveness . . . [and] the development of a surprisingly complex personality."[12]

Two somewhat unusual textual uses of Itard and Victor in the journal *Mental Retardation* expose how, by the mid-1970s, both of them were firmly ensconced in the field. First, Victor was declared "the most eminent retardate" based on the relative amounts of space granted various individual cases in well-known texts and reference books on mental retardation from 1908 through 1974.[13] Second, in 1977, S.A. Warren, the journal's editor, printed a fictive "letter from an editor" to Itard, dated April 1, 1809, as an April Fools' Day joke. In it, Itard was notified that the reviewers were "impressed" with his "five years of diligence in study of the wild boy, Victor," but his manuscript was rejected (as, the fictional editor guessed, it had already been by several other

12. Sarason, *Psychological Problems in Mental Deficiency* (New York: Harper & Brothers, 1949), 336 and Sarason and Gladwin, "Psychological and Cultural Problems in Mental Subnormality: A Review of Research," in Sarason, *Psychological Problems in Mental Deficiency,* 3rd ed. (New York: Harper & Row, 1959), 577. In 1949, Sarason hailed Itard's writings as "one of the most detailed and illuminating reports dealing with an attempt to rehabilitate a defective child" (327); in 1959, Sarason and Gladwin called them "the best description yet made of the behavior of a severely defective individual" (577). For Michael H. Stone (associate director of the General Clinical Service at the New York State Psychiatric Institute), Itard was "the most celebrated pioneer" of the "humanist tradition in the psychotherapy of children." Itard's "empathic sensitivity and extraordinary devotion" towards the "severely retarded" wild boy of Aveyron "set him apart as someone uniquely 'tuned in' to the feelings of a child"; "Mesmer and His Followers: The Beginnings of Sympathetic Treatment of Childhood Emotional Disorders," *History of Childhood Quarterly: The Journal of Psychohistory* 1, no. 4 (Spring 1974): 660.
13. Jan Case and Charles C. Cleland, "Eminence and Mental Retardation as Determined By Cattell's Space Method," *Mental Retardation* 3, no. 3 (June 1975): 20. With 3,049 lines, Victor easily outdid the other contenders for the title, J.H. Pullen (702 lines), Gottfried Mind (41 lines), and "Blind Tom" (only 4 lines). *Mental Retardation* is the practitioner's journal of research, reviews, and opinions of the American Association on Mental Retardation, the *American Journal of Mental Retardation* being its scholarly research journal. The American Association on Mental Retardation is the latest incarnation of the Association of Medical Officers of American Institutions for Idiots and Feeble-Minded Persons, founded in 1876, of which Seguin was the first president.

editors) because the study was "marred by major flaws in experimental design." Itard was advised to redo it:

> select a larger sample (e.g., 60) of wild boys of the same C.A. and number of years in the woods, assign them randomly to experimental and control groups, apply the treatments again, perform appropriate statistical tests, and re-submit. You could provide better support for your thesis if you employed on each subject several standardized measures such as the WPPSI, Binet, Porteus Mazes, Lincoln-Oseretsky, ITPA, McCarthy, VRT, AAMD ABS, Reading Free Interest, Purdue Pegboard, TROCA, Bialer-Cromwell Locus of Control, and some anxiety, self-concept, and academic tests.

The "editor" sympathized with Itard's plight ("We understand that publication may be necessary to you if you are in a struggle for University tenure") but reminded him that tenure was granted "on demonstration of a national reputation, preferably a good one. With work of this calibre, you surely cannot expect to attain any kind of reputation." To crown the joke, Warren had the fictional editor counsel Itard to "consult one of the vanity presses" for

> someone may be interested in what appears from your excellent (if pre-scientific) descriptions to be clear indication that a profoundly retarded, asocial child can be changed to one with relatively good self help and occupational skills. The document may be of passing interest as the first of its kind to demonstrate the possibility of "educating intelligence.

Warren's tongue-in-cheek letter poked fun at and amiably criticized the field, pointing out the many ways in which Itard's reports deviated from current standards for acceptable (and publishable) research and implying that contemporary works of comparable worth could face unfair rejections to the profession's detriment.[14]

The success of Warren's joke hung upon the very fact that by then both Itard's reputation and the standard version of the story (Victor was retarded, Itard proved the educability of idiots, etc.) went unchallenged. Changing attitudes, labels, and treatment options have shaken the field of mental deficiency and retardation (now more likely to be called developmental or learning disability) in the last few decades; however, no change has shaken Itard's position as pioneer and model. In Lawrence M. Lieberman's words, "[t]he Wild Boy of Aveyron is not a model of diagnostic teaching. It is the model. . . . It is a tribute to Itard's genius that he discovered and implemented perhaps the most

---

14. Warren, "Letter from an Editor," *Mental Retardation* 15, no. 2 (April 1977): 2.

important truth of all: Education must be in harmony with the dynam-ic nature of life." Lieberman furnished "modern translations" of Itard's medico-pedagogical aims because, as a special education curriculum, they have been "occasionally equalled but seldom surpassed."[15]

We need to consider the two major alternative explanations for Vic-tor's condition. The first one is the old eighteenth-century notion, taken up by Itard himself, that prolonged isolation could cause an *acquired* type of idiocy in an originally "normal" child. As Harlan Lane put it, "[t]he obvious explanation for the differences between Victor and almost any other rural French adolescent of the same era lies in Victor's experiences during his years of isolation in the wild." As evidence of the boy's initial normality, Lane upheld his survival in the wild: Vic-tor's "deviant behavior in society" was simply the obverse of his "adap-tive behavior in the forest." And Octave Mannoni (philosopher, anthropologist, and Lacanian psychoanalyst) detected in the boy's out-standing adaptation to forest life a sign of *exceptional* (rather than defec-tive) qualities.[16] Although this view accounted for Victor's wild life, it appeared to flounder before his limited recovery after his return to society. As Itard had already surmised, two possible beginnings of answers to these questions could be that the known and unknown vicis-situdes of Victor's childhood–abandonment, abuse, murder attempt, social isolation, capture, and further neglect *within* society–might have had long-term effects (what we now call trauma) and that certain skills, like language, may only be learned in early childhood (what we now know as critical periods).

The second alternative explanation, which fully returned Victor to the domain of pathology and professional expertise, is infantile autism. The concretion of the link between Victor and autism had some inter-esting twists. First, the link can be traced back to the 1959 publication

---

15. Lieberman, "Itard: The Great Problem Solver," 566-8. Similar arguments are offered in Lorraine Graham, "Wild Boys and Idiots: The Beginnings of Special Education," *B.C. Journal of Special Edu-cation* 15, no. 1 (1991): 76–95 and Ian M.L. Hunter, "Heritage from the Wild Boy of Aveyron," *Early Child Development and Care* 95 (1993): 143–52. See Frances Lamberts and Ted L. Miller, "Itard and Language Pedagogy: A Commentary for Teachers of Children with Special Language Needs," *Lan-guage, Speech, and Hearing Services in Schools* 10, no. 4 (October 1979): 203–11 for a discussion of the relevance of Itard's philosophy, procedures and errors to speech-language professionals.
16. Lane, *Wild Boy,* 170, 178 and O. Mannoni, "Itard et son sauvage," *Les Temps modernes* 21, no. 233 (October 1965): 647–63; in English: "Itard and His Savage," *New Left Review* 74 (July-August 1972): 37–49.

of Bruno Bettelheim's "Feral Children and Autistic Children." Bettelheim advanced the theory that wild children were "severely autistic,"
but perhaps bowing to the then prevailing opinion, he made an exception of Victor: "most of the so-called feral children were actually children suffering from the severest form of infantile autism, while some of
them were feeble-minded, as was possibly the Wild Boy of Aveyron."[17]
Second, the "discoverer" of autism, Leo Kanner, who dedicated many
pages to Victor's (and Itard's) role in the history of mental retardation,
never associated the wild boy with autism.[18] Third, Bettelheim's con-
tention that parents, especially mothers, were responsible for the onset
of autism provoked an intense critical reaction on the part of other
experts. But the suggestion that wild children might indeed be autistic
proved so attractive to professionals embarking on the establishment of
a new field of practice and expertise that they adopted it even as they
rejected its first proponent. Finally, in his major work on autism, *The
Empty Fortress* (1967), Bettelheim seemed to have changed his mind
with respect to Victor's condition: "Unlike Pinel, who thought the boy
feeble-minded, I tend to agree with Itard's original opinion: that this
boy was not feeble-minded but, likely as not, was reacting to the conditions of his life with what we now would call infantile autism."[19]

The late discovery of autism raised a problem: why had it not been
identified and described before? Experts willing to dispel the notion
that autism is a disorder of our time and to demonstrate that, even if
unrecognized as such, it affected all kinds of children in all times and
places, welcomed the opportunity to latch onto Victor and Itard. Seven
years after Bettelheim's seminal article, John K. Wing and Lorna Wing
noted that "the clinical syndrome has only relatively recently been ade-
quately delineated by Kanner so that past insights, such as those of

---

17. Bettelheim, "Feral Children and Autistic Children," *American Journal of Sociology* 64, no. 5 (1959):
455.
18. See Kanner, "Itard, Seguin, Howe" and *A History.* Kanner first described autism in "Autistic Disturbances of Affective Contact," *Nervous Child* 2 (1943): 217–50.
19. Bettelheim, *The Empty Fortress: Infantile Autism and the Birth of the Self* (New York: Free Press,
1967), 371. Bettelheim had ended his 1959 article with a ruthless indictment of mothers: "feral children seem to be produced not when wolves behave like mothers but when mothers behave like non-
humans. The conclusion tentatively forced on us is that, while there are no feral children, there are
some very rare examples of feral mothers, of human beings who become feral to one of their children" ("Feral Children," 467). In *The Empty Fortress* he softened his language somewhat, but the damage had already been done, and he became anathema to most experts on autism—and,
understandably, to parents of autistic children.

Itard in 1799 and Witmer in 1920, were not recognized as more generally applicable to a substantial group of similar children." The fact that we now recognize autism and distinguish it from other disorders like mental retardation is read as a signal of *our* enlightened regard for children. In the same child whom the specialists in mental retardation conceived as palpably retarded, the autism experts spotted autism 150 years before Kanner first described and named it: "To the modern reader there can be no doubt that the wild boy of Aveyron showed most of the diagnostic features of autism–whatever the original cause. The details of his behaviour are uncannily familiar."[20] The experts were so stricken by the uncanny familiarity of these telltale details that they did not see the need to attend to the context in which they were registered and their concrete place in the overall story, even though Lane, Victor's biographer, cautioned that a conscientious assessment of *all* the available evidence afforded a more intricate picture. For Lane, "the similarities between Victor and autistic children seem to be exaggerated"–Victor's rapid mood changes were provoked by specific events, usually his transactions with people; he was not emotionally withdrawn and displayed affection for others and desire to please them; he was not obsessed with order and excelled at practical manipulation; he used a gestural language and communicated his needs, desires and feelings very effectively.[21]

In the most extended and famous discussion of Victor as an autistic child, the chapter "Lessons from the Wild Boy" of *Autism: Explaining the Enigma* (1989), Uta Frith dealt with Lane's objections summarily "in the light of current knowledge." Lane's observations did not rule out autism because they "fit older autistic children very well." Frith cited selected passages from the accounts contained in Lane's own book as evidence of Victor's "serious impairment in reciprocal social interactions," "specific intellectual impairment," "characteristic impairment of

---

20. J.K. and L. Wing, "A Clinical Interpretation of Remedial Teaching," in *Early Childhood Autism: Clinical, Educational and Social Aspects,* ed. J.K. Wing (Oxford: Pergamon, 1966), 185, 186. In the 2ⁿᵈ edition John Wing hinted that the shortcomings of Itard's theory combined with his eventual acceptance of "Pinel's opinion that the child was an idiot" were partly to blame for the late recognition of autism. Itard described "[n]early all the behavioural characteristics" which Kanner would list in 1943, but since Itard "had not realised that he was dealing with a separate syndrome . . . the chance of helping other children with the same behaviour pattern had been missed"; "Kanner's Syndrome: A Historical Introduction," in *Early Childhood Autism: Clinical, Educational and Social Aspects,* ed. L. Wing, 2nd ed. (Oxford: Pergamon, 1976), 6, 10.
21. Lane, *Wild Boy,* 176–8.

sensory attention," "lack of imaginative play," and "stereotypies." She
contended as well that the major diagnostic feature of autism, "autistic
aloneness," was evident in numerous scattered incidents of his life: "It
is as if, for Victor, minds did not exist. It follows that he is unconcerned
about the effect his behaviour has on other people's opinion of him." In
a stunning reversal, Frith argued that Victor's survival in the wild,
which Lane had wielded as solid indication that he could not have been
retarded or psychotic, was downright facilitated by his autism:

> autistic individuals seem to be peculiarly qualified–better than normal children
> are–to lead the rugged, solitary life that Victor lived when roaming the forests.
> In the case of a normal child it would be more difficult to explain why he did
> not seek refuge with people. Villagers, by all accounts, were often nearby and
> ready to help him. If he was autistic this may not have occurred to him. Perhaps
> he found it impossible to differentiate well-meaning people from creatures of
> the wild.[22]

Frith used Victor not just to substantiate autism's long lineage ("Autism
is not a modern phenomenon, even though it has only been recognized in modern times") but to buttress her stand in the controversy
about its cause. In opposition to Bettelheim's psychoanalytic view of
autism as the child's response to a pernicious kind of parenting and an
extreme environment, Frith defined autism as a congenital cognitive
and developmental impairment best understood as the inability to
mentalize or lack of a "theory of mind." Autistic children, like Frith's
Victor, are unable to "recognize the existence of other people's minds,"
lack empathy, and have great difficulty communicating with others. In
her single-minded search for symptoms, however, Frith passed over
the many details and anecdotes in the accounts of Victor's life which
exhibit a boy profoundly involved with others and attuned to their feelings and states of mind, such as his reaction to Mme Guérin's sorrow
on the death of her husband and the multiple frustrations, conflicts,
and joys he visibly experienced in his dealings with Itard.[23]

---

22. Frith, *Autism: Explaining the Enigma* (Oxford: Basil Blackwell, 1989), 20–1, 26, 24.
23. *Ibid.,* 16, 154–5. Frith called into play the *contrast* between two wild children, Victor and Kaspar
Hauser, to bring out the essential features of autism and prove that it could not be caused by prolonged deprivation of human contact. Whereas Frith distinguished between the autistic Victor and
the non-autistic Kaspar, a more recent text absorbed Kaspar too: "Many earlier descriptions of
unusual children such as those of Victor, the 'Wild boy of Aveyron' whom Itard studied . . . , and of
Kaspar Hauser reportedly discovered in 1828 . . . , insofar as they can be taken as reliable accounts,
are suggestive of the condition which Kanner so lucidly described"; Colwyn Trevarthen, Kenneth
Aitken, Despina Papoudi and Jacqueline Robarts, *Children With Autism: Diagnosis and Interventions to
Meet Their Needs* (London: Jessica Kingsley Publishers, 1996), 4.

The appropriation of Victor for autism had several side effects as well, touching on the theory of mind, child psychiatry and child psychosis, and professionalization. In connection with theory of mind, the association worked both ways: at first the lack of a theory of mind was proposed as the underlying malfunction uniting all of Victor's "symptoms"; subsequently, Victor's condition was itself probed as a means to obtain insights into the theory of mind supposedly applicable to all children. As Peter Mitchell (for whom "Viktor" [sic] was "an archetypically autistic boy") maintained in *Introduction to Theory of Mind* (1997), since autism "practically amounts to either a deficient or a deviant theory of mind," its study is "particularly relevant to investigations into the development of a conception of mind."[24] More generally, child psychiatrists saw in Victor the prototype of the psychotic or emotionally disturbed child, and correspondingly awarded Itard, for his work with him, "the distinction of being the first modern child psychiatrist."[25] In 1969, Françoise Brauner and Alfred Brauner proclaimed that, inasmuch as Victor adapted very well to stable material situations and only remained weak in social and affective predicaments, the proper diagnosis for him was not mental deficiency but child psychosis (deep problems of the personality, whose real cause is unknown and which may result in severe obstacles to intellectual development). Almost 20 years later the Brauners reserved a special place for Victor and Itard in *L'Enfant déréel,* a history of "autisms" in literature and in clinical practice.[26] Moreover, as the subdisciplines and professions ministering to "exceptional children" multiplied, more of them laid claim to Itard as *their own*

---

24. Mitchell, *Introduction to Theory of Mind: Children, Autism and Apes* (London: Arnold, 1997), 61, 57. The idea that the study of autistic children can lead to knowledge about children in general is not new. John Wing stressed this relation (through Itard) in 1976: "it is likely that further study will help not only the affected individuals and their relatives but our understanding of the development of normal children, particularly their acquisition of speech. Itard was conscious of this aspect of his work" ("Kanner's Syndrome," 13).

25. Richard M. Silberstein and Helen Irwin, "Jean-Marc-Gaspard Itard and the Savage of Aveyron: An Unsolved Diagnostic Problem in Child Psychiatry," *Journal of the American Academy of Child Psychiatry* 1 (1962): 314.

26. Alfred and Françoise Brauner, "Le 'Sauvage' psychotique de l'Aveyron," *Tribune de l'enfance* 7, no. 61 (1969): 41-50 and *L'Enfant déréel: Histoire des autismes depuis les contes de fées: Fictions littéraires et réalités cliniques* (Toulouse: Privat, 1986). For other attempts to situate Itard and Victor within the field of French child psychiatry, see D.J. Duche and M. Dugas, "La Psychiatrie de l'enfant en France hier et aujourd'hui," *Revue de psychologie appliquée* 36 (1986), 203-17 and M. Gayda, "A l'avènement de la thérapeutique des psychoses et du polyhandicap de l'enfant: J.-M.-G. Itard (pour le 150ᵉ anniversaire de sa mort," *Année médico-psychologique* 147, no. 2 (March-April 1989): 187-9.

predecessor. Dennis E. McDermott was looking for the "real founder of child and youth work"; while searching for early references to "any form of humane treatment of disturbed, delinquent, or otherwise troubled kids," he came upon Itard. In him, McDermott found "a person I could easily relate to": "He worked intensely in a residential setting. His 'client' was so unsocialized that he had been given the name 'The Wild Boy.' His methods were such models of good child care work that they are, or could be, used today." The "insightful" and "caring" Itard stands as "a credible model of professionalism for our own times." Interestingly, McDermott remembered Mme Guérin's contribution: "Perhaps future historians will be able to tell us more about Guerin, and we will be able to talk more accurately about the 'co-founders' of child and youth work."[27]

The interpretations and appropriations of Victor and Itard do not bear only upon "abnormal" children. One troublesome property of the concept of normality is that the boundary between normal and abnormal is never fixed and exceedingly permeable. Already in the first decade of the nineteenth century, the evaluators of Itard's second report tied together his work with Victor and the much more comprehensive project of childhood and youth education in general. In Itard's individualized effort to train an extraordinary child, they sensed the point of departure for attempts to bring forth the right approach to all children. Half a century later, and after having adapted Itard's program of medical education for use with large numbers of retarded children, Seguin claimed that with further adaptations, Itard's methods and principles could be fit for "the training of mankind."[28] While Seguin himself did not undertake this mission, in the early twentieth century the education of the wild boy of Aveyron was made relevant to all children by Maria Montessori, who modeled her scientific pedagogy on it. By insisting on the centrality of his work as an inspiration for her own, Montessori installed Itard as a harbinger of progressive and "child-cen-

27. McDermott, "Jean Itard: The First Child and Youth Counsellor," *Journal of Child and Youth Care* 9, no. 1 (1994): 59, 60, 70. For related uses of Itard to raise the status of professions and practitioners, see Leah Gold Fein, "Clinical Child Psychology: International Perspective," *Journal of Clinical Child Psychology* 5, no. 3 (Winter 1976): 30–5 and Donald K. Routh and Victoria del Barrio, "European Roots of the First Psychology Clinic in North America," *European Psychologist* 1, no. 1 (March 1996): 44–50.
28. Seguin, *Idiocy and Its Treatment by the Physiological Method* (New York, 1866), 23, cited in Lane, *Wild Boy,* 278.

tered" education. Like the other appropriations, Montessori's operated by fastening on selected elements of Itard's account of his work. Montessori applauded Itard's minute observation of his charge: "A student of Pinel, Itard, was the first educator to practise *the observation* of the pupil in the way in which the sick are observed in the hospitals." She hailed the experimental character of Itard's endeavors, which she saw as "practically the first attempts at experimental psychology." In Itard's writings, Montessori discerned the origin of the conjunction of medicine and pedagogy and the first intimations of the kind of early childhood education anchored in science which she would elaborate in her "Montessori Method."[29] To comprehend Montessori's pedagogical innovations, her followers and commentators also scrutinized Itard's reports, hence reinforcing the belief that they prefigured the tenets of contemporary child-centeredness. Itard "anticipated the principles and practice of twentieth century education," wrote Robert John Fynne, because he realized "the great educational role of the child's organic needs" (mental, moral, social, aesthetic, and physical); conceived the idea "of creating new needs and of making them permanent and operative for further development"; encouraged and utilized "the feeble spontaneity of his pupil," and found a place for "pleasure, interest, and imitation" in his training.[30]

For Montessori, the task of scientific pedagogy was to facilitate the individual child's development. But whereas in Itard's program for Victor's education, "development" was meant in an active sense, as *making* the child's faculties develop in a certain way through direct intervention, the creation of specific needs, and the manipulation of his environment, in Montessori's pedagogy, "development" functioned equivocally: whereas in practice, her goal was the same (active) type of development underscored by Itard, in theory she misleadingly declared that the child's development is *naturally* programmed and best takes place spontaneously under conditions of "freedom"–the very conditions scientifically made possible by her method. Montessori's work relied on (and most vividly disclosed) the conceptual and practi-

---

29. Montessori, *The Montessori Method: Scientific Pedagogy as Applied to Child Education in "The Children's Houses"* (1912), trans. A.E. George (Cambridge: Robert Bentley, 1965), 34.
30. Fynne, *Montessori and Her Inspirers* (London: Longmans, Green and Co., 1924), 127. See also Willian Boyd, *From Locke to Montessori: A Critical Account of the Montessori Point of View* (London: George G. Harrap, 1912) and Lane, *Wild Boy,* 278–86.

cal shift from the wild child, through the retarded child, to "the child."
"If a parallel between the deficient and the normal child is possible,"
Montessori observed, "this will be during the period of early infancy
when the child who has not the force to develop and *he who is not yet
developed* are in some ways alike." If development was natural and followed a single pattern in all children, it was legitimate to formulate
analogies between Victor and young children: "In the education of little children Itard's educative drama is repeated."[31]

Montessori conceived of Victor as mentally retarded *but* to her mind
there was no qualitative difference between normal and retarded children. The slippery concept of development, which authorizes analogies
between young "normal" children and older "abnormal" (retarded or
backward) children, and therefore from the "wild child" (as one form of
the retarded child) and "the child," supports not only contemporary
child-centered pedagogy but also most fields of research and practice
involving children. It made sense to psycholinguist Roger Brown to
begin *Words and Things* (1958) with the story of Victor because, he
believed, it sheds light on language acquisition *in general:* "The doctor's
methods of instruction were founded on an analysis of the basic psychology of language which is the same as the analysis on which the
present book is founded." Itard's instruction and Victor's learning provided Brown with paradigmatic examples of the psychology of language. Because he construed the relation between Itard and Victor as
the prototypical teacher-pupil or adult-child relation, Brown was able
to characterize the "Original Word Game" as "the game of linguistic
reference that Victor played with Itard and all children play with their
parents."[32]

Victor and Itard have been assigned foundational and paradigmatic
roles in the fields of mental retardation, autism, and pedagogy; consequently, *critical and alternative positions* have also proceeded by revisit-
ing and reinterpreting their story and its implications. Within the field
of mental retardation, but from a psychoanalytic perspective, Maud
Mannoni reread Itard in the course of her articulation of a psychoanalytic approach to the treatment of mentally retarded children (she was

31. Montessori, *The Montessori Method,* 44, 153.
32. Brown, *Words and Things* (Glencoe: Free Press, 1958), 4, 19. For a recent (and simplistic) discussion of Victor and Itard in relation to language acquisition, see Jerry H. Gill, *If a Chimpanzee Could
Talk and Other Reflections on Language Acquisition* (Tucson: University of Arizona Press, 1997).

dissatisfied both with the educationalist's faith in the power of education to remake the other in the self's image and with the psychoanalyst's refusal to engage with children deemed uninteresting on account
of their speechlessness). What Mannoni found "touching" about Itard's
experiment with the (retarded) wild boy was precisely that Itard strove
"to bring him into the world of speech"; still, his "preconceived ideas
about the nature of language" obstructed "his pupil's path toward his
possibilities." The main lesson Mannoni derived from Itard's "mistake"
was that professionals working with retarded children, be they psycho-
analysts, physicians, or educators, must "start first with themselves,"
that is, by questioning their own attitude to the different child: "What
was the trap into which Itard fell at the very outset? Are not his reac-
tions still a determining factor in our own relationship with a retarded
child?" Mannoni, while praising Itard for having at least attempted to
reach Victor, concluded that in the end, the relation established
between them was not "a proper human relationship"—one in which
self and other, professional and patient, adult and child, *communicate*—
but rather a relation of *submission,* a form of "subjection of the child to
the Other."[33]

In reference to autism, we have seen that experts who espouse a biological or organic explanation for the syndrome cared much less about
Itard's medico-pedagogical intervention than about Victor's symptoms
as genuine indicators of autism. For them, Itard's role was that of an
observer and recorder, and the success or failure of his experiment was
secondary relative to whether he did or did not comprehend that Victor's diagnostic features were different from those of a mentally defective child. This understanding of Victor's story bespeaks a static
conception of autism as a disorder which resists treatment or ameliora-
tion. From the periphery of the field, Douglas Biklen, a proponent of
"facilitated communication" and defender of an unorthodox view of
autism, returned to Victor and Itard in the section "What Is Required
in Order to See the Person?" of his 1993 book Communication
Unbound. Facilitated communication assumed that what causes the
autistic child's mutism or unusual speech was not a cognitive disorder
but "apraxia," namely the inability to have the body do what one wants

---

33. M. Mannoni, "A Challenge to Mental Retardation," in *The Child, His "Illness," and the Others*
(New York: Pantheon, 1970), 207, 208. This chapter first appeared in November 1965 in a special
number of *Esprit* on "L'Enfance handicapée."

without help from others. Biklen did not challenge the view that Victor was autistic or disabled, yet he did not dwell on the question of diagnosis or the boy's symptoms. On the contrary, he was interested in pinpointing what exactly permitted Itard to "observe, educate, and understand Victor with optimism" even though the boy's appearance and behavior seemed to portend lack of ability and no susceptibility to improvement. Biklen cast Itard as someone who faced 200 years ago the same quandary faced today by facilitators: what is the proper attitude to be adopted before a child who appears strange, uncommunicative, disabled? According to Biklen, Itard was not daunted by Victor's strangeness because he believed in educability and was willing to entertain "multiple possible explanations for what he observed." While performing his educational task, Itard seized upon "evidence of competence" as a sign that "other abilities of a similar nature could and would follow" and took Victor's responses to be "as much a reflection on Itard the teacher as on Victor's innate or learned qualities." Biklen's generous reading extended to the boy, too. Through Itard's efforts and Mme Guérin's "warm, persistent spirit," Victor became "a caring, expressive, competent person in their eyes and possibly in his own as well." In Biklen's opinion, the facilitator must bring to the relation with autistic and other seriously disabled children the same personal traits that allowed Itard to relate to and communicate with Victor despite his odd appearance and distressing behavior.[34]

From the point of view of pedagogy, some critics reviewed Itard's reports for clues as to the ambiguities and misunderstandings inscribed at the very heart of modern education. For Octave Mannoni, the problem with Itard (and his followers in special and early childhood education) was that his arbitrary preconceptions prevented him from seeing the real child before him. Itard failed to realize that Victor was not "a

---

34. Biklen, *Communication Unbound: How Facilitated Communication is Challenging Traditional Views of Autism and Ability/Disability* (New York: Teachers College Press, 1993), 180, 182. Facilitated communication has been attacked as unscientific and invalid by the experts in the other camp, who cannot accept that autistic people may be the real authors of the communications reported by facilitators (especially since, were these communications authentic, they would give the lie to the "theory of mind" account of autism). For attempts to answer these charges and validate facilitated communication through empirical and statistical studies, see Douglas Biklen and Donald N. Cardinal, eds., *Contested Words, Contested Science: Unraveling the Facilitated Communication Controversy* (New York: Teachers College Press, 1997). Regardless of the truth of their respective theories, the contrast between the representation of autistic people by cognitive scientists and by supporters of facilitation is striking.

blank screen" but an individual with a history and a great deal of accumulated knowledge, however unconventional. To stress the unidirectional character of the pedagogical relation instituted by Itard, Mannoni imagined a reversal of roles: "send Itard into the woods at La Caune with the savage, to see what he would learn there that would be really new to him." By clinging to his *a priori* notions and glossing over "all that his pupil had not learned from him," Itard lost the chance of being himself reeducated by his savage. Still, Mannoni warned contemporary educators and psychoanalysts that even if the advances in knowledge and theory made since Itard's time may enable them to make out the inadequacies that provoked *his* failure, "they can tell us nothing about our own."[35] In "Un admirable echec" (1995), Sophie Ernct reexamined Itard's reports as founding texts of modern education. Because Itard was a precursor of modern pedagogy, it is necessary to delve into his reports to see if they make visible the essential risks of pedagogical thinking; because Itard's reporting was detailed and careful, it is possible to make our own judgments on the success or failure of his aims, procedures, and medico-philosophical principles. Ernct even-handedly analyzed the pedagogical relation between Itard and Victor and unravelled Itard's "failure" within the terms of that relation, without having to resort to temporally or conceptually prior deficiencies in the boy. Like Octave Mannoni, Ernct admitted that our superiority over Itard—our ability to benefit from the progress of knowledge and our position of exteriority in the fact of reading—only means that we may stay clear of his mistakes, but does not protect us from committing those peculiar to our own time, of which we are unaware. Itard's reports raise questions (about the emergence of humanity, the relation between humanity and language, the foundations of education) which are still our own. But their value, Ernct insisted, lies not in the answers they may offer (they offer none), but in their power to foster thoughtfulness in contemporary readers.[36]

The story of Victor and Itard has thus been appropriated by experts and practitioners in the fields of mental retardation, autism, and child-centered pedagogy—and reinterpreted by critics within and at the margins of each of these fields. There is one more way in which the story

---

35. O. Mannoni, "Itard and His Savage," 40–1.
36. Ernct, "Un admirable echec," *Les Temps modernes* 50, no. 582 (May–June 1995): 151–82.

was rewritten, and it is through further research into and reassessment of Itard's life and work. Historians of medicine long supposed that Itard's medical contribution was restricted to his discoveries and inventions in the area of ear, nose, and throat diseases; however, since the late 1970s, Thierry Gineste, a historian of psychiatry and a psychiatrist himself, endeavored to reconstruct Itard's psychiatric contribution. Whereas the other psychiatric or psychotherapeutic renderings of the story rested on hasty, selective, or simplified readings of Itard's reports and (less often) other accounts, Gineste engaged in a painstaking reconstruction of the surviving documentary evidence. Even though Gineste's research undoubtedly revolutionized the state of knowledge about Victor and Itard, the interpretation he imposed on the evidence was a new appropriation, a myth of origins, a dogmatic epic of "great men" in pursuit of the truth arrived at through the very elision of the *child*. The title of Gineste's 1992 article, "Jean Marc Gaspard Itard: Psychotherapist of the Wild Child," gives away his viewpoint. The entire story of the wild boy was fixed with reference to a single domain: "In this climate, and according to Itard's own acknowledgment, his care of the wild child was nothing but a long psychotherapy." Gineste argued that, while Pinel and Esquirol very quickly "perverted" moral treatment (or psychotherapy) by turning it into "institutionalized policing," Itard alone, in his treatment of the wild boy, confronted its "impossible pain." Through moral treatment of a child who "would never speak, regardless of the care he was given, and who, after a relative improvement, would finish by sinking again into autism and catatonia," Itard experienced a painful encounter with *himself* which originated a "new understanding of man" and allowed him to grasp the true nature of madness. Thus Itard must be recognized not just as the founder of child psychiatry, but as one of the founding pillars of modern psychiatry.[37]

But Gineste trod on dangerous ground, because his interpretation was contingent on Itard's *silence*. After ending his involvement with Victor, Itard turned away from "mental alienation" and devoted himself to the treatment and education of deaf-mutes; according to Gineste, this was a "renunciation" prompted by the very fact that what Itard learned in his moral treatment of Victor (about himself, about "man") was "unspeakable":

---

37. Gineste, "Jean Marc Gaspard Itard: Psychothérapeute de l'enfant sauvage," in *L'enfant sauvage de l'Aveyron* (Rodez: Mission Départementale de la Culture, 1992), 64–6 and *Victor*.

it is by what is audaciously hidden in his work, rather than what is noisily explicit in it, that [Itard] remains a monument of medicine. In spite of a tradition that keeps him in the turbulent role of adolescent rebelling against the father, in fact he compels us not to be blinded by a cosmogony in which the myth of the founding father hides the truth, that which is pierced by the eyes of children, who are, as you well know, eager to know.[38]

Just as he rejected one myth (Itard as the rebellious adolescent taking on Pinel as the founding father of psychiatry), Gineste inaugurated a new one, grounded on the unspoken (as unspeakable), in which the child, "eager to know," is Itard himself—and Victor, the real child in the story, has completely vanished. In the final analysis, for Gineste, the wild boy was merely the "occasion" for Itard's momentous discovery. The paradox is that Gineste both maintained (rightly) that to understand the story of *Victor of Aveyron* "[e]verything must be taken into account" and propounded a reductive view of *Itard*'s historical significance which relied on the unsaid and unwritten.[39]

*   *   *   *

How can we account for the enduring and seemingly inexhaustible evocative power of the story of Victor and Itard? How can we explain its hold on resolute adherents of diverse and opposed schools of thought about, and practical approaches to, the care, education, and treatment of children, all of whom in some measure identify *themselves* with it, perceive in Victor's condition that of the children with whom they are concerned, and recognize in Itard's principles, goals, and procedures an anticipation of their own? What is it that makes of this story such an invitation for ongoing and unrestricted identification and appropriation? One reason is that, unlike other accounts of "wild children," Itard's reports (the main source of later readings) bear unimpeachable scientific credentials and their authenticity cannot be questioned. But there is more: the story of Victor and Itard has become a legend, the perfect embodiment of one kind of child-adult relation. It is thus incredibly easy for adults (teachers, doctors, parents) to identify with Itard as the boy's rescuer, savior, maker. The medico-pedagogical

---

38. Gineste, "Les écrits psychiatriques de J.-M.-G. Itard: A propos d'un manuscrit inédit intitulé Vésanies (1802)," *Annales médico-psychologiques* 147, no. 2 (March-April 1989): 185.
39. Gineste, "Jean Marc Gaspard Itard," 66 and *Victor,* 17.

legend encircling Victor and Itard is so irresistible that it overshadows all other elements of Victor's life. Ultimately, with few exceptions, the appropriations and rereadings of the story presuppose and reproduce the glorification of Itard—at the cost of devaluing, debasing, or simply forgetting the wild boy:

> Whether Victor was normal or retarded, Itard won. . . . If normal, then it is thanks to Itard that we have an extensive and perceptive account of bringing the "savage" part way back to civilization. Compared to him, the lowliest Australian bushman or African Pygmy is highly civilized and surrounded by a thick sheath of cultural and social behavior. On the other hand if Victor was organically (or ever functionally) retarded, then Itard performed an almost uncanny feat of redeeming the unredeemable, of finding a place for a stone the builder rejected. Either way he was the miracle worker of his era.[40]

In an age of mass media, it would be unwise to ignore (and hard to exaggerate) the impact in the story's reception and endurance of Truffaut's *Wild Child,* singly responsible for making many people fall in love with it. On that account, Truffaut's explanation of his decision to play the role of Itard is both powerful and instructive:

> I feel that if I had given the role of Itard to an actor, this would have been of all my films the one that would have satisfied me the least, because I would have done only technical work. All day I would have been telling some man "Now take the child, make him do this, take him there" and that is what I wished to do myself. . . . From the day I decided to play Itard, the film took for me a complete and definitive meaning. . . . I felt that the role was more important than that of director, because Doctor Itard manipulated this child and I wanted to do it myself; but it is likely that there were also deeper meanings. Up until *The Wild Child,* when there were children in my films, I identified with them, while here for the first time I identified with the adult, the father.[41]

The story of Victor's afterlife exposes unresolved anxieties surrounding the disciplinary configuration of childhood in modern sciences and professions and debates on the proper way to treat, educate,

---

40. Roger Shattuck, "How Much Nature, How Much Nurture?" (review of H. Lane's *The Wild Boy of Aveyron*), *New York Times Book Review* (May 16, 1976), 30. It is difficult to escape the allure of the legend. Thus, even as Lane forewarned readers that the "legend of the wild boy captures a certain conception—or one should rather say, misconception—of the pupil and the teacher, the child and the pedagogue," he availed himself of it when he introduced his book as "a moving story about how a man and a boy helped each other in the search for knowledge, and how that search changed their lives and ours" (*Wild Boy,* 163, 6).

41. Truffaut, *Truffaut par Truffaut,* ed. D. Rabourdin (Paris: Chêne, 1985), 115, 116. It must be kept in mind that while barely fictionalized, Truffaut's film is not (and was never intended as) a historical document.

cure, train, or more generally *relate to* children. It sheds light on how the disciplines understand and construct their history and on how *the child* figures in disciplinary histories. Victor's numerous textual incarnations underscore the movement from *wild child* (as exception, monster or aberration) through *abnormal child* (object of psychiatry and special education) to *normal child* (object of developmental psychology, progressive pedagogy and compulsory education) and reveal how each of these instances contaminates and complicates the other two. First assimilated to the abnormal child–retarded, deficient, insane, deviant, disturbed, disabled–the wild child came to function as an adequate representative of children in general because in the sciences of childhood the categories of ordinary and extraordinary, normal and abnormal are singularly slippery and the boundary between them extremely fragile. Yet normality is not an inherent quality with which the child is born, but the product of a particular kind of intervention. This is another way of saying that all children (and all development) are somehow abnormal, that knowledge about children is indistinguishable from intervention, and that the dominant form of this intervention is *normalization.* Every child, like the wild child, is a subject *to be normalized.*

In *The Taming of Chance,* Ian Hacking argued that the statistical "laws about people" which emerged in the nineteenth century obtained their power from the idea of the normal: "People are normal if they conform to the central tendency of such laws, while those at the extremes are pathological. Few of us fancy being pathological, so 'most of us' try to make ourselves normal, which in turn affects what is normal."[42] Victor transcended his own time and place in large part because his life coincided with the first adumbrations of the idea (and power) of the normal; however, since unlike most of us he did not try to *make himself normal,* he also uncovers the limits of the normal. Never fully "tamed," the wild child resists normality as a concept and a principle for the intervention of adults in the lives of children.

---

42. Hacking, *The Taming of Chance* (Cambridge: Cambridge University Press, 1990), 2. The rise of normality as a key concept in thinking about people must be related to the growing role of the modern state in the welfare of people (as individuals and as a population) outlined by Michel Foucault in Volume 1 of *The History of Sexuality* (1976), trans. R. Hurley (New York: Vintage, 1990), especially in Part 5, "Right of Death and Power over Life."

Chapter 4

TROUBLED IN PARADISE: A CRITICAL REFLECTION YOUTH, TROUBLE, AND INTERVENTION

Janet L. Finn

Introduction

In November 1997, a professional, suburban New Jersey couple had their 17-year-old son transported against his will to Paradise Cove, a "specialty school for troubled teens" located in Western Samoa (Giegerich, 1998). Troubled by their son's ability to "push the behavioral envelope," frustrated with the inability of half a dozen psychologists and psychiatrists to get through to him, and fearful that "he was on a nonstop path to jail or death," the couple opted to pay nearly $3,000 a month for his year-and-a-half-long stay in Paradise Cove. Their son was one of nearly 300 youth receiving offshore, tough-love treatment in this self-described "therapeutic boarding school" tucked away in an obscure corner of paradise. He is one of thousands of "defiant teens" in the U.S. who have been sent by their parents for offshore rehabilitation in a growing network of private, for-profit boarding schools. Why are some parents spending tens of thousands of dollars a year to place their children in these distant locations? Why would middle- and upper-class parents be willing to pay for the containment of their own children at a time when activists are decrying the punitive treatment of poor youth and youth of color and the increasing penchant for pathologizing and criminalizing youthful behaviors and young people themselves? How have particular discourses of trouble come to wield such power and warrant such drastic forms of intervention? What hope for change do exotic sites offer? According to the promotional literature of various facilities, the therapeutic benefits of "culture shock," strict disciplinary practices, and positive peer culture offer parents a marketable option for their children's salvation. However, I suggest that both the questions and the answers are much more complicated. They call for a historical, political, and cultural analysis of the making of adolescence, trouble, and professional intervention.

In this chapter, I critically examine a history of interlocking discourses and practices regarding youth, trouble, and intervention in the context of capitalist development and class formation in the U.S. from the mid-nineteenth to the late twentieth century. I consider how particular constructions of youth in need of containment and control map onto the ideologies, discourses, and practices of various helping professionals over time. I trace the invention and elaboration of the concept of adolescence in relationship to a range of practices that have served to both pathologize adolescence and discipline adolescents. In turn, I explore Margaret Mead's cultural critique of the dominant Western view of adolescence, which she offered from the perspective of Samoa circa 1926 and question the ways in which tropes of cultural difference move through historic and contemporary constructions of adolescence and pathology (Mead, 1928). I consider contemporary discourses of youth and trouble and the interventions that shape them, and I pay particular attention to the proliferation of private, for-profit youth containment and treatment facilities in recent years. I return to the opening example and inquire into this curious and contested practice of offshore placement of (some) troubled youth in Paradise. I reflect on the discursive power at work in the construction of youth as so troubled and troubling that such drastic disciplinary measures are not only deemed to be warranted, but framed as a measure of good parenting. What is at stake in these constructions of youth, trouble, and treatment? What might they tell us about adult fears and anxieties? What are the implications of these practices for young people themselves? Let us turn now to the "youth problem" in historical perspective.

The Making of Youth and Trouble: Mid-Nineteenth Century Perspectives

Capitalism, Class, and Danger

Kett (1977) argues that images of deviance have historically been typified by "lower-class" youth and deployed to represent a threat to the safety and morality of "proper" (i.e., middle-class) youth. Such class-based constructions of youth were coming into vogue by the mid-1800s as the cleavages of class-differentiated society in the U.S. were being carved. The rapid growth of industrial capitalism, accompanied by rapid urbanization and immigration were provoking convulsive changes in social life. In the 50 years following the Civil War, the U.S. workforce shifted from a 60 percent agricultural economy, to 70 percent nonagricultural, with mass rural to urban migration (Ehrenreich, 1985). Millions of foreign workers and their families immigrated to the U.S. Political and economic power became more concentrated in the hands of a few.

The working classes embodied the consequences of industrial capitalism's brute force as they adapted to new divisions of labor, exigencies of the factory floor, and changing family roles. Working class families faced a precarious existence marked by low wages, unsafe housing, and social exclusion in the country's rapidly expanding urban centers. Survival likely depended on the collective labor contributions of men, women, and children. Women's and young people's casual labor was often central to family subsistence, and it demanded their presence in the streets as peddlers, scavengers, and at times, sex workers (Baron, 1990, p. 15). From the mid-1800s, we see a growing public concern for unsupervised youth and the need to contain and control them. As populations of young immigrants grew, so did images and fears of the "dangerous classes" of urban youth, poised to prey on the "innocent" young men migrating to the city from the countryside. Youth counselors wrote advice books targeting an audience of young men of the emerging middle class, warning them of the dangers of city life and their risk for seduction into a world of vice and temptation at the hands of lower-class youth.[1] As Kett (1977) and Griffin (1993, 2001)

---

1. The concept of youth has historically been a strongly gendered concept associated with masculinity and male experience. A number of scholars have critically addressed the gendering of youth. See for example Griffin (1993; 1997), McRobbie (1991), and Adams (1997).

have argued, these writings represented youth for the emerging middle class as a time of innocence and a stage of transition from childhood to adulthood. The success of that transition was rooted in self-discipline. Lower-class youth, in contrast, were represented as inherently dangerous, corruptible, and potentially corrupting; they were an affront to Victorian images of childhood innocence and a potential threat to that innocence (Griffin, 1993, p. 101). Given their presumably limited capacity for self-discipline, they were seen to be in need of social control. Moreover, these emerging ideologies of youth incorporated racialized notions of Euro-white superiority that equated constructions of whiteness with normalcy (Griffin, 1993, p. 14). Thus, particular class-based images of troubling youth were also racialized images, and they became synonymous with danger and fear. Lower-class youth were, by definition, a source of potential trouble, and thus in need of disciplinary intervention. And by mid-century, a cadre of reformers was poised to respond to that need.

Containment, Control, and Contamination

Social reformers of the mid-nineteenth century engaged in heated debates regarding the control and containment of these troubling youth. Some worried about their risk of further degeneration if placed with adults in poor houses or asylums. They advocated for containment in special institutions where young people would be separated from "noxious moral influences," and where their character could be re-formed through the structured practices of daily routine, labor, and surveillance. Early youth institutions utilized uniforms, strict schedules, fixed programs of activities, and heavy-handed moral instruction as the preferred modes of intervention (Boyer, 1978; Katz, 1986; Rothman, 1971). Other reformers saw the only hope for the salvation of troubling youth in "binding out," whereby the threat of idleness would be replaced by mandatory labor. Practices of the times reflected contradictory beliefs about potential for "reform" versus ongoing need for containment and control.

Reformer Charles Loring Brace (1872) utilized a discourse of contamination and contagion to evoke the threat posed by the "dangerous classes" of youth in New York. Brace's treatises on youth and danger reflect a mix of pity for and condemnation of the children of poor immigrant families and the fear of the potential social and political force of this group as it comes of age. Brace writes: "These boys and girls, it should be remembered, will soon form the great lower class of our city. They will influence elections; they may shape the policy of the city; they will, most assuredly, if unreclaimed, poison society around them." In effect, these dangerous classes posed an immediate risk to "innocent" youth and perhaps an even more formidable risk to the social order as they reached adulthood and exerted their collective will. Brace called for aggressive social control of these risky young people for their own moral well-being as well as for the general good of society. Brace initiated a plan for the "moral disinfection" of urban centers through the "placing out" of poor immigrant youth with rural farm families. Their contaminating influence was thus removed from urban space, and through the osmosis of daily life, they were to absorb the morals, values, and discipline of "proper" family life.[2]

The first part of our story, then, is one of the emergence of a class-inflected construction of both youth and trouble as part of the cultural politics of difference and the making of subjectivity within nineteenth century industrial capitalism. Both the ideologies of trouble and the disciplinary practices of containment were shaped by the heuristics of fear embodied in the immigrant other (Giddens, 1994; Briar-Lawson, Lawson, Hennon, & Jones, 2001).[3] In short, "youth" was constituted as a class-based category that needed to be contained, both to reduce risk of social contamination through contact and to ensure its proper place and trajectory in the political and economic order of things. In conjunction with this construction of youth and trouble, we see the emergence of a class of professional "disciplinarians" preoccupied with the creation of systematic, institutional responses to troubling youth.

---

2. This discussion is based on excerpt of previously published work (Finn, 2001, pp. 170–172).

3. I borrow the notion of the "heuristics of fear" from Giddens (1994) who uses the term in reference to one of the forces at work in contemporary globalization, wherein people have an anxious awareness of large-scale problems that humanity has created and that affect people everywhere (see also Briar-Lawson et al., 2001). I argue that the heuristics of fear has a much longer trajectory in the making and marginalizing of forms of difference. What that fear maps onto and the differences that make a difference may vary over time, but the heuristics of fear remains a powerful force in the meaning and power of difference and oppression.

Coming of Age in the "New" Century

Youth and Shifting Technologies and Politics of Knowledge

By the early twentieth century, a confluence of forces was shaping the social construction of both youth and trouble. Child labor laws and compulsory public education were configuring the time, space, and special status of childhood and youth. Discourses of care and control were being articulated through a new agenda of progressivism finding institutional expression in the creation of the juvenile court and child welfare systems. Ideas about children and youth were developing hand in hand with specialization in the social sciences, emerging ideologies of efficiency and scientific management, and practices of diagnosis, testing, and measurement. Studies of psychopathology, personality development, and individual differences captured the imagination of the emerging helping professions in the early 1900s. A range of helping professions (social work, child guidance, mental hygiene, education), embracing a "scientific" approach to diagnosis and treatment began to concern themselves with the welfare of "at-risk" children and the discipline of risky youth. At the same time, there was growing preoccupation with "normal" childhood and the need for professional guidance in child-rearing. Intervention work was becoming a growing concern (Ehrenreich & Ehrenreich, 1979; Heiman, 2001; Jones, 1999).

This expansion of interventionist work can be understood as resulting from the interplay of mutually amplifying forces. First, with the rise of monopoly capitalism came increased production of consumer goods, the need for an expanded consumer market, and the demand for a ready labor force of new producers and consumers. Within this context, a new "professional class" of workers positioned as "middlemen" between labor and capital began to emerge. They engaged in "intervention" work, that is, the diverse tasks of developing the knowledge and technologies to expand production and consumption; preparing future producers and consumers for their place in the new century; and creating buffers for some of the human consequences of the contradictions of capitalism (Ehrenreich & Ehrenreich, 1979; Heiman, 2001, pp. 278–280). Their work was a key component in the production of new kinds of workers, citizens, and consumers through the application of new forms of labor discipline, regulation of the activities and intimacies of family life, and promotion of desires and dispositions (Harvey, 1989). Taken together, these practices shaped and responded to the cultural logic of early twentieth century capitalism.

Many interventionists turned their attention to youth and the shaping of young people's proper trajectories to adulthood and place in the social and economic order. Some appropriated knowledge from the biological sciences and applied it in the social realm, often in problematic ways, as exemplified by Social Darwinism, the eugenics movement, and an infatuation with tests and measurements that served to justify and reinforce racist, classist, and gendered assumptions about difference. Fears about the deviance of "dangerous classes" of urban youth found new forms of expression in the vocabulary of reform, and interventionists called for a specific system for the care and control of delinquent youth (Sutton, 1988). It is on this stage that specific theories of both adolescence and deviance were articulated and disciplinary practices were elaborated and justified. As Shook (2002) argues, the concept of "delinquent youth" emerged in tandem with the "discovery" of adolescence at the beginning of the twentieth century.

The Invention of Adolescence and the Elaboration of Trouble

Psychologist G. Stanley Hall (1904) is widely credited with the "invention" of adolescence at the turn of the last century. In his two-volume treatise entitled *Adolescence, its Psychology, and its Relations to Physiology, Anthropology, Sociology, Sex, Crime, Religion, and Education,* Hall put forth his view of adolescence as a biologically driven time of stress and storm. Further, Hall offered a recapitulation theory of adolescence wherein he argued that adolescence was a "second birth" and a critical measure of human progress. Hall held that the development of the individual paralleled the development of the race and that adolescence was thus key to racial and cultural betterment (Adams, 1997). His notions served to both justify and promote racialized notions of biological determinism regarding youth and deviance. Hall gave form and content to adolescence as a dynamic and salient social category to be variably developed, diagnosed, and disciplined by the nascent social sciences and helping professions. The very concept of adolescence was charged from the start with the portent of pathology and shaped by assumptions of biological determinism. Hall employed an alarmist discourse of adolescent turbulence, setting the stage for the pairing of adolescence and pathology and thus the need for professional intervention. From Hall's perspective, it seems that all adolescents are vulnerable to corruption and in need of guidance as they negotiate the turbulent transition to adulthood. However, poor and working class youth are at risk by virtue of their heredity, while middle-class, "white" youth are vulnerable to the corrupting potential of the world around them. Thus there is a protean nature to Hall's concept of adolescence and its relationship to trouble, wherein adolescence becomes the Other that is both vulnerable and dangerous, at-risk and risky. Hall's construction reveals more about adult anxieties regarding youth than it does about the actual experiences of young people. And it may tell us more about the political struggles involved in the making of new social subjects within the cultural logic of early twentieth century capitalism than about the hormonal struggles involved in the making of an adolescent.

Determining Deviance

Hall had wide-ranging influence in the emerging fields of child guidance and juvenile reform, and he was very influential in the eugenics movement. His work inspired troubling new directions in professional discourse and practice regarding the containment and control of "deviant" youth—generally those marked by differences of race and class. For example, according to Natalia Molina (2000), the California Bureau of Juvenile Research, informed by Hall's theory of recapitulation, introduced eugenic practices into state institutions for the control and containment of troubled and troubling youth. Researchers sought to identify genetic causes of delinquency and genetic links between delinquency and feeble-mindedness. They employed batteries of tests and measurements in attempts to unearth the hereditary roots of delinquent behaviors. They took particular interest in the presumed genetic "deficiency" of immigrant families and employed Mendelian charts to map out the inheritance of trouble, targeting Mexican families in California. The Bureau was successful in developing segregated Mexican schools and went so far as to propose the building of a "colony" to contain those with IQs of less than 70 in order to assure that they did not reproduce (Molina, 2000).

Places of youth confinement became sites of surveillance where professional interventionists brought moral judgment and "scientific" observation to bear on the scrutiny of young "deviants." The power of this gaze is forcefully illustrated in the work of psychologist Arthur MacDonald, a protégé of Hall, who proposed a study of the physical and mental characteristics of delinquents to the U.S. Senate in 1908 (MacDonald, 1908 in Bremner, 1970). MacDonald's appeal to Congress for funds to establish a laboratory for conducting anthropometrical measurements of juvenile delinquents was ultimately unsuccessful, but his discourse offers a glimpse into the thinking influencing public policy regarding youth and trouble in the early 1900s. MacDonald writes:

> In the study of man the individuals themselves must be investigated. As the seeds of evil are usually sown in childhood and youth, it is here that all inquiry should commence, for there is little hope of making the world better if we do not seek the causes of social evils at their beginning. . . . The time has come when it is important to study a child with as much exactness as we investigate the chemical elements of a stone or measure the mountains on the moon. . . . As an illustration of such investigation I give the following plan: To study 1,000 boys in industrial schools, ages from 6 to 15; 1,000 boys in reformatories, ages 15 to 30; this investigation to consist in a physical, mental, moral, anthropological, social, and medico-social study of each boy, including such data as . . . age, date of birth, height, weight, sitting height, color of hair, eyes, skin; first born, second born, or later born; strength of hand grasp, left handed; length, width and circumference of head; distance between zygomatic arches, corners of eyes; length and width of ears, hands and mouth; thickness of lips, measurements of sensibility to heat and pain; examination of lungs, eyes, pulse and respiration; nationality, occupation, education, and social condition of parents; whether one or both parents are dead or drunkards; stepchildren or not, hereditary taint, stigmata of degeneration. All data gathered by the institutions as history and conduct of inmates might be utilized. (MacDonald, 1908 in Bremner, 1970, p. 562)[4]

MacDonald's proposed project encapsulated both the anxieties around troubled youth and the fixations with bodily form and "defective ancestry" that informed much of the professional discourse and intervention of the times. His discourse exemplifies the seductive power in the melding of containment and surveillance with the authority of science and the moral and political imperative of corrective intervention.

---

4. It is interesting to note the flexibility of the category of youth here in terms of age span. The fuzzy boundaries of chronological age and the concept of youth has added to the concept's ambiguous power.

Through the micropractices of measurement and classification judgments about the deviance and justifications about the containment of particular groups of youth could be made.

Some professional reformers took a more optimistic, growth-oriented perspective on troubled youth. For example, William Healy, a pioneer in the investigation of juvenile delinquency, the formation of the youth court system, and the child guidance movement, advocated for an individualized, case study approach to the diagnosis of troubled and troubling youth. He argued for the need to consider the various influences—social, psychological, hereditary—that shape the delinquent. Healy contended that troubled youth were also malleable and thus salvageable (Healy, 1915). Healy called for preventive efforts to guide children away from the potential dangers of delinquency.[5] Healy's work was influential in promoting the rehabilitative perspective on discipline in the emergent juvenile justice system.[6] While Healy helped shift the focus toward social and environmental factors that contributed to adolescent "trouble," views informed by biological determinism and other racialized forms of testing and measurement continued to capture the popular and professional imagination (cf. Burt, 1925). In sum, early twentieth century images of youth and trouble were fraught with tensions and contradictions that mapped nineteenth century anxieties onto twentieth century science. On the one hand, evocative references to "seeds of evil" and "stigmata of degeneration" paired the heuristics of fear regarding particular classes of young people to the truth value of emergent technologies of knowledge and modes of intervention. The deviant other could be scrutinized and contained, hopefully before spreading its taint to the vulnerable innocents. On the other hand, an optimistic, if somewhat anxious, view of all youth as malleable and therefore both vulnerable to corrupting influence and salvageable with proper guidance and discipline was being advocated. Both views promoted the cause of modern, scientific intervention and the expansion of the helping professions' involvement with all youth. And both were

---

5. Healy's work also reveals ways in which representations of adolescent trouble are marked by gender. While delinquent boys were discussed in terms of stubbornness, disorderly conduct and, at times, mental slowness, the most troubling aspect of female "deviance" was their sexuality.

6. The institutionalized practices of the juvenile justice system, which expanded rapidly in the early twentieth century, helped to establish adolescence as a new social category and legitimize the role of the state and intervention professionals in their care and control (Shook, 2002).

informed by class, race, and gender biases in the determination (and conflation) of risky and at-risk youth.

From its creation, the concept of "adolescence" represented a charged cultural trope through which larger anxieties about normalcy, difference, and deviance moved. As Adams states (1997), the concept of adolescence was constituted as a "funnel of [adult] fears" regarding society at large (Adams, 1997). The concept of adolescence came of age alongside early twentieth century shifts in industrial capitalism toward mass production and consumption and the concomitant demand for new social subjects socialized to new dispositions and desires. It became the interventionists' crucible for forging adults and their trajectories and containing and controlling the behaviors and bodies of those who deviated.

The Cultural Politics of Adolescence and the Inter-war Years

Margaret Mead's Challenge

Assumptions about adolescence as a biologically determined time of stress and storm were challenged by the cultural inquiry of anthropologist Margaret Mead. Mead was a student of the eminent North American anthropologist Franz Boas, a champion of cultural relativism. Boas used ethnographic inquiry to challenge the premises of scientific racism and question the logic of biological determinism (Stocking, 1982). Under Boas' direction, Mead set out to study the relative influence of biological and cultural factors on the experience of puberty.

Margaret Mead set sail for Samoa in 1924, a time of heightened interest in youth, consumerism, and progress in the wake of World War I. She spent several months in what she describes as the most "primitive and unspoiled part of Samoa" attempting to grasp the social organization and cultural meaning systems at work and to come to understand the experience of "adolescence" from a Samoan point of view.[7] Mead observed social interactions, participated in cultural life,

---

7. Mead herself seemed to be somewhat seduced by the imagined native community of Samoa. She was traveling to a Samoa arbitrarily divided by competing Western powers looking to secure strategic military sites in the Pacific. Mead's Samoa is under the administrative authority of the U.S. navy when she arrives, and it has a long history of Christian missionary presence. These colonizing and imperializing influences are bracketed out of her account.

and conducted interviews with Samoan girls in her effort to illuminate their experiences of coming of age. Her work was ahead of its time in her attention to the experiences of young people on their own terms and to the gendered nature of that experience. Mead published the results of her inquiry in *Coming of Age in Samoa* (1928), a popular account of adolescence that countered dominant views of biology as destiny, the universality of Western meaning systems, and Hall's view of adolescence as a period of "stress and storm."

Mead painted a picture of seamless, integrated village life in Samoa in which young people were valued members. She contended that Samoan young people, especially girls, experienced adolescence as a time of freedom and sexual experimentation that was socially constructed as normal rather than deviant. With this greater sexual freedom, Mead argued, Samoan teens were not repressed, and thus there is not a struggle between adults and adolescents. Instead, they enjoyed a freedom of social and sexual expression denied youth in industrialized societies who were "hurried along in life." Mead concluded that "adolescence represented no period of stress or crisis" in Samoa, and thus that adolescence is not, by nature, a time of stress and storm, that stress is socially, not biologically driven (Mead, 1928, p. 214). In contrast, Mead argued, young people in America come of age in a context of social and sexual repression. From the rigidity of infant feeding schedules imposed by the professionalizing of parenthood, to the disciplinary agendas of schooling and religious indoctrination, young people live pressured lives. In addition, she argued that the emphasis on consumption, acquisitiveness, and choice, the pitfalls of modernization, exacerbated the stresses of coming of age in America. In short, adolescent angst in the modern industrial world is largely a product of the disciplinary practices deployed in families, schools, and other contexts of social life that shape young subjects for their place in that world. In a sense, adolescence was the embodiment of the tensions and contradictions of twentieth century industrial capitalism.[8] Mead called for a rethinking of educational practices, less authoritarian child-rearing, and the normalizing of sexuality and youthful sexual experimentation as strategies to ameliorate the stress and storm of American adolescence.

---

8. Mead does not make direct reference to capitalism. This is the author's interpretation of her critique.

Mead opened a space of contestation regarding the meanings of adolescence, development, and sexuality. She posed a direct challenge to Hall and his followers. From Mead's perspective, the efforts of the interventionists were producing rather than responding to the turbulence of adolescence. However, Mead's work contained its own contradictions. Even as she argued that the phenomenon of adolescent stress and storm was more a product of culture than nature, she invoked static, naturalized images of Samoa and Samoans that reinscribed linear, modernist notions of "progress." Mead utilized a discourse of difference and the trope of the "simple, primitive" ways of Samoan life to articulate values of tradition, family, and social integration, and contrast them with the pitfalls of the modern, "civilized" world. That is, she positioned a fixed image of the premodern Samoan "Other" as foil to the perils of modern society, it disciplinary tactics, consumptive ways, and constricting views of coming of age. While psychologized models of adolescence and development prevailed, Mead captured the popular imagination. Her work offered something of a corrective to the prevailing preoccupation with adolescence and risk and the sense of moral panic surrounding images of troubled youth at the heart of the professional interventionists' work. In many ways, her work became a benchmark ethnography for using the trope of the "primitive" as a lens through which to critique contemporary Western society. And, for better or worse, Mead helped inscribe the impression of the Samoan cultural other on the American imagination of adolescence.

Youth, Politics, and the Interwar Years

The interwar years constituted a new era in the shifting logics of twentieth century capitalism. It was a time of economic crisis and social struggle. With the onset of the Great Depression, the vulnerabilities of capitalism were exposed. Its future was in jeopardy, and it needed the right mix of labor discipline strategies and state intervention to survive (Harvey, 1989; Gramsci, 1988). The future of "unoccupied youth" also became a growing concern of the state in the wake of massive economic dislocation and social protest. In this scenario, all youth were at risk of an uncertain future. New social and labor legislation was enacted to respond to the crisis, and the state took a more interventionist role in the lives and futures of youth. For example, the National Youth Administration was established in 1935 to expand the education, technical training, and employment opportunities for young people (Bremner, 1970; Hawes, 1997). Young people themselves began to make claims as citizens and assert a collective political voice. The growth of state intervention also expanded the space and specificity of professionals preoccupied with young people. While sociologists turned their attention to the study of youth gangs among the poor and working classes, psychologists and social workers focused on child guidance, psychodynamic perspectives on young people's development, and the emerging notion of the inferiority complex as precursor to both neurotic and delinquent behavior (Bremner, 1970; Nybell, 2002). Control of youthful impulses and sexuality remained central to the concerns adult interventionists. Ironically, as young people themselves were organizing to challenge the post-Depression alignment of capital and the state and establish their own collective political voice, war intervened, rendering the "youth problem" and their potential threat moot for a time (Bremner, 1970; Enright et al., 1987).

Postwar Promises and Problems of Youth

The postwar years saw a new configuration of capitalism, supported by state intervention, a long postwar economic boom, and a privileged workforce, reach maturity. The preeminence of U.S. political and economic power on the global scene fueled a national sense of confidence and possibility. However, the surface promises of post-war progress thinly masked the underlying fissures in U.S. society and the growing discontent among groups who had been excluded from the American dream. Adams (1997) argues that youth came to symbolize what was both good and bad about postwar years. On the one hand, youth were emblematic of postwar progress; on the other, discourse of the "youth problem" revealed white, middle- and upper-class anxieties about growing social unrest and the potential volatility stemming from social and economic inequality. Once again we see the power of protean imagery of youth as promise and problem, reminiscent of the days of Charles Loring Brace.

New psychosocial theories of adolescent development were emerging in the postwar years. Erik Erikson's classic theory of psychosocial development conceptualized adolescence as a period of identity formation, wherein young people "tried on" on future adult roles (Erikson, 1959, 1968). Those who failed to properly negotiate this phase would likely experience a sense of inferiority and a crisis of identity, troubling precursors to delinquency. Erikson's model located adolescent development soundly in the dominant postwar, middle-class script of upward mobility achieved through successful, sequential negotiation of the challenges posed at each life stage. Erikson provided the psychosocial correlates for postwar capitalism, reinforcing beliefs in a proper trajectory for development and explaining failure in terms of individual deficits or circumstances rather than in structural inequalities (Erikson, 1968; Griffin, 1993).[9] In contrast, African-American psychologists Kenneth and Mamie Clark were challenging the class and race boundaries of Erikson's theory and redefining the sense of "inferiority" experienced by poor children and children of minority groups in terms of structural inequalities and exclusions rather than personal deficits. Their work informed the emerging civil rights movement and the landmark 1954 decision against public school segregation, Brown v. Board of Education (Markowitz & Rosner, 1996; Nybell, 2002). Despite these significant challenges, the dominant professional discourse on youth and trouble continued to focus on individual rather than structural deficits and interventions.

The postwar years also saw growing attention to theories of family (Hartman & Laird, 1983). Theories of childhood bonding and attachment offered a renewed focus on the mother-child relationship. This work provided the theoretical scaffolding for speculation regarding the linkages between maternal deprivation and juvenile crime. Researchers became preoccupied with questions of "attachment." Griffin (1993) notes that, "John Bowlby's speculations on connections between maternal deprivation and juvenile crime (1968) generated a boom in studies on working-class family life, which implicated 'working mothers' in the development of 'delinquency' and 'deprivation,' incorporating psychological, social, and cultural (but not structural) themes into the ubiquitous 'broken home thesis.'" Once again, larger structural questions were ignored and views of white, middle-class ideal types informed

---

9. Nybell (2002) notes that: "Things began to change in the 1950s when the notion of inferiority that was a central construct of child guidance was dramatically politicized. In the ground breaking case of Brown vs. the Board of Education, the "inferiority complex" . . . .

inquiry and obscured the ways in which these constructions of youth and pathology were shaped along lines of race, class, and gender difference. "Troubled" youth in need of containment and control were once again largely "other" youth. These ideas infiltrated understandings of adolescence in the postwar baby boom and the parenting practices of the middle class. Likewise, they were readily taken up by the professional helpers dedicated to guiding young people through the rough waters of adolescence.

By the 1960s, the professional discourse of transmitted degeneracy had been supplanted by a kinder, gentler view of the process as one of transmitted deprivation via the "broken home" and the concomitant pathology of the poor single mother. Growing preoccupation in the 1960s regarding the "culture of poverty" and the "pathology" of the black, female-headed family served to further racialize constructions of risky youth. These heavily psychologized representations were challenged by the political mobilizations of the civil rights movement and the War on Poverty. Some professionals and youth advocates were articulating the connections among poverty, racism, and the physical and mental well-being of children and youth and calling for radical new directions in the practice of intervention that championed community action and structural transformation (Cloward & Ohlin, 1960; Nybell, 2002; Kepel, 1995). Despite these efforts to locate discourses of youth and trouble in a larger social, political, and historical context, the efforts of helping professionals remained largely focused on individualized, psychologized models and the concomitant disciplinary practices of individual care, containment, and control.[10]

The 1960s also saw a growing concern for the mental health of young people and the link to delinquency. The neglect of children's mental health was coming to be viewed as a harbinger of future problems, when that troubled child grew into a troubling youth. A number of mental health experts had articulately argued the link between childhood poverty and emotional and behavioral problems of young people. However, questions of political economy were soon bracketed out of the discussion, and it was a more individualized, depoliticized, and medicalized view that came to define a national "crisis in children's

---

10. See Nybell (2002) for an insightful summary of this period and a detailed examination of the depoliticization of the problem of children's mental health.

mental health" by 1966. Professional concern focused broadly on children "at risk" and the need for detection, diagnosis, and intervention. For example, in 1969 the Joint Commission on Mental Health reported that "using the most conservative estimates, the National Institute of Mental Health estimates that 1,400,000 children under 18 needed psychiatric care" (Joint Commission, 1970). In sum, the 1960s was a decade marked by political activism, and the voices and actions of young people were central to struggles on multiple fronts, from the war on poverty and civil rights to the free speech and antiwar movements. In spite and because of these struggles, anxieties about troubled youth and discourses of individual pathology continued to capture the imagination of professional helpers. While a new alarm had sounded regarding the mental health of all young people, old practices of care, containment, and control continued to differentiate troubled and troubling youth along axes of race, class, and gender. At the same time, that new alarm resurrected old fears that all youth are potentially "at risk," harboring the as-yet-undetected seeds of pathology.

Youth, Trouble, and the Postwar Professional Middle Class

The postwar discourses and practices regarding youth and trouble need to be read against shifting postwar constructions of class. Barbara Ehrenreich (1989) contends that the Professional Middle Class (PMC), emergent in the early twentieth century, came into its own as a subgroup of the middle class in the post- World War II years. According to Ehrenreich, the PMC is a group whose social and economic status is based on education, whose work is professional or managerial in nature and characterized by relative autonomy and often accompanied by the power to manage or judge others, whose "capital" is knowledge and skills, and who rely on consumption to establish status (Ehrenreich, 1989, pp. 12–15). The PMC encompasses a broad range of professions, incomes, and prestige, from the low-end professionals such as teachers, social workers, and middle managers to the high-end professionals such as engineers, doctors, and lawyers. In other words, they are the professional interventionists. Ehrenreich sees the PMC as a deeply anxious group who identify their success with their self-discipline, and who fear loss of control, inner weakness, and the risk of downward mobility.

Ehrenreich argues that, in the wake of 1960s activism, the PMC focused its anxieties on the problem of its children, and interpreted youth protest as a symptom of overly permissive upbringing and a lack of proper discipline. Presumably, the postwar generation had taken Margaret Mead's child-rearing advice to heart, and the results were proving problematic. Freedom from social and sexual repression and the loosening of rigid child-rearing practices were coming to be seen not as solutions to the problems of modern society, rather they were coming under scrutiny as part of the problem. Parents feared that their privileged children lacked the self-discipline to meet the rigors of PMC expectations and were thus at serious risk of falling into lower-class behavior, and eventually, life paths. Further, the very making of the PMC as a privileged class demands intensive preparation and gate-keeping practices to restrict entry. Ehrenreich argues that, ironically, the very "barriers that the middle class erected to protect itself make it painfully difficult to reproduce itself" (1989, p. 83). Their own children were thus at risk of being denied full adult status as members of the PMC.

As the PMC was coming into its own, another significant shift in the logic of capitalism shook its foundations. Economic crises rocked the world capitalist system in the early 1970s. Over the past quarter century, we have experienced a shift to what some refer to as "late capitalism," characterized by the increasing concentration of capital, especially in the hands of multinational corporations, the growth of flexible and mobile labor markets, weakened unions and greater pressure on workers, a decline in older industries, a surge in the service economy, and new forms of marketing and production that are again shaping new kinds of workers and consumers. According to Ehrenreich (1989), the PMC's dreams of upward mobility have been replaced by a chronic fear of falling. They are anxious not only about their children's future but also their own. The expansion of the service economy of late capitalism has sustained and even bolstered the financial status of some sectors of the PMC, but this has not allayed their fears regarding their own and their children's futures. The volatile economic conditions disrupt their certainties of the present and hopes of the future. PMC parents anxiously struggle to reproduce postwar scripts for getting ahead and convince themselves of their truth value in order to assuage the "terror of downward mobility" (Ortner, 1991). It seems that the postwar American Dream is in crisis, even for those who considered it their birthright, and many middle-class young people are unlikely to attain let alone surpass the lifestyles of their parents. PMC children have become foci of adult fears of falling. "Deviance" is no longer limited to "other" youth, but a possibility for their own as well. PMC fears of falling and producing the deviant other feed practices of "saving their young" via interventions of care, containment, and control. Their fears are fostered by the dominant popular and professional discourse that frames virtually all children as "at risk" for manifesting some yet unknown, unnamed form of pathology.

Expanding the Market of Trouble and Treatment

In recent years, we have witnessed a heightened preoccupation with troubled and troubling youth and the proliferation of new forms of pathology, diagnostic categories, and intervention strategies by which to classify, contain, and cure them. Discourses of risk and dangerous permeate both popular and professional constructions of adolescence, and notions of risky and at risk youth are increasingly conflated (Finn & Nybell, 2001; Stephens, 1995). Since the late 1970s, adolescent pathology has become a major growth industry in an expanding service economy as ever increasing proportions of young people are being deemed in need of care, containment, or control. As I have argued elsewhere, we are experiencing a medicalization of youthful difference, defiance, and distress such that adolescence itself has become equated with pathology (Finn, 2001). However, the forms of intervention continue to play out very differently along class and color lines through separate and unequal systems of care and control. The commitment to due process, diversion, and deinstitutionalization that shaped juvenile justice in the late 1960s and early 1970s has shifted to more punitive, get- tough policies, with young people of color bearing the brunt of the punishment (Austin et al., 2000; Feld, 1999; Krisberg & Austin, 1993; Males, 1996; Poe-Yamagata & Jones, 2000). For example, between 1987 and 1996, the number of white youth in detention facilities rose 18 percent, while the number of black youth in detention rose 71 percent. This period also saw an 80 percent increase in the number of minority youth in prison. Between 1980 and 1995, the proportion of black youth to white youth in custody rose from 28 percent to 40 percent (Austin, Johnson, & Gregorian, 2000; Males & Macallair, 2000).

The arena of adolescent mental health was also expanding exponentially. In 1982, it was being reported that "at least ten million children are in need of mental health services, and many more have yet to be identified" (Knitzer, 1982). By 1986, there were more than 150,000 young people age 10–17 in inpatient psychiatric care for mental disorders. And between 1987 and 1996, the rate of psychotropic drug use in the treatment of child and adolescent disorders had tripled. Thus in 20 years time, childhood itself had been identified as the fertile breeding ground of adolescent pathology. For example, in 1995, the Carnegie Council on Adolescent Development declared that half of America's 10–14 year olds are "at risk" due to their problem behaviors (Males, 1996). It seemed only a matter of time before trouble reared its head in that volatile passage to adulthood.

These expanding indicators of youthful pathology coincide with a proliferation of new psychiatric diagnostic categories by which to label their troubles in terms of disease. Along with this move came a shift in hospital regulatory practices resulting in greater scrutiny of medical services. Adolescent psychiatric treatment remained a relatively unregulated arena, and hospital management specialists encouraged strategic moves into this relatively undeveloped treatment niche. A proliferation of diagnostic possibilities accompanied a rapid expansion of adolescent psychiatric bed space in the 1980s (Gaylon, 1985; Philips & Jemerin, 1988). The clientele competing for these spaces were largely white, middle- and upper-class youth whose parents' health insurance covered the bulk of the costs. Aggressive marketing campaigns promoted the need for residential treatment to parents and professionals, feeding their fears. Meanwhile, poor youth and youth of color continued to be disproportionately represented in state-based, juvenile correctional facilities. As Mike Males (1999, p. 12) writes: "(K)id-fixing services erupted to meet the market. They were of two kinds. Prison gates opened wide in the 1980s to receive tens of thousands more poorer teens, three-fourth of them non-white. . . . At the same time, mental health and other treatment centers raked in huge profits therapizing hundreds of thousands of health-insured children of the affluent, nearly all white." By the mid 1980s, placements of white youth in juvenile detention facilities had significantly declined while their placement rates in psychiatric facilities and private residential treatment programs soared. For-profit youth care was on its way to becoming the 25 billion dollar a year industry that it is today (Kearns, 1998, p. 4).

The bull market in treatment for troubled teens has been fed and sustained by the fevered pitch of popular media and professional discourse of youthful menace. Near hysteria surrounds the various depictions of youth as violent thugs, druggies, super-predators, and suicide risks, who are constructed as basically to blame for a "national moral melt down" (Males, 1999; Zimring, 1998). Recent articles in magazines such as *Atlantic Monthly* voice fear and loathing over the coming of the "Adolescent Apocalypse" (Powers, 2002). Powerful protean images of youth as pathology are at work here, serving to heighten the anxieties of parents, professionals, and the public regarding their potential volatility. While racialized and class-based images of dangerous youth remain prevalent, fears are growing regarding the violence within those young people previously presumed to be "innocent"–middle- and upper-middle-class white youth from suburbia and Middle America "on the right track" to adulthood. While placement rates in treatment and disciplinary facilities soar, communities are increasingly becoming sites of youth discipline through the surveillance and restriction of young people in privatized spaces such as shopping malls, enforcement of strict curfews, and zero tolerance policies in schools. These practices further blur the boundaries of at-risk and risky youth, of "us" and "them," and thus heighten anxieties of PMC parents regarding their own young. As Males (1996, 1999) argues, young people in the U.S. have become targeted as the scapegoats for a host of social, political, and economic ills. The net of potential deviance has been broadly cast and the PMC fears of falling run deep. As these fears and discourses map on to one another, parents of the PMC come to see the confinement of their "own" as well as "other" youth to be not only viable but also loving options.

Troubled in Paradise

In recent years, parents with means have been offered an ever-expanding choice in containment options for their troubled and troubling teens. Residential treatment programs employ diverse monikers, ranging from boot camps to wilderness camps, boarding schools, and "specialty schools for troubled teens," whose residents are by and large the offspring of the PMC. They explicitly appeal to concerned parents whose teens had been destined for success until they veered off course

(Finn, 2001). A number of these facilities have been established in "exotic" and out-of-the-way places, from remote communities in the Rocky Mountains to isolated beaches of Mexico, Jamaica, and Samoa. (For the purposes of this discussion, I will be focusing mainly on facilities located in Samoa.) The facilities variably describe "culture shock," separation, and immersion, along with strict discipline, respect for authority, and "positive peer culture" as key components of treatment. Placement in one of the facilities costs between $30,000 and $50,000 annually, with average stays of 1 to 2 years. Thousands of young people have been removed from their families and communities and placed, often against their will, in one of these schools at the behest of their parents (Giegerich, 1998; Constantinou, 1998; Shirk, 1999). Some youth and their families offer testimonies of transformation regarding their experience of removal and containment. Others are embroiled in legal battles regarding placement involving parents', children's, and states' rights (Cohen, 1998; Kilzer, 1998; MacNamara, 1999; Shaffer, 1994). In the following discussion, I attempt to unpack and examine what these programs offer, how their discourse of intervention maps onto parental fears, and why they have become a viable, even seductive option. I explore some of the principles and practices that drive these offshore placement facilities; consider some of the tensions and anxieties that fuel parental decisions to have their children "abducted" and contained; address some of the resistance efforts mobilized by young people themselves against these practices of containment; and reflect on the meaning and power of these facilities in the context of late capitalism and the pathologizing of adolescence.

Principles and Practices of Offshore Treatment

CULTURE AND CONTROL: Offshore "specialty schools for troubled teens" share common principles and practices. Similar to Margaret Mead, they draw heavily on the cultural trope of the traditional, and "primitive" life ways of island culture and images of a premodern cultural "other" in their critique of contemporary youth trouble. In sharp contrast to Mead, however, they emphasize the therapeutic value of separation, isolation, and "culture shock" as necessary correctives to overly permissive and indulgent parenting in the U.S., which is framed as a key part of youth trouble (A Better Way, no date; Teen Help,

2000). Youth are transported to a remote island setting and inculcated in premodern, naturalized values of loyalty, hierarchy, and authority. Programs emphasize the value of ascetic living, where young people are stripped of their creature comforts and are "forced to come to terms with a situation that is completely foreign to their experiences" (A Better Way, n.d.). As comforts are stripped away so, presumably, are the dispositions and desires shaped by overly permissive parenting, a sense of entitlement, and overconsumption. For example, one program based in Western Samoa highlights the "natural therapy" of Polynesian culture and immersion in its "gracious, friendly and unspoiled" ways as part of the process of instilling new attitudes and values (A Better Way, n.d.). Program promotional materials describe how youth will live in grass huts, sleep "Samoan style" using mats of the floor, and get accustomed to a diet of "basic, humble food" as part of the "treatment process." Promotional materials make frequent reference to the therapeutic value of the unhurried, uncluttered ways of life where the self-involved individualism and materialism of U.S. culture is stripped away and youth come to accept humility, family loyalty, and community as "supreme values" (Teen Help, 2000; Giegerich, 1998; A Better Way). The permissive parenting of the postmodern world is rejected and in its place is a program purportedly grounded in traditional values marked by a paternal voice of authority. In effect, the facilities appropriate and re-imagine Mead's "primitive" cultural other as a site from which to critique "postmodern" parenting.

Curiously, while extensive claims are made about the corrective power of cultural simplicity and traditional authority, the programs seem to at best borrow superficial trappings of cultural difference, such as having boys dress in the Samoan "lava lava"–a simple fabric wrap that covers the lower body–as part of their shock therapy approach (Beck, 1998). Moreover, some of the programs, while physically located in remote island locations, are separated from the surrounding cultural community by security fences. Much like interventions of earlier times aimed at the "dangerous classes," they emphasize containment, strict discipline, and highly structured routines to combat idleness. Their detailed daily routines reflect more a boot camp approach than an "unhurried and unspoiled" island cultural influence. For example, a "typical day" for youth placed in "A Better Way," a self-described "special needs boarding school" located in Western Samoa," consists of the following schedule. As one commentator summarized: "The daily schedules are packed, the rules are firm, and every little privilege has to be earned" (Beck, 1998, p. 5):

7:00 am Wake Up
7:30–7:45 Room Checks
7:45–8:10 Breakfast
8:10–8:15 Clean Up
8:15–8:30 Goal Group
8:30–11:15 School
11:15–12:15 Therapy Group
12:15–1:00 Lunch and Chores
1:00–2:15 School
2:30–4:30 Gymnasium Fitness Program
4:30–5:30 P.E. Time on Campus
5:30–6:00 Shower and Prep for Dinner
6:00–6:30 Dinner
6:30–7:00 Chores
7:00–8:00 Positive Peer Group
8:00–8:30 Journals/Study Hall
8:30–9:30 Free Time/Reading
9:30–9:45 Reflections Group
9:45–10:00 Prep for Bed
10:00 pm Lights Out

In contrast to Margaret Mead's use of the primitive cultural trope as an opening for challenging repressive practices and championing youthful freedom and experimentation, these programs invoke notions of "culture" that play on stereotypes of cultural difference and emphasize discipline, control, and tradition. "Culture" becomes the means for calling for more rather than less discipline. They tout the power of a radical change in environment, spartan surroundings, and a highly disciplined approach to child rearing as keys to treatment success. In effect, they are using offshore sites that allow for low-cost, low overhead operations, unencumbered by the regulatory oversight of stateside youth facilities, to contain young people in tightly rule bound systems of behavioral control. Some of their promotion language is very telling. For example, one Samoan-based facility warns parents that youth "must come to terms with a situation that is completely foreign to their experiences" and then reminds parents of the value of island isolation, noting that "we have them where we want them" and "it is impossible to run away." They turn Mead's critique on its head as they deploy cultural tropes to justify more, not less, discipline and control. Culture becomes the marketing ploy for selling containment, discipline, and punishment at a hefty price to desperate parents.

DISCIPLINING THE SELF: Another key component of the offshore boarding schools is the structuring of the disciplined self. The strict behavioral programs are part of an overriding belief that young people, through the daily *habitus* of participation in regimentation, rules, and routines, will come to internalize these external values and disciplinary practices and become self regulating bodies.[11] In addition to the closely monitored daily schedules, youth are expected to conform to detailed rules covering every aspect of life. They progress through level systems, earning and losing basic privileges depending on their disciplined performance. Contractual arrangements between the facilities and the youths' parents permit staff to use physical restraint or force if necessary, to bring youth in line with the rigid programmatic expectations. Promotional materials of the offshore facilities stress the goals of making youth "internally motivated," restoring their "self-worth," and building a "stronger sense of self." Testimonials from parents and youth published in the promotional literature repeatedly speak to this transformation of the self from a rebellious and defiant teen to a goal-oriented and self-regulating "young adult." As one youth stated: "You are stripped of your freedom here and take pride in earning it back." As previously noted, youth are not only stripped of their freedom, but of their own clothing, hairstyles, and other markers of their individuality, further enforcing both conformity and the concept of foreignness where youth are no longer in control of their surroundings. These programs ascribe to a self-as-container model of personhood wherein a young person can be emptied of contrary defiance and refilled with confidence and self-control through a practiced *habitus* of discipline in which external values become internalized in a contained space. Stripped of their sense of entitlement, these youth can then be inculcated with new dispositions and desires informed by loyalty and deference to authority. It is the belief, then, that these self-regulating bodies will be able to withstand external pressures and maintain their internalized disciplinary practice upon release from the facilities and return home.

---

11. I borrow the concept of *habitus* from Pierre Bourdieu (1977, 159–197).

A key part of the process is the engagement of youth in the discipline of one another. The concept of Positive Peer Culture (PPC), a somewhat questionable practice premised on engaging youth in peer discipline, is put to practice as part of the treatment strategy. Through the PPC approach, young people are enlisted in ongoing surveillance of one another and confronting youth for violation of program rules, and they have a role in the disciplinary process for violation of rules. For example, Paradise Cove in Western Samoa promotes their "Teen Leadership Program" wherein youth participate in the discipline process of other youth as part of their own leadership development. By taking on disciplinary responsibility over other youth, residents are able to earn their way through progressive program levels. In theory, PPC has been touted as a tool for teaching responsibility and encouraging youth participation. In practice, positive peer culture risks placing youth in difficult power positions such that one's own ability to gain rights and move toward freedom is through practices of informing on and punishing others. Some youth describe the experience of being bullied by others as part of the "treatment" process. Thus, one's success in the program is measured not only by how well one follows the rules, but also by how well one enforces them. While the program discourse praises the values of loyalty and authority, the everyday practice suggests that success is measured by the disciplined performance of unquestioning loyalty to authority. One moves from privation to privilege not only through self-discipline, but also through active participation in the discipline of others.

Why Discipline and Punish? Troubled Parents of Troubling Youth

What forces are at work that make these offshore boot camp schools a not only plausible but appealing option for largely middle- and upper-middle class parents struggling with their difficult teens? How is it, when youth rights advocates decry the unjust treatment of poor youth and youth of color who are recipients of the most punitive and coercive interventions in systems of youth containment and control, that parents of more privileged youth are willing to pay dearly for the containment of their own children? How is it that parents are willing to go outside the country in order to control their own troubling children? I contend that this phenomenon is more than a late capitalist rendition of "out of sight out of mind." I suggest that there are several forces at work here shaping parental beliefs and practices, and I examine them in turn: the (new) heuristics of fear; the ideological power of corrective intervention; the class-based appeal of boarding schools; and the cultural value of difference linked to distant esoteric knowledge.

HEURISTICS OF FEAR: First, the turn to offshore treatment needs to be understood within the class-based heuristics of fear associated with late capitalism. While "other" youth have historically been the icons, indices, and symbols of fear, the important shift here, among the PMC, is toward fear not only *for* but also *of* one's own children. Parents who have opted for distant "behavior modification programs" share a discourse of desperation and heightened sense of panic. For example, the concerned New Jersey couple cited in the beginning of this chapter employ a hyperbolic discourse of fear in their claims that their son was "on a nonstop path to jail or death" while in reality his offenses had been relatively minor and had not resulted in any criminal charges. Rather, they read fear and danger in the nuances through which their son showed them he was "not himself." It was "only a matter of time" until their son "collided with the law." Curiously, these parents and others voice an *anticipatory* fear of what *might* be were they not to take "desperate measures" on their child's behalf. Their anxieties are fueled by the ubiquitous popular and professional discourses that construct "youth" in general as a category of pathology and conflate notions of "risky" and "at risk" in the process. The marketing strategies of offshore treatment facilities play to these fears and fuel anxieties of what might befall their offspring. For instance, The "Teen Help" website offers the following propaganda that plays to the heuristics of fear:

"In the next 24 hours . . .
   1,439 teens will attempt suicide
   2,759 teenage girls will become pregnant
   15,006 teens will use drugs for the first time
   3,506 teens will run away. (Teen Help, 1998)

In part, parental discourses reflect their fears of their offspring out of control. However, there seem to be more complicated fears in play here as well. For instance, there appears to be a fear of humiliation resulting from run-ins with the police, or the humiliation of having one's private struggles and shortcomings of parenting be publicly exposed. I suggest that the fears of these largely PMC parents regarding their young are intimately bound to their own "fears of falling"

(Ehrenreich, 1989). Their sense of panic resonates with their own frenetic efforts to maintain their position in a precarious service economy. Their defiant teens are not just kids who push the behavioral envelope. They are also reminders of parental vulnerability, both literally and figuratively. Not only do their children threaten the truth value of the postwar middle-class script of "getting ahead," they also pose liabilities for family solvency. For example, the New Jersey father stated that the costs of placement were well worth it and "only a fraction of what the legal fees might have been" had his son continued along his path toward trouble. It seems a powerful heuristics of fear is at work painting a broad brush of trouble over youth in general and bringing that fear into the most intimate of spaces as parents come to see and fear their own children as "other" and in need of containment and control.

CORRECTIVE INTERVENTION: Second, the appeal of offshore treatment facilities needs to be considered in light of the powerful ideology of corrective intervention. I have made the case that the pathologizing of youth is a historical and political process that has developed in mutual amplification with the expansion and legitimization of the interventionists. I have outlined the emergence of the PMC as a professional class carving out its identity and socioeconomic niche in the realm of intervention. Their professional identity, practice, and sustainability are predicated on the truth value of corrective intervention (Sarri & Finn, 1992). Their beliefs are rooted in the modernist possibilities of progress through the application of professional knowledge and skills to planned, rational change efforts. And yet, this foundational belief system itself seems fraught with doubts and ambiguities at present. Parents refer to the need to "take extreme measures" and to make "last ditch" efforts to "save" their children from themselves. They speak of "losing faith" in mainstream psychological intervention and of having exhausted all the standard professional treatment options. For example, a Maine couple who sent one of their sons to a facility in Jamaica and the other to Samoa reported: "The school system, psychologists, the judicial systems—no one could help us. We could feel him slipping through our fingers" (Beck, 1998, p. 3). Their fear of "slippage" may not only be about their children, but also about the solidity of their own foundation as a professional class. In short, they voice doubts about the forms of professional intervention that have been developed, elaborated, and advocated by the PMC. They are both skeptical of and beholden to the modes of intervention they have produced. They are coming to doubt their own abilities as parents and the capacities of their class to manage the current crisis of youth and trouble. Their language of "losing faith" and hoping to "save" their children speaks more to the power of religious salvation than to the healing power of mere professional interventions. Facing a crisis of faith in their own parenting practices and professional interventions, some parents are seeking answers in the reinvention of authoritative traditions of discipline. In this dark night of the PMC soul, some parents are engaging in desperate measures that both reinforce and challenge their reason to be.

The marketing strategies of offshore treatment facilities play to these doubts and ambiguities. On the one hand, they speak to the professionalism of their staff, and on the other, they question the power of "softer" professional interventions to make a difference. In contrast to earlier notions of troubled youth as "bad seeds" and the products of inherited degeneracy, these facilities emphasize that the youth they work with are not "bad kids." Rather they are suffering the consequences of overly permissive child-rearing, and of social systems that did not hold them accountable. The facilities make it clear that the youth they serve are essentially "good kids" who have gotten off course. They praise parents for having the courage to consider a "tough love" approach, and to love their children enough to go outside of mainstream practices. They question the efficacy of systems that emphasize the rights and voices of youth over the power of discipline, and they offer intervention grounded in "traditional" values and practices. The treatment discourse offers a contrast to modernist professional intervention through its emphasis on tradition, authority, loyalty, and discipline. The approach suggests a "premodern" paternalism as antidote to societal practices that have gone soft on youth. In ironic contrast to Margaret Mead's claims regarding coming of age in Samoa, the spokesmen for offshore treatment market the cultural value of discipline, punishment, and sexual repression as hallmarks of successful passage to adulthood in the postmodern age.[12] The cultural other

---

12. Sexuality is not explicitly addressed in the informational materials of the facilities. However, the rigid scheduling and surveillance of everyday life, sex segregation and the strong subtext of heterosexuality as norm suggests that a discourse and practice of sexual repression infiltrates "treatment." It is interesting to note that some of the websites criticizing these facilities also offer scathing critiques of "reprogramming" centers that focus on "deviant" youth sexuality. Some critics suggest ideological if not practical links among these various treatment programs.

becomes the trope for traditional values and the position from which to critique the excesses of permissive parenting run amuck.

BUYING THE BOARDING SCHOOL: Third, I suggest that these facilities appeal to anxious parents through the cachet of the boarding school image, long a marker of coming of age for members of the elite classes. Offshore placement sites tend to emphasize the language of "boarding school" rather than "treatment facility" in their promotional literature. In part, this may serve to remove them from scrutiny by those charged with oversight of youth treatment facilities. However, I suggest that there is a class-based appeal here wherein the stigma of pathology is softened by the seduction of tradition. Parents of the PMC are rejecting the interventions developed and championed by their professional peers in favor of that venerable tough-love tradition of the boarding school. They are choosing to remove their children from home, friends, and community in the hopes of a transformative experience in these distant crucibles. In their book *Preparing for Power*, an ethnographic study of elite boarding schools in the U.S., Cookson and Persell (1985) argue that these schools are crucial to the development of both social networks of power and the structured experience of privation through which young people of the elite class develop their sense of privilege, entitlement, and obligation. A key component of boarding school power lies in the presumed character-building experience of austerity. In short, elite boarding schools have maintained a belief in the power of tradition, authority, and privation as key components for socializing children of privilege for their place in class-based society. Offshore treatment facilities employ a similar discourse, appealing to the power of tradition, discipline, and privation as necessary correctives to the overly egalitarian, permissive, and consumptive practices that arguably characterize contemporary middle-class family life. They thus market to desperate parents of the PMC a long-standing elite recipe for success. It is a model that responds to the class-based desires and anxieties of the PMC. By submitting their children to a regimen of discipline and deprivation, parents can hang on to the hope that they, like the elites, are preparing their children for power, and enabling them to respond to the challenges of the postmodern world. In turn, if parents' worst fears of falling are realized, they will have done well to prepare their troubled offspring for the privations and uncertainties awaiting them amidst the vagaries of late capitalism.

DISTANCE AND DESIRE: Finally, I contend that distance itself is part of the appeal of offshore placements. On the one hand, geographic distance heightens the seductive power of cultural difference and belief in transformative possibility associated with esoteric knowledge obtained at a price from "other" worlds. The construction of treatment in terms of separation; immersion in a liminal space marked by absence of status, homogeneity, humility, simplicity, and obedience to authority; and reintegration of the transformed self encodes fundamental cultural scripts regarding rites of passage (Turner, 1974; Kottak, 1994). I suggest that the pairing of exotic, distant locales with the cultural weight of ritual creates a salient sense of transformative possibilities that parents are willing to embrace. On the other hand, the very notion of geographic distance shrinks with the compression of space and time in the postmodern world (Harvey, 1989). Global flows of people, goods, and images have made the exotic accessible. Global travel is a form of status recreation among the privileged classes, and the third worlding of travel, another spin-off of an expanding service economy, has become an acquired taste and another marker of status. Thus the placement of one's child in a distant, exotic site can be seen as a logical extension of class-based dispositions and desires under late capitalism. In sum, the discourses and practices of these facilities gain their power through a dynamic push and pull of the cultural politics of youth trouble and treatment under late capitalism. They both fuel and respond to the heuristics of fear, offer hope for youthful futures grounded in the truth value of tradition, and appeal to the desires, dispositions. and aspirations of an increasingly anxious professional middle class.

Contestations and Resistance

Over the past five years, offshore youth facilities have been the targets of criticism, and placement practices have prompted a rash of investigative reporting and professional and popular debate on youth, trouble, and treatment. A few high-profile legal battles regarding custody and youth rights have brought a number of these facilities to the attention of mainstream media. Emotionally charged accounts that pit desperate parents against defiant kids and pose "do the means justify the ends?" questions have appeared in major newspapers, weekly news magazines such as *Time* and *Newsweek*, and on the prime time television program *48 Hours*. These reports variably feature youth and parents decrying the fear tactics and militarized approaches to treatment or offering testimonials of the positive impact of such desperate measures. For example, one news report noted that "Teen Help uses sophisticated marketing to offer parents the hope of extricating their teens from a downward spiral." One parent is quoted as saying: "Kids are violent and they're scary and parents are not empowered to do anything. . . . They're not given any support and they're given all the blame. All you have to do is look at Littleton. What a terrible example. Who helped these parents?" (Kilzer, 2000). Another writes: "This is a crazy time we are living in—where kids are taking assault rifles to school and killing their classmates. The problems for a teenager in today's society are so much greater than they were when we were growing up. The problem isn't going away. When does it stop? If it is going to change, it will change one kid at a time. My daughter is now part of the solution."[13] *Time* writer Adam Cohen (1998) asks whether these facilities are camps or jails and whether parents are violating the rights of their own children when they ship them to these camps and schools. Facility spokespeople defend their professionalism and denounce criticism of their methods as groundless complaints by troubled teens forced to give up their privileges.

However, reports of abusive treatment of youth in some offshore facilities and the death of a youth in one such facility in 2000 prompted calls for more systematic investigation of their practices (Kilzer, 2000). Some youth advocates and youth care professionals have raised questions about the ability of these facilities to operate outside of the scrutiny and oversight of governmental and professional regulatory or licensing bodies. They have expressed frustration at the lack of access to and accountability of these facilities. In 1999, in response to growing public concern, the U.S. Department of State issued a "Fact Sheet on Behavior Modification Facilities" that cautioned parents as follows:

> In recent years there has been a growth of facilities around the world for the treatment of minors with drug/alcohol and discipline problems. These overseas treatment centers are known as "BEHAVIOR MODIFICATION FACILITIES." Parents enroll their children in these facilities in the hope of improving their behavior. The Department of State is aware of facilities in Jamaica, Mexi-

---

13. "Barbara," parent, quoted in testimonials, www.galaxymall.com/youth.teens/testimonials.

co, and Samoa. There may be facilities in other countries that have not come to the attention of the U.S. Government.

U.S. citizen parents who place their children in these facilities typically sign a contract for their child's treatment that authorizes the staff to act as agents for the parents. These contracts often give the staff blanket authorization to take all action necessary, in their judgment, for the health, welfare and progress within the program for the children. The facilities isolate the children in relatively remote sites, restrict contact with the outside world and employ a system of graduated levels of earned privileges and punishments to stimulate behavior change. Communication privileges of the children may be limited.

The Department of State has no direct knowledge of the corporate or legal structure of these enterprises nor of their precise relationship to each other, including ties to organizations in the United States. Though these facilities may be operated and staffed by U.S. citizens and populated primarily by U.S. citizen minors, the country where the facility is located is solely responsible for compliance with local safety, health, sanitation and educational laws and regulations, including all licensing requirements of the staff in the country. These standards, if any, may not be strictly enforced or meet the standards of similar facilities in the U.S. (U.S. Department of State, 1999)

While the State Department's caution is understated, other critics have been much more pointed. For example, Alexia Parks, of Boulder, Colorado, conducted her own investigation of these facilities and published her exposé entitled *An American Gulag: Secret P.O.W. Camps for Teens* (2000).[14] According to the *Rocky Mountain News*, Parks "led a national movement to expose the network of religious and secular compounds that incarcerate American teenagers both in the United States and in places as remote as Western Samoa" (Kilzer, 1998). Parks describes her journey into a world of containment and control and denounces the practices of forcible removal of youth from their homes and communities, "brain-washing" tactics of behavior change, and practices of incommunicado isolation and physical restraint that violate human rights. Parks' critique has been cited and quoted by a number of youth-oriented websites that have taken up watchdog roles. For example, the IntrepidNet Reporter offers a series of web articles that critically examine the marketing and treatment tactics of these facilities, champion youth rights, and raise serious questions about the increasingly global nature of the youth containment industry. Another website, Libertarian Rock (2001), describes the facilities as "teen

---

14. Parks published earlier versions of her work via Internet, and it generated further debate and investigation by both mainstream journalists and youth activists and advocates.

concentration camps" and offers specific advice to young people on "How to Stop Your Abduction." They write:

> When you go to sleep tonight, you may not have to set your alarm because two big guys are going to wake you up, force you into their car, and then drive you to a teen concentration camp. You can prevent your abduction and possibly ensure your ultimate escape by visiting the website of Teen Aid, an organization that protects the civil and human rights of teens. (Libertarian Rock, 2001)

Another internet site, "Free Youth," an "online forum for the Youth Rights Movement," has published a scathing critique entitled, "Prison Camps for Defiant Youth." They write:

> Picture yourself on a tropical island, with palm trees and a warm sun, and tourists on vacation. Now picture yourself looking at those things through a barbed wire fence and an armed guard at your back. This is the fate faced by hundreds of youths per year that are sent to prison camps overseas by their parents. . . . In remote facilities far from the public eye, in countries with little or no laws on human rights, young people are threatened, illegally restrained, and beaten, all to get them to submit to the will of the parents. . . . Like a horse trainer who must break the spirit of a horse to make it rideable, these facilities crush the will to stand strong in youth [to] make them servile. Human beings are treated as animals. These prison camps claim they teach "morals" and "values." But whose morals? (Russell, 1999)

The internet has become a key site for communication among young people and youth advocates who are organizing resistance to the offshore containment of youth as a form of "care." Through their efforts, they are resisting the totalizing and individualizing practices through which youth as a group are pathologized and through which intervention is depoliticized. They are reclaiming a political voice, recognizing youth rights, and the reenvisioning the politics of youth, trouble, and treatment.

Conclusion

I have argued the need for a cultural, historical, and political perspective on the making of youth, trouble, and intervention in order to understand contemporary discourses and practices. I have attempted to demonstrate the ways in which the discourses and practices regarding youth, trouble, and intervention have been both mutually constituting and mutually amplifying. Throughout this discussion, I have illustrated the protean nature of the concept of youth as it is differentially mapped onto adult anxieties and images of pathology and possibility, often blurring the boundaries among "normal," "risky," and "at-risk" youth along the way. Further, I have attempted to show that these discourses and practices must be understood in the context of the shifting logics and inherent contradictions of capitalism and the concomitant making of new social subjects. But it is not enough to simply make these arguments. Those of us who engage in professional intervention work with youth need to critically reflect on the "certainties" that shape our theory and practice and the ways in which we ourselves are disciplined to be certain kinds of practitioners who produce and respond to certain kinds of clients. We need to interrogate the relationship between our practices and the individual and collective consequences for young people with whom we work. Grounding in a cultural, historical, and political perspective needs to be a key component in the formation of the next generation of helping professionals so that they may become critically reflective practitioners who continually interrogate the meaning, power, history, context, and possibility of their practice (Finn & Jacobson, 2003).

I concur with Adams (1997) that youth serve as funnels for adult fears. However, we need to seriously examine what sorts of youth are defined and targeted in terms of what kinds of fears at what moments in time. As Sharon Stephens argues: "the labeling of some youth as pathological because they deviate too far from the script, i.e., they are too political, rebellious, or sexual, is not new. Nor, as we have seen, is the pathologizing and control of adolescents in the 'dangerous' classes and racial and ethnic groups. What does seem to be new is the extent to which all youth are now going into the 'pool of pathology' to be subsequently fished out with different sorts of nets" (Stephens, 1997, in Finn & Nybell, 2001). Both popular and professional discourse regarding poor youth and youth of color is growing increasingly punitive, as are the practices of confinement and control. For example, the growing ease and volume of transfers of juvenile offenders to adult courts, especially when they are young people of color, suggests that some groups of young people are viewed by adults as no longer warranting a place in childhood. Other youth, such as those shipped to offshore treatment facilities by their parents, are still viewed as salvageable. But we must confront the question, salvageable for what? What sorts of youth and adults are being produced through our interventions? Stephens argues that "[T]he sorts of adults now needed are individualized, depoliticized, flexible subjects. The pathologization of adolescence and its related modes of treatment may be one way to get from here to there" (Stephens, 1997, in Finn & Nybell, 2001).

Let's return to the question of the offshore containment of relatively privileged youth. Perhaps the pendulum of parental leniency has swung to the side of permissiveness, as some would argue. Perhaps, in an effort to offer young people "less hurried lives" and freer spirits, some have ended up rudderless and in need of firm guidance. But we need to look carefully at what is at stake in the disciplinary alternatives posed by offshore treatment facilities. These programs promise to mold young people to be loyal, servile, and deferent to authority. They are to be self-disciplined bodies who are also willing to engage in the surveillance and discipline of others. These disciplinary practices fit with a cultural logic of late capitalism and the concomitant practices of making new social subjects suited for the flexible, just-in-time labor force needs of a global economy. Moreover, these are depoliticized subjects; they structured as particular kinds of workers, consumers, and family members, but they are denied the rights and social experiences of citizenship. What does it mean to be stripped of one's sense of citizenship and the accompanying responsibilities and obligations? What prices will these disciplined and disciplinarian bodies pay for their rigorous rite of passage? We know little of the long-term personal and social consequences of these interventions. How does removal and separation from one's family, peers, and community and the accompanying access routes to the adult world affect one's life chances? What are the ripple effects among other young people when their peers are "disappeared" by their parents and their absence shrouded in secrecy? What sorts of lasting marks might these drastic measures make on parent-child relations, parenting practices, civic engagement, and the future of professional intervention? In what other ways will the bodies of young people be commodified to meets the demands of an expanding service economy? We in the helping professions need to promote dialogue and debate regarding these questions and concerns. It is a dialogue that must include the voices and views of young people themselves. Moreover, we need to take seriously the political critique and resistance generated by young people through their diverse, emergent range of networks and movements. Young people are raising fundamental questions about the ongoing construction of youth as trouble such that their full personhood is denied. They are angry and claiming the right to resist and be heard. It is time for adults to listen.

BIBLIOGRAPHY

A Better Way (no date). Adolescent residential treatment services. Online at www.abetterwayrts.com. accessed 6/4/02.

Adams, M. (1997). *The trouble with normal: Postwar youth and the making of heterosexuality in Toronto.* Toronto: University of Toronto

Austin, J., Johnson, K.D., & Gregorian, M. (2000). *Juveniles in adults prisons and jails: A national assessment.* Washington, DC: Bureau of Justice Assistance.

Baron, A. (1991). Gender and labor history: learning from the past, looking to the future. Introduction (pp. 1–46) In A. Baron (Ed.), *Work engendered: Toward a new history of American labor.* Ithaca: Cornell University Press.

Beck, R. (1998). A family's tale of renewal. *Boothbay Register,* Boothbay Harbor, ME, 16 April, 1–3. Accessed at boothbayregister.maine.com/1998-04-16/family_tale.html.

Bowlby, J. (1968). *Attachment.* London: Pelican.

Boyer, P. (1978). *Urban masses and moral order in America, 1820–1920.* Cambridge, MA: Harvard University Press.

Brace, C.L. (1872). *The dangerous classes of New York and my twenty years work among them.* New York: Wynkoop and Hollenbeck.

Bremner, R. (Ed.) (1970). *Children and youth in America: A documentary history* (Vols. I–III). Cambridge, MA: Harvard University Press.

Briar-Lawson, K., Lawson, H., Hennon, C., & Jones, A. (2001). *Family-centered policies and practices: International implications.* New York: Columbia University Press.

Burt, C. (1925). *The young delinquent.* New York: D. Appleton.

Cloward, R., & Ohlin, L. (1960). *Delinquency and opportunity: A theory of delinquent gangs.* Glencoe, IL: Free Press.

Cohen, A. (1998). Is this a camp or a jail? *Time,* 26 January 151(3). Online at www.time.com/time/magazine.1998/dom/980126/family. Accessed 6/4/02.

Cookson, P., & Persell, C.H. (1985). *Preparing for power: America's elite boarding schools.* New York: Basic Books.

Costantinou. M. (1998). Unwilling teen's stay in Jamaica debated. *San Francisco Examiner,* 8 January. Sfgate.com/cgi-bin/aritcle.cgi?=/examiner/archives/1998/01/08. Accessed 6/4/02.

Ehrenreich, B. (1989). *Fear of falling: The inner life of the middle class.* New York: Pantheon.

Ehrenreich, B., & Ehrenreich, J. (1979). The professional managerial class. In P. Walker (Ed.), *Between labor and capital.* Boston, MA: South End Press, 5–45.

Ehrenreich, J. (1985). *The altruistic imagination.* Ithaca, NY: Cornell University Press.

Enright, R., Levy, Jr., V., Harris, D., & Lapsley, D. (1987). Do economic conditions influence how theorists view adolescents? *Journal of Youth and Adolescence, 16,* 541–549.

Erikson, E. (1959). *Identity and the life cycle: Selected papers.* New York: International Press.

——. (1968). *Identity, youth, and crisis.* New York: Norton.

Feld, B. (1999). *Bad kids, race, and the transformation of the juvenile court.* New York: Oxford University Press.

Finn, J. (2001). Text and turbulence: Representing adolescence as pathology in the human services. *Childhood, A Global Journal of Child Research. 8*(2): 167–192.

Finn, J., & Nybell, L. (2001) Introduction: Capitalizing on concern: The making of troubled children and troubling youth in late capitalism." In J. Finn & L. Nybell (Eds.), *Capitalizing on Concern: Special Issue of Childhood, A Global Journal of Child Research, 8*(2), 139–146.

Gaylon, S. (1985). The coming of the corporation and the marketing of psychiatry. *Journal of the American Academy of Child and Adolescent Psychiatry, 36:* 154–59.

Giddens, A. (1994). *Beyond left and right: The future of radical politics.* Stanford, CA: Stanford University Press.

Giegerich, S. (1998). The last resort for troubled son. *Asbury Park Press,* 15 November, pp. A1, A4. Asbury Park, NJ.

Gramsci, A. (1988). *An Antonio Gramsci reader: Selected writings, 1916–1935.* Edited by D. Forgacs. New York: Schocken Books.

Griffin, C. (1993). *Representations of youth: The study of youth and adolescence in Britain and America.* Cambridge: Polity Press.

——. (1997). Troubled teens: Managing disorders of transition and consumption." *Feminist Review, 55* (1), 4–21.

——. (2001). Imagining new narratives of youth: Youth research, the "New Europe" and global youth culture. *Childhood, 8*(2), 147–166.

Hall, G.S. (1904). *Adolescence, its psychology and its relations to physiology, anthropology, sociology, sex, crime, religion, and education* (Vol. I). New York: Appleton.

Hartman, A., & Laird, J. (1983). *Family-centered social work practice.* New York: Free Press.

Harvey, D. (1989). *The condition of postmodernity.* Oxford: Basil Blackwell.

Healy, W. (1915). *The individual delinquent: A text-book of diagnosis and prognosis for all concerned in understanding offenders.* Boston, NA: Little, Brown.

Hawes, J. (1997). *Children between the wars: American childhood, 1920–1940.* New York: Twayne Publishers.

Hebdige, D. (1988). *Hiding in the light.* New York & London: Routledge.

Heiman, R. (2001). "The ironic contradictions in the discourse on generation X, or how "Slackers" are saving capitalism. *Childhood, 8*(2), 274–293.

IntrepidNet Reporter. (1999). Specialty schools for defiant teens. Accessed at intrepidnetreporter.com/TeenHelp/pow.htm, 6/4/02.

Jones, K. (1999). *Taming the troublesome child: American families, child guidance, and the limits of psychiatric authority.* Cambridge: MA: Harvard University Press.

Joint Commission on Mental Health of Children. (1970). *Crisis in child mental health: Challenges for the 1970s.* New York: Harper and Row.

Katz, M. (1986). *In the shadow of the poor house: A special history of welfare in America.* New York: Basic Books.

Kearns, R. (1998). Finding profit in at-risk kids. *Children's Voice,* Fall, 4–5, 14–16.

Kepel, B. (1995). *The work of democracy: Ralph Bunche, Kenneth B. Clark, Lorraine Hansberry, and the cultural politics of race.* Cambridge, MA: Harvard University Press.

Kerr, J. (1999). (Un)equal justice: Juvenile court abolition and African Americans. *The Annals of the American Academy of Political and Social Science, 564:* 109°125.

Kett, J. (1977). *Rites of passage: Adolescence in America, 1790–1970.* New York: Basic Books.

Kilzer, L. (1998). Children Were Isolated and Hogtied, They Report. Denver, CO: *Rocky Mountain News,* 15 November, accessed at www.teenliberty.org, 6/4/02.

——. (2000). Desperate measures. Denver, CO: *Rocky Mountain News,* Online at www.denver-rmn.com/desperate/site-desperate/0702desp4. Accessed 6/4/02.

Knitzer, J. (1982). *Unclaimed children: The failure of public responsibility to children and adolescents in need of mental health services.* Washington, DC: Chldren's Defense Fund.

Kottak, C. (1994). *Anthropology: The exploration of human diversity* (6th ed.). New York: McGraw-Hill.

Krisberg, B., & Austin, J. (1993). *Reinventing juvenile justice.* Newbury Park: CA: Sage.

Libertarian Rock. (2001). Teen concentration camps: Stop your abduction. Online at www.libertarianrock.com/topics/teencamp. Accessed 6/12/02.

MacDonald, A. (1908) Juvenile crime and reformation, including stigmata of degeneration, 60 Cong., 1 Sess (1908). Senate Doc. 532, pp. 16–17. Washington, DC. In R. Bremner (Ed.) (1970), *Children and youth in America: A documentary history* (Vols. I–III). Cambridge, MA: Harvard University Press.

MacNamara, M. (1999). Love or betrayal?" Diablomag.com/archives/DM9902. Accessed 7/08/02.

Males, M. (1996). *The scapegoat generation.* Monroe, ME: Common Courage Press.

——. (1999). *Framing youth: 10 myths about the next generation.* Monroe, ME: Common Courage Press.

Males, M., & Macallair, D. (2000). *The color of justice: An analysis of juvenile adult court transfers in California.* Justice Policy Institute.

Markowitz, G., & Rosner, D. (1996). *Children, race, and power: Kenneth and Mamie Clark's Northside Center.* Charlottesville: University Press of Virginia.

McRobbie, A. (1991). *Feminism and youth culture: From "Jackie" to "Just Seventeen."* Boston, MA: Unwin Hyman.

Mead, M. (1928). *Coming of age in Samoa.* New York: Dell.

Molina, N. (2000). Wanted: Women to play future citizens of America–Mexicans and Japanese need not apply. Paper presented in session entitled "Bodies, Soil and Statistics: New Perspectives on the History of Medicine and Science in 20th Century California." Western History Conference, San Antonio, TX, November, 2000.

Nybell, L. (2002). *Remaking children's mental health: On children, community, and care in reform.* Ph.D. Dissertation University of Michigan. Ann Arbor, MI.

Ortner, S. (1991). Reading America: Preliminary notes on class and culture. In R. Fox (Ed.). *Recapturing anthropology: Working in the present.* Santa Fe, NM: School of American Research Press.

Parks, A. (2000). *An American gulag: Secret P.O.W. camps for teens.* Eldorado Springs, CO: Education Exchange.

Philips, L., & Jemerin, J. (1988). Changes in inpatient child psychiatry: Consequences and recommendations. *Journal of the American Academy of Child and Adolescent Psychiatry, 27:* 397–403.

Poe-Yamagata, E., & Jones, M. (2000). *And justice for some: Differential treatment of minority youth in the juvenile justice system.* Washington, DC: Building Blocks for Youth.

Powers, R. (2002). The apocalypse of adolescence. *The Atlantic Monthly, 289*(3), March, 58–74.

Prout, A., & James, A. (1997). *Constructing and reconstructing childhood* (2nd ed.). London: Falmer Press.

Rothman, D. (1971). *The discovery of the asylum: Social order and disorder in the new republic.* Boston: Little, Brown.

Russell, J. (1999). Prison camp for defiant youth. *Free youth: Online Forum for the Youth Rights Movement,* Issue 1. Online at www.oblivion.net. Accessed 6/12/02.

Sarri, R., & Finn, J. (1992). Child welfare policy and practice: Rethinking the history of our certainties. *Children and Youth Services Review, 14:* 219–236.

Shaffer, L. (1994). Paradise Cove. *Woodbury Reports Archives, 31,* December. Woodbury Reports, Inc. Accessed at www.strugglingteens.com/archives/ 1994/12/np01 .html, 6/4/02.

Shirk, M. (1999). It's cheap, but it is good for kids? *Youth Today,* June, p. 22.

Shook, J. (2001). Examining constructions of childhood and adolescence through the lens of the juvenile court. Unpublished paper. University of Michigan, School of Social Work, Ann Arbor, MI.

Stephens, S. (1995). *Children and the politics of culture.* Princeton: Princeton University Press.

——. (1997). Discussant's comments on "capitalizing on concern," panel session presented at the American Anthropological Association Annual Program meetings, Washington, DC. Cited in J. Finn & L. Nybell (2001), Introduction, *Childhood: A Global Journal of Child Research, 8*(2): 142.

Stocking, G.W., Jr. (1982). *Race, culture, and evolution: Essays in the history of anthropology.* Chicago: University of Chicago Press.

Sutton, J. (1988). *Stubborn children* Berkeley: University of California Press.

Teen Help Adolescent Resources. (2000). Support for families with teen challenges. Online at http://vpp.com/teenhelp. Accessed 8/20/02.

Turner, V. (1974). *The ritual process.* Harmondsworth, England: Penguin.

Zimring, F. (1998). *American youth violence.* New York: Oxford University Press.

Chapter 5

CLARITY, RITES, AND CHILDREN'S SPACES OF DISCIPLINE

STUART C. AITKEN AND JOEL JENNINGS

> I have had to get in a kids face, and some think it is kind of funny. So once you get the little class-clown's attention, or the class leader, and you break them, you've pretty much broken the whole class and you have their attention. And that is what you need to get is their attention.
>
> First Mate of the *Euterpe*

The children mill around on the wharf, laughing and clowning, full to the brim with boisterous excitement. The *Euterpe,* a nineteenth century square-rigged, iron-hulled sailing ship towers above them, casting long shadows in the morning sunlight. Necks strain as young heads tilt back to capture the grandeur and majesty of the 120 foot main mast with its sails flapping gently, seemingly beckoning the youngsters to come on board. Young minds are filled with pirate ships, buccaneers, cutlasses, canons, treasure maps, broadsides, and navy battles. This is a fourth grade field trip and the dock is awash with an air of youthful energy and expectations of adventure on the high seas. The reverie is broken by the yells of a large bearded man whose appearance on the gangplank had gone unnoticed. He holds a big belaying pin in one hand. On his broad belt are a knife, a marlinspike, and sailor's string. He looks like one of the more salubrious characters from *The Princess Bride* or *Treasure Island.* This is going to be fun. But his voice is intimidating, and he is yelling at the kids:

All hands for the barque *Euterpe!* I am the First Mate aboard the *Euterpe.* I have been ordered by the Captain to muster a crew of experienced sailors for the long voyage to New Zealand, Australia and eventually the West Coast of America. . . . You ugly bunch of ne'er-do-wells are mine. . . . What a sorry sight of sailors you are. . . . I doubt if many of you will survive.

The children are not sure how to react to this haranguing. It is more intense than they expected. Most are not used to verbal abuse of this kind, and they are not sure that they deserve it. Some snigger, others look awkwardly at parents for help. The parents are a little unsure. The first mate shouts and bullies the kids into one line and then parades before them, eyeing each suspiciously. One boy starts sniggering and the mate pounces on him verbally. The "class clown" is singled out and reduced to tears. The other children are silent, attentive, and working very hard not to draw attention to themselves. This is a form of collective discipline that few of them have ever experienced. Some of the parents are apprehensively looking at the teacher. She has been here before and offers a reassuring nod. After the crew muster, the first mate marches the children up the gangplank and onto the ship. They are entering a bounded space of rules, discipline, and hierarchical order with an edge that is palpable and, at least for the moment, none too reassuring.

With this essay, we engage the disciplining of children's minds and bodies through an educational program where children become sailors for 18 hours aboard the *Euterpe* in 1874. The indomitable spaces of maritime law are recreated as a context for the children's educational experience. The *Euterpe* is moored in San Diego Bay throughout the program, which is directed and produced by San Diego's Maritime Historical Society. This living history program is designed for fourth and fifth grade students, and covers the San Diego City Schools' requirement for a fieldtrip in these grades. Originally, the *Euterpe* was designed as a merchant vessel but later transported immigrants from Europe to America. Sailing at the height of European emigration and the growth of the U.S. as a global power, the ship transported men, women, and children in cramped and unsanitary conditions.

Our concern is not solely with this highly successful educational program that effectively "bootcamps" children into the context of late nineteenth century maritime rules, but more generally with the way the program reflects and refracts contemporary social and spatial constructions of childhood. What is it about the disciplining, clarity, and hierarchy of ship space that is so appealing to teachers, parents, and, at least by the end of the program, most child participants? While it does not endorse many of the excesses and abuses of late nineteenth century maritime rules, we recognize that the "living history" program is a window on how contemporary society constructs childhood and disciplines children. What does the program's popularity say about the spaces of contemporary childhood? Enthusiasts for the program highlight it as a panacea for society's ills, including school violence and low SAT scores. This notwithstanding, a deeply disturbing hierarchy of patriarchal dominance and discipline undergirds the program as it attempts to authentically recreate nineteenth century maritime law and space.

Although we initially focus on children's experiences aboard the *Euterpe,* this essay is ultimately about the everyday spaces of children, and the disciplinary rules that are encoded in those spaces. Space, we argue, offers a combination of mixed and contradictory messages about children's identity, their cooperation in an adult world and what constitutes a rite of passage. There is clearly dissonance between the program that is in large part inspired by the historical and geographical context of the *Euterpe* and the children's everyday lives. A paradox is contrived that reveals a series of anxieties and tensions in the lives of the young participants and those who care for them. We argue that discipline in a child's world—in the home, the classroom, and the neighborhood, or in the hyper-commercial festival places of malls and kid-theme restaurants—is often hidden or unfairly meted out, without explanation or contingency. The *Euterpe* offers something different. For the children who participate in the living history program, it is a working space and following rules is a matter of life and death. What the children get from this, in combination with the experiences of their daily lives, is complex and contradictory. It marks what some postcolonial theorists call a hybrid space, for it combines unlike parts that, for many children, give rise to anxious and ambivalent identities. We find this fantastic co-occurrence in space/time of identities and discourses that might be thought of as mutually exclusive of great interest. We use interviews with staff aboard the *Euterpe,* children, teachers, and their parents, and in-class focus groups to argue that the program's success, both educationally and experientially, hinges in large part on the creation of a safe space within which children explore responsibility, accountability, and teamwork in the context of clear communication and explicit, hierarchical rules.

In what follows, we introduce the terms "living history" and "living geography" as contexts for understanding the times and spaces of children's everyday lives as they are constructed by adults. We argue that these histories and geographies are disciplining, and use the *Euterpe* program as a foil to understand them better. First, we construct the living history program aboard the *Euterpe* as a rite of passage, or a liminal space where children get to play with their identities. Later in the chapter, we argue that liminality is a day-to-day occurrence and that everyday rites of passage are also about disciplining. For many children and their parents, this disciplining is so mundane that it goes unnoticed, but it is nonetheless powerful and problematic. In the body of the chapter, we discuss the less subtle transformations that accompany the 18-hour participation in the living history program. We then focus on the ways that rites of passage are disciplining. We end the chapter by speculating on the subtler disciplining rules and mores that are embedded in everyday spaces. To set up these discussions, we begin with a brief account of the geography of rites of passage.

Sites of Passage

> . . . the passage from one social position to another is identified with a *territorial passage*, such as the entrance into a village or a house, the movement from one room to another, or the crossing of streets or squares.
>
> van Gennep 1960, 192.

In the early twentieth century, when the *Euterpe* was actively giving immigrants passage to the United States, Arnold van Gennep (1909 (1960) introduced the concept of a rite of passage to describe those rituals and practices that define the various stages through which individuals' pass on life's journey. As the epigram above suggests, passages are about territories or places, and sometimes they are as mundane as walking through a door. According to Gennep, three processes mark a rite of passage: separation, transition, and incorporation. Oftentimes, these processes or stages are associated with rituals. For van Gennep, separation was usually into a sacred world and it was always a geographical area or place, in what Matthews (2003) calls a site of passage. This place took on the characteristics of liminality, or "threshold," and it is here that transitions take place. A ritualized or liminal space is about ". . . the doffing of masks, the stripping of statuses, the renunciation of roles, the demolishing of structures" (Turner 1969, 26). The third process, incorporation, represents a return, transformed, to the profane world.

The *Euterpe* is presented here as a liminal space. Children separate from their familiar worlds on the wharf. The fierce first mate, shouting rules and regulations in their faces, presents a hard, granite-like demeanor that goes beyond their toughest teachers. The first mate is the children's initial encounter with the program and the experience suggests something different. So, as the children board the ship there is a sense that anything may happen. They have entered a domain of transition. It is a place where they are required to forget the masks of identity that they previously wore, where they have to hide their status and roles, where the structures of their familial life are cast asunder. But, of course, they never forget, so in what follows we attempt to articulate the hybridity of children's experiences as part of the program and how the spaces of childhood play out in a myriad of ways on the decks of the *Euterpe*.

The Euterpe program challenges children's understanding of authority and rules. It estranges them from access to a "received" Western tradition of power and identity, where parents and teachers are for the most part nurturing and where legal structures protect against physical and emotional abuse. As Homi Bhabba (1994, 219) puts it, hybridity is about "how you survive, how you produce a sense of agency or identity in situations in which you are continually having to deal with symbols of power and identity." The first mate is clearly a symbol of power: he embodies ship's rules and, as far as the children are concerned, metes out dire consequences if those rules are not adhered to. In the face of this powerful encounter, which is as much about the ship as it is the first mate, children are forced to realign customary boundaries and, we will argue, a new sense of social possibilities is attainable.

When drawing on the notions of liminality and hybridity, it is important to recognize that there are multiple childhoods and a myriad of different transitions. It is important to note also that transitions to maturity are not unproblematic. Amongst some feminists, for example, rites of passage are critically assessed as transition rites (e.g., birthing rituals, barmitzvahs, marriages) that are symbolic and focused with a particular intent. The intent, they argue, is not only a rite of passage but also a rite to patriarchy, and this rite is locally contingent (Homans 1994; Aitken 1999). Feminist concern highlights the success of the *Euterpe* program as hinged upon a hierarchical and overtly masculanist chain of command that attempts to "break" young minds and bodies. As such, it elaborates a patriarchal order than many of us fight to eradicate. Alternatively, it may be argued that in our feminist rush to judge the excesses of disciplinary and authoritarian structures and spaces as patriarchal, we throw out other values embodied in these sites of passage. Later, we speculate that the seemingly nurturing places of schools, daycares and, especially, commercial fun-zones discipline in ways that are much more insidiously contrived to inculcate the machinations of a patriarchal capitalism onto young minds and bodies. We wonder if there is any chance for hybridity in these spaces. This, we argue, is about the rules and regulations that discipline living space. Before we elaborate on those everyday spaces of childhood, we focus on living history and some of our concerns regarding educational programs based on attempts to authenticate history that purportedly enable children to experience some truth about the past.

Disciplined Through Living History

It is beyond the purview of this essay to elaborate on the development of living history museums. It may be argued, however, that some of the well-known early sites such as Colonial Williamsburg (sponsored by John Rockefeller, Jr.) and Greenfield Village (sponsored by Henry Ford) grew out of a perceived need to preserve the legacy of modernity, elitism, and Anglo-American values (Leon & Paitt 1989; Snow 1993). With few exceptions, they depict the lives of middle- and upper-income protestants in agrarian settings and they were established to preserve a specific set of values against a perceived tide of change with a new wave of immigration in the early twentieth century. Living history museums' struggles to balance the necessities of attracting tourists, producing profits, and re-presenting history are well documented (Leon & Rosenzweig 1989; Snow 1993; Handler & Gable 1997; DeLyser, 1999). More importantly, for our purposes here, are the reasons behind the development of educational programs related to a sense of authentic history. One of the instructors on the *Euterpe* described the program's authenticity this way:

Authenticity, well the *Euterpe* is original. It isn't a mock up ship, it hasn't been modified in anyway, she is original. She is 138 years old, uhh I believe the ship herself represents a lot, because she did carry immigrants, because she did carry cargo. So we don't have to make believe on anything. The program has been adjusted to the ship. It's really surprising that the kids really do know that they are on an actual ship that goes to sea. You can feel the ship, you can hear the ship, and the ship can talk to you . . . kids do take that in.

But history is always rehistorized as it is recreated in educational living history programs. That children should touch aspects of the past says more about adult views on what society needs today than it does about the truth of past representations. Living history traditions generate the spaces of a past "other" through the generation of spaces of "self" and of "our" culture. Just as second and third generation American's wanted to distance "American" culture from the values and culture of new European immigrants, so too living history museums distance people of the past from our current state of development. David Sibley (1995, xi) argued famously that "the human landscape can be read as a landscape of exclusion" and we add that representations of the past may be read not only as landscapes, but also timescapes of exclusion. Living history museums, created out of a sense of development and difference, provide not so much a window to the past, as a mirror to observe specific kinds of social reflections.

Dydia DeLyser (1999) points out that authenticity is important only in so far as a program's participants' images and values are authenticated. Although there is a substantial debate on how authenticity is constructed, the verity of any program rests with the evaluation of participants. As sociologist Erik Cohen (1988, 378) argues, the question is not whether participants have an authentic experience, but whether their experience is endowed with authenticity in their eyes. For fourth and fifth graders, the authenticity of the *Euterpe* is not necessarily about immigrant life in 1874. Young imaginations turn on pirates, naval battles and the romance and grandeur of square-rigged sailing ships:

Interviewer: Ok. Good. So why do you think they made you stand nightwatch? Matt?

Matt: To watch out for pirating and things like that . . . and um like . . . the icebergs and Titanics and the water. . . .

(Matt, fifth grade)

"Well, I . . . well, I thought the ship was going to be red because I saw it on TV . . . but I never thought it would be this magnificent, I never thought it would be this much fun." (Matt, fifth grade).

Aboard the *Euterpe,* a space of legitimacy rather than authenticity (this is a large ocean going vessel that was built a long time ago) is all that is needed for youngsters to experience a maritime past of their own imaginations.

Another, equally important, aspect of authenticity are the values imparted by a program's staff of educators, and the dissonance between those values and the expectations that the children bring to the program. An important point about the ways that the instructors construct the social setting of *Euterpe* during the program is that they speak to contemporary adult views on what children need. Michael, a second-year instructor, spoke at length on his interests in raising children's awareness of class histories:

> I really emphasize the class structure, like this is where the first class passengers live and I try to give them the whole full life for what immigrants were like. And I say, look it, this is what they had to go through. They didn't know what they were getting themselves into. This is their conditions they had . . . and then I say like, well how is it on your farms right now? And when I say their farms I mean their homes. Wow [they say] we have it pretty easy.

One of the issues that may be raised about some living history programs is that they glorify and romanticize the past. In places like Colonial Williamsburg and Greenfield Village, there is a clear value judgment that many aspects of the way of life disclosed in these "traditional" places and periods are preferable to those of here and now. There is another discourse at work in the *Euterpe* program that may be equally problematic. An alternative tendency is to see in past times the absences of our present (this is what they had to go through and we don't). Another instructor, Hector, had this to say about absences that define our present:

> The program is to demonstrate how life was. How good they really have it. Life was expendable back then, they had no rights. . . . When they leave the ship in the morning . . . they may be dragging their feet a little bit, but I think when they get home and get into their comfortable bed, and they get three meals a day, and they get clean clothes and clean socks . . . and then of course parents, parents learn how they can do dishes. . . .

The conditions and artifacts of the nineteenth century immigrant define a lack that enables the moral high ground of a "normal," better present for the children who participate in the program.

For some educators on the *Euterpe,* the pedagogy is not about constructing a better present but an equivalent one. Michael goes on to note that it is important for him to relate past experiences of immigrants to current injustices. He points out that although it is easy to cast judgment on past eras, there is just as much evidence of poor conditions in our own time:

> . . . so I feel like a lot of them, their like thinking about it and I think ya know if you can stretch and that is the foundation for building a good kid, ya know. . . . For me I think that, umm, I am more of a person who is progressively into trying to find, uhh, ways for all peoples not to be marginalized. . . . They [immigrants] went through some hard times, and I try to say there are people struggling with this even today. . . .

The living history program is an educational venue for disciplining children's minds, not only in terms of the immediate experience of being on board a ship, but also by incorporating larger discourses that span geographic eras and scales.

And yet it is to the immediate experience of discipline on the decks that the children respond to rather than the larger disciplinary concerns of Michael and other educators. This too, according to the staff of the *Euterpe*, is about "stretching and making the foundation for a good kid." The official script and experiential elements included by instructors during the program demonstrate an awareness of the formative capacity inherent in this kind of discipline. The *Euterpe* program is an intersection of teachers who desire to instill discipline in their school classes, parents who want their children to appreciate the things they have in their everyday lives, and instructors who want to make a positive impact on a child's future. Children are the recipients of a struggle to shape and stretch (read discipline) the identities of young people.

Overt discipline and the role of the first mate throughout the program is perhaps the most easily defined underlying disciplinary theme in the program. Instructors, and the *Instructor Training Manual and Program Curriculum* (Spearal, 2002) alike identify the dominant first mate character as central to the success of the program:

> *Training Manual:* This is probably the most vital part of the program. Here the First Mate sets the tone to the entire program. The muster must be carried out correctly in order for the rest of the voyage to run smoothly. The First Mate must capture the students' attention and set the scene and expectations ashore before the "lads" ever come aboard. The first mate must be *firm, confident, clear* and *organized.*

> *Hector:* When I go out there and start yelling and screaming at em- they forget everything they have been told and they are going to do exactly what I say.

Jenny: But when they come on board it is very much more dramatic for them because they are dealing with the first mate, who is a very strict disciplinarian and who is very noisy and loud and in their faces.

Michael: Alright, well we first shock them to start them off, we establish the hierarchy which is a fun thing, they're pretty shocked about what happens, and the first mate does that.

Hector: And then we pull the cat o' nine tails out of the bag, a nice orange bag, which is traditional, which lays on the rail, and hit it on the sun cover on the ship, and they all jump back about a foot, and we put it back in the bag and tell them it is up to them not to let the cat out of the bag.

Kathy: So the first thing that happens: they say oh shit, what did I get myself into?

There is significant tension between the latent threat of violence as demonstrated by the first mate and described by the crew, and the nurturing educational environments that elementary schools generally try to achieve. The children's response to their meeting with the first mate confounds this tension:

(John, fourth grade): Well, it was kind of mean, to like right when you get to the ship, like they are just picking you up off the streets and then right when they come over there they start yelling at you like you are their little catch or something.

(Mike, fourth Grade): We learned about the First Mate's cat. . . .
Interviewer: Right. Which is the cat o' nine tails?
Mike: That lives in a bag. I got really freaked about it, I did not want to get, get real bad around her . . . cause I did not want to be hit.

Is it the barely repressed violence of the first mate that inspires discipline, or the clear communication and explicit explanation of shipboard rules? This question notwithstanding (although it is an important question) there is, nonetheless, an elaboration of vocal and physical violence that would get any fourth or fifth grade teacher fired. The *Euterpe* instructors' threatened violence is permissible because this is a re-enactment of nineteenth century maritime values. Teachers, parents and instructors know that this is a fiction, albeit a seemingly authentic one, and that the children will not be hurt physically. But the quotes above suggest that the possibility of violence is real to the children.

Extending Foucault's (1975) conceptualization of the executioner representing the wrath of an impinged king to the first mate and captain provides a lens for understanding the violence of the first mate in a different context. It may be argued that the *Euterpe* program provides an opportunity to move beyond the violence of patriarchal hierarchy, not towards discipline through some form of panopticon, but rather towards stretching, through dialogue. One of us discusses the importance of dialogue as part of children's play elsewhere (Aitken, 2001), suffice to point out here that we see it as an internal tension that relates to the relations formed between children, adults, and their environments. And on the *Euterpe* it is also a very real dialogue between the children and the crew (including the first mate) that is joined on the second day of the program. The program is not about overt violence, nor is it about surveillance through some kind of panoptican. Unlike Bentham's prison, there is no surveillance of sailors, nor are the children separated from each other. Rather, the violence is a threat that highlights the life or death consequences of making mistakes on board a ship. It is a clear communication of the need for vigilance and "getting it right." We will elaborate on the importance of children "getting it right" in a moment, but from the perspective of a nineteenth century sailor, mistakes are deadly. The living history program is not successful because of threats of violence, but because it presents children with different ways of understanding their environmental and their own internal dialogues. In this sense, the *Euterpe* is a site of passage. What needs fuller elaboration are the ways that the processes of ritual—and the liminal spaces of transition—inculcate discipline (read stretching) and the ways that this disciplining empowers children.

Disciplined Through Ritual

An intending sailor should have above all things good health, and be stout hearted. Men, for the next year this ship is your entire world and you will find it to be a small one indeed. On board it does not matter where you are from or who you are. You men are equal to each other. It would be wise to pull together and get along. A man who comes to work on board should be prepared to do anything at first that comes to his hand; and he should try and adapt himself to the ways of a new situation in which he has placed his lot. You will have many things to unlearn and also to learn. You must put aside your old ways and be willing to accept the new ones, if you can truly accomplish this you may indeed succeed here. (*Euterpe*, Letters and Logs of a British Emigrant Ship, quoted in Spearal, 2002, p. 9)

This epigram was written in 1870s, but it is quoted in the instructor's training manual. As such, it sets the scene for the liminal space created on board and it presages the program's rituals surrounding separation, transition and incorporation.

Separation

After the first mate has secured the undivided, and likely trepid, attention of the young sailors on the wharf, he delivers the crew muster. As part of muster, the boys and girls are degendered into long and short-haired sailors. The children are told that there were no women sailors in the nineteenth century as women were deemed to make the female ship jealous and bring bad luck. Their ritual journey began with the children facing a seemingly tyrannical first mate and learning that they belong to him, both in body and in mind. They are now told that they are neither girls nor boys, but sailors. As part of their journey, this is the ritual separation from all that they have known about themselves. Gender is often one of the first things that children have to "get right," and it may be argued that the relative fixity of other identities (e.g., ethnicity, class) follows (Yelland & Grieshaber, 1998; Aitken, 2001). Yelland and Grieshaber (1988, 3) argue that despite the importance of "getting it right," children learn to move between and adopt different gender positions for purposes of strategic advantage. Selection from a multiplicity of available discourses and positions because there are different things at stake in different situations suggests a calculated hybridity. By requiring children to cast aside the gendered aspects of their identity, the living history program exacerbates this hybridity because the children have no discourse to draw upon. But the decks of the *Euterpe* are awash with discourse.

Ostensibly, gender is not part of the *Euterpe's* living history program, but it is clear that gendered norms pervade many aspects of ship life. The educator/actors on the program are both men and women, including the fierce first mate. But the nested hierarchy of command–played by men and women–to which the children are introduced at the crew muster is clearly a patriarchal order. The lazy, fun-loving though effective second mate, for example, is introduced as a social balance to the dominant first mate, while the nurturing persona of the ship's cook counterweighs the captain's stern "scientific" persona with his ship's tales and witchdoctor medicinal concoctions. The children respond to this hiearchical discipline irrespective of the gender of the crewmember, but it is interesting to note that ship's cook, whether male or female, is always a matriarchal figure. The young sailors learn that each of the ship's officers fill an important and clearly defined role within the social hierarchy of the ship's daily functioning. The captain pilots the ship through dangerous seas, guiding the cargo and crew safely to California, while the first mate, as a vital link in the chain of command, ensures that the crew carries out the duties assigned by the captain. Likewise the second mate and ship's cook help train the new apprentices, develop their knowledge of seagoing lore, and provide nurturing when required.

The crew muster, in addition to gender-bending, contains vital rules establishing the *modus operandi* for the rest of the 18-hour field trip. This, too, is about separation and the creation of liminal space:

> There are a multitude of dangers inherent in life aboard ship. If you have the will for survival and self-preservation, or you wish to return to your farms one day, you must learn to understand and obey all orders before meeting the captain.
>
> When you are asked a question and you wish to answer in the affirmative, you are expected to answer "Aye Aye," is that clear?
>
> . . . You will at times be given a long list of detailed instructions and orders. You must listen to all instructions, otherwise you will not be able to successfully complete the tasks given to you and some one may get hurt. Is that clear?
>
> . . . Soon you will meet the captain, your commander and ruler for the entire voyage. When you are in the captain's presence, all hats must come off! Should the captain look at you, your hat comes off!
>
> You men better be ready to work hard and work together!

(Spearal, 2002, pp. 42-43)

With the crew muster, the scene is set for something different that anticipates rules, work, collaboration and a clear structure of authority. When the first mate explains to the children that the captain is the lord and master of the vessel, and that his word is law aboard the ship, his order serves the double purpose of establishing a clear chain-of-command, while also establishing, in a less defined context, the highest social level of the ship's nested hierarchy. The muster also integrates important safety instructions with social norms. So, for example, the children are told to keep their hands out of their pockets, feet apart, and knees bent to prevent injury in case of a swell rocking the vessel at the same time as they are told to remove their hats in the captain's presence. The important point here is the intermingling of safety issues and social traditions in a obfuscating manner, inspiring children to accept social constructions which reinforce a specific hierarchy along with the larger issues of safety and responsibility. By raising children's awareness of their surroundings, while creating an atmosphere of suspended liminal reality, the first mate next invites the children to explore the ship's environment. The explorations occur, not only within the physical space of the ship, but also through the social constructs of traditional shipboard life.

Transition

Following the muster and crew introductions, the children set about tasks and they continue working at various shipboard tasks until they leave the ship at 9:30 a.m. the following morning. These tasks, or challenges as they are identified in the training manual (Spearal, 2002), are designed to force children to work together to overcome physical and intellectual barriers and confrontations. The first mate, for example, instructs the young sailors in the construction of a boatswain's chair. He leads a crew of children to a tangled pile of lines and several blocks lying on the deck near the main mast. His instructions are brief and clear. "The captain has ordered the mast cleaned . . . you men must rig these lines to the boatswain chair so the linehandlers and deckhands can haul each other aloft and scrub the mast." With the first mate keeping a careful eye on the developments, the deck is soon awhirl with the reaving of lines and the hoisting of blocks. An improper placement of a line brings the first mate into action with further instruction. If the line is not properly riven, he explains, your crewmates could fall to the deck and be seriously injured. Unbeknownst to the sailors, the first mate ties a safety line to the boatswain chair, which will be handled by a parent when the sailors sit in the chair. As the rigger crew completes the boatswains chair, the first mate, pleased with their efforts and teamwork leads the crew in a boisterous "Hip, Hip, Hooray!"

The captain, meanwhile, guides two crews working to maneuver a barrel around his favorite chair in the hold below. The task behind this

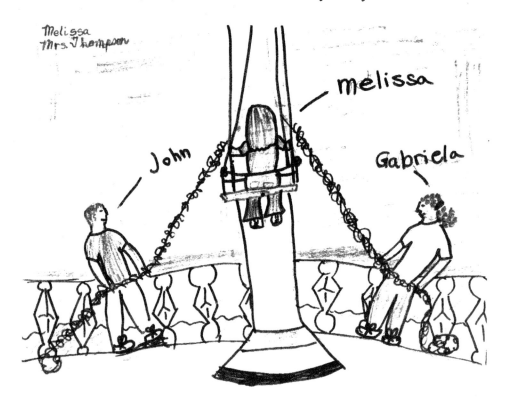

Figure 5.1. Child's sketch of the botswain's chair.

ritual is to develop the crew's ability to work together to accomplish something that none of the children would be able to accomplish alone. The captain tells the children that the barrel is empty, but it still weighs 100 pounds. The two crews practice moving the empty barrel in anticipation of moving heavier cargo "later in the voyage." The captain provides the crews with several challenges, for example, touching the side of a board standing on end (without knocking it over), before he seats himself on the chair. A mate, his face several shades of pale, struggles to coordinate a halyard line crew and two preventer line crews simultaneously, all the while ensuring that the barrel does not even brush the captain's regal backside. White knuckles and blisters often accompany the sailors' success, but so also does a sense of achievement at accomplishing a difficult and dangerous task.

Later in the program, the second mate trains the children to lay aloft ten stories above the deck in high and rolling seas, while the cook pre-

Figure 5.2. The captain's barrel task.

pares his crew of helpers for the frightening task of serving the captain dinner in the saloon. The second mate, despite his scurvious nature, does not suffer foolish sailors lightly when it comes to training and safety. He leads his crews down below to the hold where they encounter the training yard, a royal yard kept in the hold for training new crewmembers before they are sent aloft (the children do not actually ascend ten stories). The second mate provides important instructions about *laying out* on the yard when you are 110 feet above the ship's deck: "Communication is the key. When you lay out on the yard, you ask permission from the men already out there. You say 'Laying on starboard or laying on port', because these *footropes* move, and you can bounce that man right over the yard and down to the deck." And then, the young sailors are told, the cook will have spaghetti the next night, because they will have to scrape that man off the deck with a spatula. Meanwhile, in the galley, the cook instructs his crew about serving dinner to the captain:

You will line up, and each of you will hold a dish to take to the saloon. As you walk out on the deck, the other crew's will be lined up for dinner. You will show them the fine dinner the captain is having (chicken, salad, vegetables, and pie for desert). When you present your dish to the captain, you will answer any questions he has, and then you will return and serve the rest of the crews their *rat stew*. The captain gets better food because he is better educated and ranks the highest on the ship. If there are leftovers from the captain's table, you may get to share them, if you work hard clearing the captain's table. Is that clear to everyone?

The transition period is when the children are introduced to new ways of knowing and doing. It foments skills that are about "getting it right," but it is also, and more importantly, about working as a team and taking responsibility. Instructors expect children to forget past identities so that they can work together effectively during the program. But any outsider watching the children at work with the boatswain's chair or the captain's barrel task will not fail to recognize that this is also about play. In short, the children are working hard at play. And what they get from the overtures of the first mate and other crewmembers is that this is serious work, and so most are responsible around their tasks, and they seem to work/play well together.

An extended discussion of the importance of child work and responsibility is beyond the scope of this chapter. Suffice to say that researchers have recently focused on the importance of incorporating children more with the productive world rather than sequestering them completely in reproductive activities such as school, day-care, and recreation. The modern construction of childhood in Western society is more often than not about shielding children from taking serious responsibility and excluding them from the productive world of adults and work. The Factory Laws of the nineteenth century were put in place to stop child labor and, laudably, to protect young people from injury and exploitation. But researchers recently point to some of the problems in Western middle-class society of excluding children from the productive sphere of work (cf. Robson, 1996; Roberts, 1998; Aitken, 2001). Our point here is that the liminal, transition space of the *Euterpe* is in large part about the right to work and participate responsibly in serious contexts; that the world of work has important lessons to teach children.

The children's identities are ostensibly wiped away when they become long- and short-haired sailors during the crew muster. What follows are a series of tasks that require discipline, responsibility, and cooperation. Everything that the first mate sets up at the outset is reflected here, in how the children work together. As they work together, the children learn how to solve problems and to function as a team. Here are two girl's responses to this core part of the program:

> Well, they told you how to do it, and then I did it wrong and they told me to do it again (Hillary, fifth grade)

> And what I really like about the work, I like everything we had to do down there, it was all work. We had to pull something out and I was like working really hard to pull it out because it was dark. . . . And you pull right there, you pull and it's really hard work and like if you can't do it other people will do it for you, other people will help you and it's called cooperation (Adie, fifth grade)

The larger context of children "getting it right" that we articulated earlier is about accepted societal norms and the construction and fixity of identities. It is an aspect of childhood that feminists and poststructuralists rightly criticize. The other part of "getting it right" is about communication and camaraderie, responsibility and jointly experiencing problems and solving them satisfactorily:

> I thought it was fun, but I kinda thought it was scary. But then I kind of got over it because all the mates were holding me up. (Jean, fifth grade)

Adie had this to say about teamwork and responsibility:

> I like the work because you have to work with other people and we work closely and that comes to be better than just working by yourself. . . . It's all about teamwork. . . . Then like we go do our jobs and it's my responsibility to tell them right and wrong. Like you're not supposed to be doing that, or stop doing that, or do that. And it's not being bossy or anything, it's being really responsible and that is what we did. (Adie, fifth grade)

There comes a point in the program when the children are called on to take up the responsibility not only of working together, but of leadership. Adie continues:

> When the captain called all the five mates he was explaining to us he was counting on us to be responsible because we are each responsible for everything they do, because what if they told us to go somewhere which is dangerous we have to tell them to do this so they won't get hurt. . . . We're just doing safe and fun things (Adie, fifth grade).

The space of the ship is liminal in the sense that is a ritual place of transition. It is unfamiliar to the children at first and so, we argue, it heightens their acuity and, by so doing, enables the crew to establish new ways of knowing. This transition is in large part into the world of work with its attended needs of responsibility and teamwork. The transition begins with the crew muster, but the physical presence and structure of the ship is also part of this new awareness:

> *Interviewer:* Do you think that your life is more structured off the ship or here on the ship?
>
> *Jorge:* On the ship.
>
> *Interviewer:* And why do you think that?
>
> *Jorge:* Well, because then I am here on the ship I hear better and I pay more attention. Not like in class.
>
> (Jorge, fifth grade)

The point that we want to end this section making is that rites of passage are about sites and liminal spaces; and space makes a difference. One of the reasons that the living history programs works is because the space of the *Euterpe* is unique. As one young participant put it:

> The difference is—on the ship you are, well you are not actually on a house you are in a ship which is floating in water—and what happens is it is a little different because yes there are people taking care of you but they expect you to do the work no matter what. (Lisa, fifth grade)

The ship functions through a set of spaces—decks, forecastle, galley, first-class cabins and working, bilge and rope room—that exude rules, which may not be immediately obvious to the untrained and undisciplined, but they are nonetheless crucial for the survival of all on board. The transition period is about learning these rules, but it is also about working together and taking responsibility.

Incorporation

Children continue to work into the night, standing an hour-and-a-half watch on the quarterdeck to insure the ship is not boarded or starting to sink. Waking in the morning offers no respite: the galley crew, armed with pots and pans designed for maximum cacophony, rouses the other children sleeping quietly in the 'tween decks. Only following breakfast and morning wash-down are the children slowly reacculturated into their everyday lives with opportunities to ask the captain and crew questions and relate their experiences to their lives off the ship. One of the instructors explains this important process:

> Because in the morning the captain and the cook will bring them back into modern time and question-answer time where kids ask certain questions and we are totally up front with them. If they have any questions we answer them. And

Figure 5.3. Girl's sketch comparing ship life with home life.

many questions are about the ship, and is the ghost story real and does it go out sailing? And how they could possibly become part of it. We explain that they must be 18 and [then] they can come down and learn how to sail this beautiful ship.

Incorporation is about the children reinserting themselves back into there seemingly normal lives. It is about the staff dropping their roles and celebrating with the children their experiences, their learning, and their work.

All rites of passage require spaces for separation, transition, and incorporation. Some researchers are concerned about a seeming lack of rites in contemporary Western society. Mythologist Joseph Campbell (1972) famously argues that contemporary society suffers when it no longer sanctions specific rites of passage. Michael Meade (1996, 27) speculates that our lack of rites is associated with a form of mass denial that may relate to increases in random violence and drug abuse, and to the confusion in personal, gender, and national identities. One of us argues elsewhere that these charges are problematic because they leave unquestioned the social order, scale, and space from which rites derive their power (Aitken, 1999, 105). We argue below that rites are still important, that they are powerful, that they surround us everywhere, and that the processes through which they manifest themselves today are understated and the outcomes are veiled. We argue with John Schouten (1991, 49) that in materialistic, commercial, wealthy societies, rites of passage are often subtle or hidden. Individuals may choose to mark their passage by consumption patterns, developing new roles by what he calls "disposition and acquisition." What he does not consider is the space of disposition and acquisition, and the liminality associated with those spaces. We asked children to compare ship-board life with their everyday life, to get a sense of how disciplining works elsewhere, and to what end. In the balance of this chapter, we use the *Euterpe* program as a foil to understand more fully the liminality of children's spaces in contemporary Western culture, what precisely they are transitioning into, and the part played by disciplining in that transition.

Disciplined Through Living Geography

The production of space—its design, manufacture, and how it is imagined—is also about the production of rules. The space of the *Euterpe* is an unending series of rules that children are required to learn quickly or suffer the consequences. Elsewhere, children learn rules in a myriad of ways: whose chair not to sit on at home, how to approach the teacher, where to put the dirty laundry, when to switch off the television, when and where to pull out the homework, what parts of the neighborhood are safe and what parts should be avoided. What we turn to here is the idea that the production of space is also about disciplining young minds and bodies:

> [When I'm not on ship] I get up and then get dressed in my room and then get my stuff and go to school, and we play until the bell rings and then we go to class and do our reading and then after that we might do art or something like that, and then recess and then we come back and do reading, and then we have math. And then after math we have lunch, and then after lunch we have science and that's all [for school]. I go home and do my homework and go to bed. (Michael, fourth grade)

Sometimes rules are important for the safety of children and they are communicated clearly, but often they are intertwined insidiously with the comfort of adults and they are always part of the machinations of social reproduction. In everyday life, children know that their parents and their teachers have authority, but that authority is not always clearly delimited the way it is on board the *Euterpe*. As one boy put it when questioned about how the ship's experience compared to his classroom:

> Uhmm, I think it is much funner [on ship]. . . . Well the teachers [in the classroom] are much nicer than the first mate, cause you don't want to mess around with him. But Mrs. Richmond at our school is like, um, kinda, kinda mean. No offense! But, um, if I compared both of them I think I like this one would kinda be the best, "'cause you get to learn what you are supposed to do on a ship and how to do different things." (Matt, fifth grade)

Children dance around fuzzy authoritarian edges and weave their own interpretations of social reproduction:

> *Interviewer:* So tell me about what it was like when the First Mate came off the ship on the first day?
>
> *Grant:* I think . . . I was going to like it here
>
> *Interviewer:* Oh, really?
>
> *Grant:* Yeah, I like being yelled at. I always get yelled at
>
> (Grant, fourth grade)

In the early 1990s, geographer Dennis Wood combined talents with linguistic psychologist Robert Beck to articulate a sense of how physical spaces, from public plazas to private homes, inculcate spatial rules that impinge upon the lives of children (Wood & Beck, 1990, 1994). They argued that a child's built environment–crib, room, home–is a social construction that defines lived experience by providing a forum through which sensations can be contextualized and socially produced. Space is never merely a container of activities, then, but it is always an active part of the production of those activities and of itself. As we argued above, the space of the *Euterpe* in combination with the actions and attitudes of the educators, produces comaraderie, teamwork, responsibility, and leadership. But everyday spaces are often delimited precisely to contain the activities of children, and unlike on board the *Euterpe,* what is produced is frequently enervating. For example, many inner-city schools look like fortresses in efforts to provide safety for children but also to contain and delimit boundaries beyond which children cannot wander. Security guards and custodians police the entrances to public skateboard parks and commercial day-care spaces or "fun-zones" designed specifically for children.

Subtle rules of discipline are encoded in commercial fun-zones where competition and gambling are prominent imparted values: if children spend more money playing the games, competing with each other and the technology, then there is a chance that they will earn more tokens to redeem for toys. These enterprises are a shameless commodification of children's lives, designed and promoted by what Barry Glassner (1999) calls a "culture of fear" to provide a safe haven from the seeming dangers of the street. That all this focus on young people is based on a carefully constructed market is more than ironic at a time when, in poor inner city neighborhoods, minority youth are policed in a different manner and actively prevented from congregating. And so, lower-class, inner-city youths are also targets for competitive consumption, but rather than being sequestered in kid corrals, they are increasingly surveyed and disciplined on the streets in true Foucaultian fashion. As toddlers, kids, and youths grope for meaning from their kid-corralled and surveyed experiences, planners zone secure suburban neighborhoods, and developers build gated residential citadels for those who can afford them.

And the story does not end there. Subtle rules are encoded within a home's physical elements so that seeming neutral space is understood as a stimulus that is also an embodiment of one or more "voices," such as capitalism, social constructions of gender, or concepts of social class. Adults who live in the house respond intuitively to these rules (as, more often than not, do visitors), but the presence of children makes them explicit because the room is a site of passage, and implicit knowledge of the rules is a sign of maturity. Indeed, home rules always operate at the intended level of action which is, precisely, the child: "Don't stand so close to the fire, how many time do I have to tell you?" "Get up and give Dad his chair, he's had a hard day at the office." "Don't run around your bedroom like that, it creates a racket down here." "Keep your dirty hands off the walls." These rules highlight commonplace values such as social hierarchy, quietness, cleanliness, and aesthetics that protect middle-class sensibilities. Children see a field of rules that define, for adults, a nest of comfort. And the rules are hidden in images of comfort to the extent that children ultimately embrace their worth.

Not only is the space of middle-class comfort the consequent of a massive contrivance, its means and ends are neither simple, nor is it straightforward or direct (Wood & Beck, 1994, 26). The image of domestic propriety is that of a mother, a father, and their two children lounging comfortably in a room heated by a crackling wood fire as the snow falls outside. Perhaps they are sipping hot chocolate as they wile away the time playing a game of Monopoly. Familial bliss is encapsulated in the home, safely secured in a quiet neighborhood of similar houses and families. The snow deadens the sound of global exploitation and corruption that enables this scene. The comfort requires that these voices of capital–from the electricity provided by the environmentally unsound and potentially unsafe fission of uranium to the threatening presence of American warships protecting supplies of oil in the Persian Gulf–melt and disappear as quietly and conveniently as the falling snow against the chimney. And disciplining children's propensity to disrupt and disturb this comfort is part of the process of deadening, of quieting problematic voices. The important geography here is that the structures of meaning, the rules for kids and the comfort of adults, do not originate in the fire-heated serenity of the room but in the larger structures of the global economy.

It is the obfuscation of this larger designation of young people's lives that intrigues us and draws us to the clarity of rules aboard *Euterpe,* and their intent. We understand that this is a stretch, but it is an important one given what we see as the complex, subtle and hidden meanings of capital in the lives of many children. A generation of scholars raised on Foucault understands implicitly how societal power is imbued in surveillance and discipline, but what we are trying to highlight here is that rules are also about bodies in places and actions in space. By so doing, we argue the need to take the Foucaultian project beyond that of understanding discipline through surveillance to understanding more proactive forms of social transformation that target material bodies and take control of social and spatial reproduction.

REFERENCES

Aitken, S.C. (1999). Putting parents in their place: Child rearing rites and gender politics. In E.K. Teather (Ed.), *Embodied geographies: Space, bodies and rites of passage.* New York and London: Routledge.

——. (2001). *Geographies of young people: The morally contested spaces of identity.* New York and London: Routledge.

Bhabba, H. (1994). *The location of culture.* New York: Routledge.

Campbell, J. (1972). *Myths to live by.* New York: The Viking Press.

Cohen, E. (1988). Authenticity and commoditization in tourism. *Annals of Tourism, 15:* 371–86.

DeLyser, D. (1999). Authenticity on the ground: Engaging the Past in a California ghost town. *Annals of the Association of American Geographers, 89:4.*

Foucault, M. (1975). *Discipline and punishment.* New York: Vintage Books.

Handler, R., & Gable E. (n.d.). *The new history in an old museum: Creating the past at Colonial Williamsburg.* Durham and London: Duke University Press.

Homans, H. (1994). Pregnancy and birth as rites of passage for two groups of women in Britain. In C. Maccormack (Ed.), *Ethnography of fertility and birth* (2nd ed.). Prospect Heights, IL: Waveland Press.

Leon, W., & Piatt, M. (1989). Living history museums. In W. Leon & r. rosenzweig (Eds.), *History museums in the United States: A critical assessment.* Urbana and Chicago: University of Illinois Press.

Leon, W., & Rosenzweig, R. (1989). *History museums in the United States: A critical assessment.* Urbana and Chicago: University of Illinois Press.

Matthews, H. (2003). The street as a liminal space: The barbed spaces of childhood. In P. Christensen & M. O'Brien (Eds.), *Children in the city: Home, neighborhood and community.* London and New York: RoutledgeFalmer.

Meade, M.. (1996). Rites of passage at he end of the millennium. In L. Mahdi, N. Christopher, & M. Meade (Eds.), *Crossroads: The quest for contemporary rites of passage.* La Sall, IL: Open Court.

Roberts, S. (1998). Commentary: What about children? *Environmental and Planning A., 30,* 3–11.

Robson, E. (1996). Working girls and boys: Children's contributions to household survival in West Africa. *Geography 81,* 403–7.

Schouten, J.W. Personal rites of passage and the reconstruction of self. *Advances in Consumer Research, 18,* 49–51.

Sibley, D. (1995). *Geographies of exclusion.* London and New York: Routledge.

Snow, S.E. (1993). *Performing the pilgrims: A study of ethnohistorical role-playing at Plymouth plantation.* Jackson, MS: University Press of Mississippi.

Spearal, J. (2002). *Instructor training manual and program curriculum.* San Diego: Maritime Museum Association of San Diego.

Turner, V.W. (1969). *The ritual process: Structure and anti-structure.* London: Routledge and Kegan Paul.

van Gennep, A. (1960). *The rites of passage.* Trans. M.B. Vizedom and G.L. Caffee. London, Routledge and Kegan Paul. First published in 1909, *Les Rites de Passage.* Paris: Noury.

Wood, D., & Beck, R. (1990). Do's and don'ts: Family rules, rooms and their relationships. *Children's Environments Quarterly, 7* (1), 2–14.

——. (1994). *The home rules.* Baltimore and London: Johns Hopkins University Press.

Yelland, N., & Grieshaber, S. (1998). Blurring the edges. In N. Yelland (Ed.), *Gender in early childhood.* New York and London: Routledge.

Chapter 6

MELANIE KLEIN, LITTLE RICHARD, AND THE PSYCHOANALYTIC QUESTION OF INHIBITION

DEBORAH P. BRITZMAN

I

For those outside the psychoanalytic field, encountering the language of Melanie Klein and her work with children is a strange, if not shocking affair. If a reader thinks of her interpretations of the child's play as literal, considers her case studies as her attempt to anchor causality through the Freudian fiction of psychical structure, or supposes her theories of psychical life install the very pathologies they claim to reveal, then one may as well not read Klein at all. And yet Kleinian theory presents contemporary readers with a dramatic theoretical conundrum. Klein begins her narrative of the subject not with a discussion of how external reality influences or affects it, but instead with the poiesis of psychical reality, of an inner world of object relations. Hers is a narrative that entangles theory and its origins with a biological drive she called the epistemophilic instinct, the drive to know, to master, to control. By hitching the fate of knowledge to the fecundity of the unconscious drive, distinctions between epistemology and ontology are no longer the matter; left over is the shadowy internal world of phantasy as the first means and resource for encountering the world of others. This resource is precocious, already a bizarre puppet world of theories.

No wonder Klein takes learning away from education and instead supposes that learning occurs in confrontation with the drive. It is not that the outside world cannot matter, but Klein imagines preconditions for its encounter, namely the anxiety of the internal world of object relations. She thus can raise the crucial question of how both the internal and external worlds can be known at all. Thinking, interpretation, and narrative emerge from and are marked by this anxiety. The difficulty of learning is not so much clarified by Klein's general insistence upon the power of an asocial death drive. Yet this pressure afflicts the subject, prior to her or his capacity for language and understanding, with a persecutory anxiety so profound that it can feel as if the attack comes from the outside. What reduces the opacity is Klein's claim that the confusion between bodily boundaries, of what is inside and what is outside, of the self and other, provokes an excess of meaning. There can then emerge both psychical representatives of anxiety and the capacity to think about them. These creatures can be thought of as personifications of anxiety and defenses against it. Klein will call the precocious group that arrives before knowledge of the world, phantasy, and thinking about them will constitute knowledge. So the drive is the conveyer for both the subject's destruction of objects *and* her first resource for meaning itself. Klein will dedicate her theory and practice to elucidating these phantasies because her commitment is with how insight into anxiety allows the self more flexibility for interpreting the stakes of constructing reality. Good and bad, inside and outside, self and other, reality and phantasy, these are the object relations of the capacious Kleinian subject.

If, then, we have something like meaning before we have understanding, Kleinian speculation opens the ostensibly settled question of what biology can signify if the problem of making psychical significance is where we must begin. Klein raises meaning, or knowledge of reality and phantasy, as the first terrible problem and so she attributes something original and frustrating to the infant: a lively, desperate, paranoid, and an urgent struggle to mean and to understand. Biology is no longer a clichéd destiny. Instead it is a symbol for that mythic battle, the movement of meaning with relating: how even the barest flutter of significance emerges from and is marked by the violent recursiveness of terrifying literalness, how interpretation undoes concrete representations to make room for symbolization, how thinking can come close to atonement, or thinking of the other. Klein's theorem may go something like this: *where deprivation was, there frustration, symbolization, gratitude, and reparation shall become.* There can be for the human a tolerance for language, interpretation, and so for a metaphoric freedom. This is what Klein means by poignant thinking. And she insists upon language and narrative for working through the confines of infantile reality. For Klein will maintain that perceptions of reality as only stringent and punishing are projections of an internal world of object relations. The rigidness is preserved through a fear of interpretation and so of psychological meaning. These fears are what Klein means by inhibition and why she is concerned with difficulties in and obstacles to psychical freedom.

Working with some Kleinian conundrums, the theme I will develop in this chapter is the psychoanalytic idea of freedom as it plays out in theory and in analytic practice. Klein links this freedom to the capacity to think about phantasy, to value interpretations, and take pleasure in psychological meaning. I will suggest that Klein's theories on inhibition and narrative offer a different way into our contemporary debates on the status of the concept of psychological freedom during times when we seem to be more adept at describing social processes of normalization and subjection than we do in describing the problem of learning to live and what it can mean that we are susceptible to both conscious and unconscious forces. Indeed, critical theories of the subject emphasize the ways we are affected through external processes and so explain our susceptibility to discursive design as the sum total of events. Interiority is thus viewed as an afterthought; psychological significance becomes a ruse of social structure. Klein's theories challenge this docility, even suggesting that if inhibition can be the royal road for the subject to normalize herself, it is also a lively, aggressive, and powerful dynamic and in that sense, a nascent challenge to docility. I explore this paradox throughout and suggest that Klein's theories of learning can be thought of in three registers: as a response to historical and cultural circumstances that supposed women and children were incapable of intellection, as psychoanalytic arguments with Anna Freud over the question of what the child is capable of accepting in the psychoanalytic setting, and last, as clinical provocations to the child and to theory itself.

While there is great difficulty in making a context for Melanie Klein's clinical practice, particularly because of her interest in speaking in a language of archaic anxiety, it is clear what Klein's practice and theories were responding to in the world of child analysis: the influence of education, or better, the belief that education, if properly conducted, can cure neurosis and inhibition and can prevent the future of neurosis. Adam Phillips (2002) ties the quest to determine childhood, education, and cure to the desire to systematize. He argues that the concept of childhood is one procedure of knowledge:

> In simple terms, the Freudian child suffers, so to speak, from an intensity of desire and an excess of vulnerability; and it was not, as Aries was among the first to show, that this was news about childhood. The news was in the need, beginning in the eighteenth century, to make the child an object of systematic knowledge. (151)

The news is the need. The systematicity of knowledge must pass through the distortions and condensations of the unconscious, thereby marking knowledge with affect: obsession, fetish, anxiety, and paranoia, for instance. In Allan Bass's (1998) view, systematicity is not just a codification or procedure of knowledge but a structure of defense: "Whenever one finds systematicity, one can, from a psychoanalytic point of view, ask the question of what unbearable piece of reality is being defended against by means of the system" (426). This is the news that put education into question, and where the Kleinian theory of knowledge begins.

II

Melanie Klein (1882–1960) was responding to something within her own generation, perhaps in this return to Klein we are responding to something in ours. There are those biographic details that open and may serve as an emblem of, but not the explication for, the early twentieth century. As a daughter of the Jewish Enlightenment, the *Haskala*, she began with great faith in education. She had hopes for herself to be a medical doctor but instead, by 1903, married a business man, Arthur Klein. Then over the next ten years came three children, along with what might have been a return of a deep depression. Around 1914, Klein entered psychoanalysis with Ferenczi in Budapest; there she practiced in that new field of child psychoanalysis as well. During that first part of the twentieth century, Klein has moved from country to country, language to language, through different psychoanalytical theories. The reasons are dramatic: depression, civil war, family obligations, constraints, analysis, and finally, her work. Perhaps there was also a need for recognition or escape. By 1919, Klein is a member of the Budapest Psychoanalytic Society; by 1921, she had moved to Berlin, joining that Society, and in 1924, another analysis with Karl Abraham. A year later there was Abraham's premature death. By 1926, Klein divorces and emigrates to London. These idiomatic events, now residues of history, also congeal in her theory, or perhaps they set the stage for what her theory of object relations will become.

In his discussion of Klein's legacy, J.B. Pontalis (1981) thought her theories attempted to work toward a difficult question: "what holds the child back?" (95). Some contemporary commentators of Klein's theory and life such as Grosskurth (1986), Likierman (2001), and Kristeva (2001) consider the concept of inhibition as her core dilemma. It is a question, Pontalis suggests, that exceeds *savoir faire*, resting in neither knowledge of the object nor with the subject-presumed-to-know:

> If in her first text, Melanie Klein's attention was held above all by the child's inhibitions, it was because they assumed an exemplary value for her: the child had more to say for himself than what he actually said. This was why she refused to see this or that "characteristic" of the child as a deficiency that . . . one should relate to his nature . . . . She therefore chose not to define the conditions which should be fulfilled by child analysis, but to submit psychoanalytical theory and methods to the disconcerting text of the child's speech. (95–96)

Here then is a practice with children that counters application and adjustment, that refuses to define itself prior to its own events. It is also other to education and child-rearing because its problem is psychic freedom, with what holds one back from thinking about one's thoughts, with how inhibition is the self's means of normalization, and theory's defense against affecting itself. Yes, Klein will say. Inhibition is the self's defense, a means for the ego to reduce anxiety, but also, to reduce the world. And yes, there is a certain tragedy. The strategy for warding off anxiety only accrues more, so the cost is as severe as the reality it diminishes. Where there is anxiety there may be theory, but it is a theory that is precarious, dangerous, and paranoid.

Let us try to place Klein's theory of inhibition alongside much that inaugurates our age of testimony: the emancipation of women, the right to divorce, the Jewish problem, diaspora, exile, genocide, human rights, all forces that come under the sign of what Kristeva (2001) called, in her study of Klein, "The Psychoanalytic Century." It is the century of affect, subjectivity, and narrative, a century of sublation, of preservation and overcoming. But it is also the century of the return of the repressed, of suffering, thinking, and so, of the unconscious. If the Psychoanalytic Century is one of witnessing and testimony, it is also qualified with trauma and negation. In our own age, where depth psychology is dismissed as an imposition on the subject, and so where interior life is reduced to an afterthought, to a discourse effect, or denigrated by critical theory as illusion (Adorno, 2001) and, where the depressive society dulls our capacity for revolt, passion, and Eros (Kristeva, 2002; Roudinesco, 2001), Klein's theories of authority, knowledge, and psychical life are there to remind us of the consequences of eschewing the elaboration of psychological knowledge for adults and children.

Yet it is difficult for the self to accept and elaborate psychical reality and this idea, too, is part of her theory. Klein places resistance not in processes of learning, but in designs of phantasy. There is the refusal to know. In resistance, one can glimpse the terrible volatile nature of unconscious anxiety: when phantasy cancels reality, when there can be a world of no difference. Pointing this out takes language and meaning to its limits. She understands the fragility of psychological significance, how easily it can get lost, become wrong-headed, collapse into itself. To see the world as more than an imposition or as a reflection of one's own internal reality, to encounter reality not as a sealed fate but as a problem of interpretation requires a return to that other world, phantasy. This return will require the capacity to enter nonsense, to speak the language of a puppet world of theory. Kristeva (2001) gathers this discourse of madness under the sign of Klein's stunning achievements: Klein accepted that there was something foolhardy, ridiculous beyond compare, in psychical life and articulating this could only be done through performing the absurdity of language and desire. The paradox and achievement are that Klein took psychical life so seriously that she could see at its heart something deeply foolish and then human.

Some of the terms she would lend to this foolhardiness, this urge for theory to wrap the world tightly, this urge against all rational odds, sound like tin to the sensitive ear. By the middle of her career, Klein would no longer assert her theory of the epistemophilic instinct, or the sadistic grounds of the desire to know. It would be her commentary on the problem of where knowledge comes from. And so this drive, what could be awkwardly spoken of as "the highest flowering of sadism" (Petot, 1990, 186) was an attempt to describe both the internal devastations of control and the omnipotence, when not knowing equates with danger, when danger means helplessness, when helplessness means annihilation. And yet, without this terrifying danger, there would be no reason to press knowledge into shape. Klein will place her theory of inhibition in this conundrum and counterintuitively view inhibition's withdrawal as necessary and as paranoid, as devastating on its own accord but also as capable of being influenced even as it influences. Inhibition will hold one back. Against all odds, Klein will call it forth.

Certainly inhibition is a form of intellectual withholding. But holding back from what? Adam Phillips's (2002) essay, ironically titled, "Against Inhibition," takes us in one direction with a story of education: a teacher encouraged a student, who eventually became a famous poet, to explore through narrative his rather violent fantasy of crushing babies' heads. The idea was that putting feelings into words dissipated the violence but also that words were of a different order than actions, even if the words described despicable actions. This writing was "against inhibition," a way to explore the difference between reality and phantasy, the difference between omniscience in thought and woeful disregard in life, but also the narrative becomes a way of getting around the problem of imagining forbidden things.

Klein's sense of inhibition began with the problem of only imaging forbidden things. In her narrative, inhibition is an attack, a murder of curiosity, because inhibition is a heightened state of being plagued by too many answers. "Where there was a text," writes Phillips (2002), "there will be a set text. Inhibition—the whole sado-masochistically staged drama of it—is like a ruse of the ego in its relentless project of negating the unconscious" (73). One can inhibit the self so there is no otherness. Inhibition is thus emblematic of profound negativity, a wish to destroy one's creativity, a hatred of not knowing, what Kristeva (2001, 84) considers as a particular dilemma of subjectivity, that there can be "a phobia of being." Here is normalization in its most devastating and intimate sense, the loss of curiosity, the fear of reality, the denial of phantasy. Something in the drive to know negates itself and so Klein leaves us with a theoretical tension: if we have knowledge before we have something like understanding, what unbearable reality must knowledge defend itself against? Her response is the fear of what is already there: the death drive.

Jacqueline Rose's (1993) return to Klein begins with one of the key dilemmas a theory of death poses to social thought: if death has psychical meaning then the child, and everyone else, is always embroiled in spinning, projecting, and fleeing meanings marked by inescapable negativity. "What seems to be outrageous," writes Rose in her discussion on the status of negativity in the work of Melanie Klein and hence on the problem of subjectivity and politics,

> –paradoxically harder to manage than death as a pure force, as something which assaults the subject from outside–is this internalization of death into the structure. If death is a pure point of biological origin, then at least it can be scientifically known. But if it enters into the process of psychic meanings, inseparable from the mechanisms through which subjects create and recreate their vision of the world, then from where can we gain the detachment with which to get it under control? (160)

Because of the unconscious, knowledge will always be a magnetizing problem, calling things it never intended. And objectivity will have to accept this as well in order to reach its own difference from dissociation and stasis. It will mean not only the acceptance of subjective meaning, but also the courage needed to comment upon that.

Without an awareness of the workings of phantasy, itself a problem of objectivity, there can be no reality, only compliance to an unforgiving authority. This is the painful experience of inhibition, where the encounter with authority repeats something archaic: helplessness, hatred, paranoia, anxiety, and so the potential. John Phillips (1998) argues that Kleinian knowledge begins at this extreme:

> The Kleinian notion of knowledge must be considered in terms of her account of its *possibility*. . . . A deeply objective knowledge in the Kleinian sense demands a knowledge of phantasy itself, as well as an understanding of the inhibiting power of authority. Without this the "reality principle" is just another tyrannous master, because the phantasy of omniscience remains undiminished. For Klein, objective knowledge is a step towards understanding of phantasy. (163)

Klein's knowledge is paradoxical. Objective knowledge comes as close as possible to understanding the paranoid state of subjectivity and what makes it so susceptible to authority, rigid conceptualizations, and intellectual inhibition. Yet objective knowledge must also be marked by these very qualities even as such knowledge is an attempt to think about thinking. Knowledge of phantasy allows for theories of reality: this is what Klein understands as objectivity, a knowledge at one degree removed from the charge of phantasy yet still affected and so able to comment upon it from the inside. The utterance does not direct activity but only calls attention to its own activity, to what it can mean to think about thinking. Thus there will also be something foolhardy about interpretation itself, even antiauthoritarian.

III

In the analytic setting, domination and normalization are indexes of unresolved conflict and ironically there they are given free reigns. While Klein thought a child's play with small toys was akin to the adult's free association, there was nothing benign. "Play exists," Kristeva (2001) suggests when speaking about Klein's work, "to the extent that it moves forward, burns, breaks, wipes, dirties, cleans, destroys, constructs, and so forth" (49). This destructive or dematerializing drama sets the terms for Klein's utterance; interpretations are meant to pull the kicking and screaming psychical states into language. If psychoanalysis puts a great deal of faith into language—as the means for complaint, free association, negation, interpretation, dialogue—Klein's interpretations point to the vulnerability at the heart of even having language at all; subjectivity is deeply at odds with reality since subjectivity is noncoincidental with consciousness of itself. So language must provoke this divide to speak of itself. Kristeva (2001) stresses the evocative: "By respecting the fantasy and interpreting it, the analyst does not establish the reality to be known or the law to be followed, but gives the ego a chance to constantly create a reality" (238). Here is the ego's second chance. While respect for phantasy will be where Klein will place the interpretation and freedom, it will also be where meaning will break down.

Contemporary readers may well find Klein's prose difficult to take because at one level Klein's writing performs a stunning literalness matched only by what she claimed in the name of the child. She (1975) tried to put into language "memories in feelings," (338) a linguistic repetition where words, too, provoke the very affectations they try to contain. Klein does what analysts must do, eroticize language, enliven it so that the subject can experience language as relation rather than as an imposition of a heartless authority. "Analysts mobilize affect," writes Kristeva (1995), "by openly presenting themselves during interpretation as a magnet of libido" (99). Kristeva goes on to describe the analyst's words as performing two functions.

> [A]n analyst fosters desire (including of course the desire to speak) despite inhibition and depression. Second, the therapist must be a *speech therapist* who maps out an individual program for each child (since "theoretical givens" do not apply to everyone) and then helps these children understand the linguistic cat-

egories that will allow them to add symbolic productions to their subjectivity. (105–106)

Where inhibition was, there desire, language, and symbolism shall become. But also, the analyst is a magnet for the analysand's hatred. In the beginning, the analyst encounters a terrible anxiety content that is bellicose, aggressive, sadistic, and paranoid that renders the inner world hostile and angry, and that is projected onto the outer world. From this compost of meanings emerges the world of object relations: concreteness, symbolization, sociality, and individual history. Phantasy will be the means for Klein to speculate on this puppet world that she will call without irony an "unreal reality" (1930, 221). Because we are discussing the experience of knowledge in psychical reality there can be no appeal to the outside as a means of explanation or motivation. It is a style the analyst Kohon (1999) describes as "a literature of excess based on interpretations" (156). It is a literature that mobilizes affect, theory's second chance.

What is repeated in play is the articulation of history and the repetition illustrates the linguistic conundrums Kleinian theory proposes. The language of psychoanalysis may use everyday words, but their usage sends meaning to the furthest outposts of sense. Words are even meant to question the scene of meaning. Language magnifies its use: dreamy, insistent, echo-like. Kristeva (1995) has described language as "a complex psychological event . . . [where] psychic representatives are displaced from affects as well as from the drama of desires, fears, and depressive fits that have a meaning for children, even thought they are unable to join the world of everyday language's coded signification" (108–109). An interpretation of anxiety, for instance, takes its residence in the performance of the phantasy that is the anxiety. As for the relational difficulty, Melanie Klein's theories are theories of phantasy–she has to imagine a time before language and education, a time that diminishes all time. If this is the anterior time of anxiety, it is also, for Kristeva (2002) a time of resistance. There is the wish not to know:

> The child's unconscious forces us to confront *another form of knowledge,* an enigmatic knowledge that characterizes the *fantasy* and that remains resistant to "enlightenment," a knowledge that does not wish to be *familiar* with the real world through learning and adaptation to reality. Such *knowledge* staves off *awareness.* (40, emphasis in original)

Klein claims she could witness the child's unconscious, what else the child says. She eschews appeals to authority, to promises of betterment, to the goodness of the child, to the best intentions of a helping relation, to morals, indeed, to all that secures the grounds of normalization. All that is left is to enter anxiety. And Klein places at risk her own intelligibility with a contact that symbolizes, repeats, and calls to attention the paranoia, aggression, depravation, and frustration that are the phantasy. If at first Klein repeats a terrible discourse, she must also make this discourse into difference, a commentary on the nature of knowing. So Klein tries on a doubled discourse, speaking simultaneously to theory and the child. This borderline discourse is what Jacqueline Rose's (1993) sees as foolhardy:

> Let's note that the genesis of the persecutory object in Kleinian thinking casts a shadow over interpretation, since, according to the logic of negation, interpretation comes as a stranger from the outside. And let's note too that if Klein makes of the analyst a fool and a fantast, it is from this place that the analyst has to try to speak, bridging the gap . . . between the baby ignorant of the external world and the scientist aware of nothing else. (169–170)

IV

By the time Klein moved to London in 1926, arguments with Anna Freud over how to conduct the analysis of children were in full swing. There were significant debates over what children were capable of and whether they could be psychoanalytically involved. If the early biographical details suggest the ways Klein was drawn to the problem of inhibition, by the middle of her life, she may have been asking something crucial of her own field: what holds interpretation back? And so from where does psychoanalysis come? Her arguments with Anna Freud suggest a radical uncertainty about the status of the concept of influence in learning and in self/other relations. And nowhere did this argument become more fantastic than when it turned to the meaning of helplessness in both psychoanalytic work and in psychical life (Britzman, in press).

Both analysts agreed that human helplessness and the utter dependency of the immature human were a structuring condition of psychical life and so carried over to relations with others. They accepted that helplessness found residency within the very beginnings of thinking itself. They diverged on the future of helplessness. Was this also influence? For Melanie Klein, helplessness enraged and frustrated the infant to such an extent that anxiety and aggression marked every moment of normal development. Anna Freud did not attribute such formative aggression or sadism to the infant and felt instead that the ego, with the help of its defenses, its actual parents, and its capacity for love, made its own second chance. Anna Freud offered "a helping hand," an ego ideal that would win the child over. She was prepared to open some possibilities through confidence building, and foreclose others by rational persuasion and the position of authority. Education, particularly as *Aufklärung*–the bringing up of childhood and culture, or Kantian Enlightenment–was the desirable influence. Klein was directly opposed to this relation with the child in the analytic setting.

If for Anna Freud there were three sources of anxiety–the object, the instinct, and the superego–for Klein anxiety was constitutional and had only one source: the death drive, and so a fear of annihilation. The difference here is rather stark. Anna Freud argued that educative measures should be joined with child analysis, for education could offer the child strategies of reality testing and, through the analyst's solicitation of the child's help, encourage the child to develop an interest in being needed, helping others, and sublimating aggression. To Klein, these needs are irrelevant in the psychoanalytic setting. Moreover, Klein viewed education as inhibition for two reasons. The internal world does not affect itself through rational appeal. But also many of her young analysands where sent to her because their education made them more miserable. Thus Klein argued that the alliance of analysis with education only repeats inhibition.

Here is the dilemma. Melanie Klein began psychoanalytic work with her imaginary as the resource for interpretation of unconscious phantasies. This orientation opened new tensions for what cure can mean and how symbolism or putting things into language actually allows for thinking, relating, and affecting one's narrative world. She made in child analysis a new psychoanalytic object, leaving the child's conscious preoccupations and listening to the child's unconscious anxiety. And this meant a radical change in her understanding of the child, the nature of knowledge, and psychoanalytic cure. Klein would come to believe that it is phantasies that inaugurate development. In the case of psychoanalytic encounter, Klein would leave her desire to mold the child's character and so abandon educational goals for the uncertainties of free association. And finally, as for knowledge, it would no longer be on the side of adaptation to reality: in this redrawing, epistemology emerges in the wake of anxiety and phantasy and knowledge becomes knowledge of phantasy, or what would later be thought of as "thinking about thinking." Petot's (1990) study of Melanie Klein's radical shift makes the argument that when Klein left the idea of education she could also see inhibition as one of its effects:

> The child's good social adaptation and success at school cannot be the goals for the child analyst; they are at most secondary . . . "normality" cannot be stated in terms of objective criteria, but in terms of liberty, fluidity, and the variety in the creation of fantasies. . . .[N]o references to external criteria can be acceptable in psychoanalysis. . . .[T]he objectives of the analysis of children can be defined only in psychoanalytic terms. (44)

The tension, as Kristeva (2002) poses the dilemma, is "the distinction between the use of the imaginary in the cure, on the one hand, and the consideration of an objective and knowable reality on the other" (75). If Klein raises the fantastic question from where does reality come, if she can put in parentheses, at least during the analytic hour, the world beyond her clinic, her answer would be just as incredible: the condition for constructing any knowledge of reality at all is the unconscious.

V

In 1961, a year after Melanie Klein's death, her case study of Richard was published under the title, *Narrative of a Child Analysis: The Conduct of the Psycho-analysis of Children as Seen in the Treatment of a Ten-Year-Old-Boy.* This analysis came to a premature end, but the notes she refined years later detail a total of 93 sessions, more than four months in 1941, along with almost all of Richard's drawings made through their analytic work. Mrs. Klein notes in her introduction that Richard's symptoms of being terrified of other children, his worries that strangers would attack him or follow him and overhear his thoughts, and his refusal to go to school began during the outbreak of World War II, in 1939. There was for Richard a profound intellectual inhibition but also an intellectual precociousness. That is, Richard had theories of the world; the problem was that he was not interested in finding out what his theories meant for him and others. He did have keen interests. Richard was an avid follower of the British navel maneuvers and the war theater. He knew many of the European national anthems and occasionally would burst into these songs at a particularly crucial moment in his play. Richard also collected with pleasure a miniature fleet of toy navel ships that he brought to most of the sessions; leaving them at home was a communication as well.

Mrs. K provides the paper, pens, and crayons Richard would use to draw. Seventy-four drawings are included in this text; their maturity and articulateness vary with Richard's emotional states. When he is mad at Mrs. K., she appears in these drawings. In one she is a triangle body with giant breasts, glaring eyes. It is the only picture he will be embarrassed over, and it is one of the few times that Klein will try to appease his worry. She will also have second thoughts and rethink her own desires in that appeasement. In another picture Richard draws a line across the middle and happily announces that whatever happens on the top of the picture matters; whatever happens at the bottom half of the picture does not. This splitting occurs throughout his drawings: empires are divided and battles are fought. There are strange starfish animals, each prong representing a family member. Sometimes the star fish are arranged in military formation. There are intricate maps and there are scribbles. Whereas the analysis begins with Richard fighting the interpretations, as the work progresses, near the end Richard begins analyzing his own thoughts.

Over the course of these 93 sessions, Richard is preoccupied with enemies, sometimes wondering, for example, if Mrs. K. and Mr. K. (who has passed away although Richard had difficulty believing that) are German spies, or even if his housekeeper is out to poison him. All these worries and their strange narratives come with a special language that Klein learns from Richard: there are Mrs. K. cruisers, big jobs, bird mummies, giants, blue-mummies, the Hitler-penis, the brute Mrs. K., lonely Rumania, "Roseman"-genital and lunatic-genital, and then many silly coincidences (such as a ship named the Vampire and Mrs. K.'s interpretation of Richard's greediness), mis-hearings that take on a life of their own, denials of symbols, and Richard's strange corrections of Mrs. K.'s interpretations.

The analysis occurred in a Welsh village where Richard and Mrs. Klein stayed during the London Blitzkrieg. Mrs. Klein rents a play-room and this means that after each session, she must pack up her materials and ready the room for other renters. Richard is quite preoccupied with this and also with what else Mrs. Klein does with her time when they are not together. Although Mrs. Klein gives readers a brief history of Richard's upbringing, the majority of the study's nearly five hundred pages are composed of Klein's notes of the sessions, taken immediately after each hour ended. These notes are verbatim ethnographic details, a curious combination of Klein's observations of Richard over the session, their reported speech, and the detours through which she and his interpretations are sent. Occasionally, Klein adds a further note years later to comment on her technique with children, tensions in practice, and problems in analyst/child relations. Readers also glimpse, through Klein's eyes, the flora and fauna of daily analysis, the detritus of interpretation, and the quotidian qualities of the analyst/analysand's relations. There are moments of great poignancy but also practical jokes that Richard plays on Mrs. Klein, such as when he gives her a jar of face cream that when opened becomes a Jack-in-the-box.

Richard is a precocious child, able to read adult desires and, by his own admission, manipulate them. Yet by the eighth session, Richard speaks of his analysis as "the work" and Mrs. Klein wonders if she had used this term or if it was his own description. Work it is and from the beginning Klein interprets deeply whatever she perceives as Richard's unconscious anxiety. Not only did children have a wide range of phantasies but these emotions for Klein refer to an internally complex world of object relations. Perhaps anticipating resistance to her method of interpreting deeply, of asking about sexual fears, oedipal phantasies, and hostile wishes, by the twenty-first session, Klein considers the benefits of her approach:

> It is in fact striking that very painful interpretations—and I am particularly thinking of the interpretations referring to death and to dead internalized objects, which is a psychotic anxiety—could have the effect of reviving hope and making the patient feel more alive. My explanation for this would be that bringing a very deep anxiety nearer to consciousness, in itself produces relief. But I also believe that the very fact that the analysis gets into contact with deep-lying unconscious anxieties gives the patient a feeling of being understood and therefore revives hope. (100)

And yet, there is still resistance to the analysis, each session reads like a tiny play, not because there is resolution, but because the sessions are composed of rapidly changing scenes, zany plots, foolhardy theories, flashes of insight, and then again, the resistance returns. Against all odds there are also feelings of being understood for both Richard and Mrs. K.

A few sessions later, Richard doubts Mrs. Klein's interpretation of his hostile wishes toward her, "Do I really think this of all of you? I don't know if I do. How can you really know what I think?" (111). Maybe he was also asking how do thoughts come to matter at all? Klein continues:

> *Mrs K.* replied that from his play, drawings, and what he was saying and doing she gathered some of his unconscious thoughts; but he expressed his doubts whether she was right and could be trusted. These doubts, Mrs K. interpreted, had come up together with his general distrust of her and Mummy, which had been more marked in the last few days. . . . Recently he had unconsciously expressed his death wishes towards Mummy and Mrs. K., and found it very painful and frightening when Mrs. K. interpreted this. But he felt relieved and happier afterwards. . . . (111–112)

What were these unconscious thoughts? For Richard, they could be about the war, both the terrible one he was living through and the internal one that fascinated him, what Klein spoke of as his internal Hitler. And when she spoke in that way, using words like "Hitler daddy" or "Hitler penis," Richard would become anxious and begin walking around the room, looking in cupboards, Mrs K.'s purse, or any closed object. On that particular day, Richard begins to squeeze a little ball between his feet and then marches around the room doing the goose-step:

> *Mrs K.* interpreted that the little ball represented the world; Mummy and Mrs K., squeezed by German boots–the goose step. In doing this Richard expressed his feeling that he not only contained the good Mummy but also the Hitler-father, and was destroying Mummy as the bad father did. Richard strongly objected, saying that he was not like Hitler, but he seemed to understand that the goose-stepping and the squeezing feet represented this. (114)

At the end of that session, as Richard is getting ready to leave the room, he turns off the electric fire and says: "Poor old radiator will have a rest. He carefully put the crayons according to sizes into the box . . . and helped Mrs K. to put the toys away in her bag" (114). After a rather poignant description of Richard bidding the room goodbye, reminding Mrs. Klein to bring his drawings back to the next session and his lingering there as the room was being prepared for the next group, Mrs. Klein offers one more interpretation:

> *Mrs K.* interpreted his fear that she might die at the weekend–the poor old silent room. That is why he had to make sure about her bringing the drawings; this also expressed his wish to help in the analysis, and thus to put Mrs K. right and preserve her. This is why he wished for Mrs. K.–the poor old radiator–to have a rest, not to be exhausted by her patients, particularly by him. (114)

And, of course, Richard is preoccupied with death, wondering in another session who will psychoanalyze him if Mrs K. dies. Richard is worried about Mrs K.'s travels to London; will she return to him? These questions come before a long break. When they return to analysis, Mrs K. believes Richard's resistance had reached a certain climax:

> While Richard at times wished to leave the room when anxiety welled up more fully and resistance reached a climax, he never actually left early. . . . What he did on a number of occasions was not to bring his fleet, which usually expressed his feeling that he had left a good part of his self and of his objects at home. The analysis of this splitting often had the effect that he brought the fleet again in the next session, and that he was able to make another step towards integration. (192)

Richard is beginning to think about his thinking, to understand that when he looks to the world he is looking through his emotional wishes, that his theories of the world are not coterminous with reality. And others can notice his communication and so allow the fleet to return, itself a good object. Richard is also learning to have a very different kind of conversation about language, where the poor old radiator is not just a radiator, but can represent his worry in their analytic work, that perhaps his badness has destroyed or taken the steam out of poor old Mrs Klein.

And so with this mismatch between memory and perception, there can also be questions. In the middle of his analysis, Richard asks Mrs. K. what grown-up's are afraid of, whether, "grown-ups are afraid of other grown-ups?" (231). But he was also interested now in psychoanalysis, "It seemed such a secret to him. He would like to get to the 'heart of it'. Mrs. K. interpreted that while he was actually interested to know all about psychoanalysis, he also wanted to find out all Mrs K.'s secrets" (231). A few sessions later, Richard returns to the topic of psychoanalysis: "Was it a rule amongst psycho-analysts that they were never to get cross or impatient? Would it harm the work? . . . Mrs K. interpreted that she stood for Mummy and he expected her to become very hostile about his desires to rob her of Daddy's good penis and devour it. But Richard also hoped that Mrs K. was not actually like Mummy, because she was a psychoanalyst and was doing this work to find out his thoughts and help him with them, and she would not be cross and he could speak freely to her" (246).

As Richard begins to ask more and more questions about Mrs K. and psychoanalysis, he slowly gets to the heart of the matter for himself.

The session occurs on a Sunday, a full seven session week. Richard wonders if analysts go to church and Mrs K. asks him if he thought it was wrong not to go to church on Sunday. This exchange begins to move slowly into other matters that Richard might feel are wrong:

> *Mrs K.* pointed out his strong doubts in psycho-analysis; he felt it to be very wrong. Because Mrs K. discussed with him matters which he thought improper and which he had even been taught to consider as improper, he felt that she was tempting him and allowed him to experience sexual desires towards his mother and herself. These desires seemed all the more dangerous to him because they are connected with hate, jealously, and destruction of his parents, whom he also loved. . . .
>
> Because she stood for the good and helpful Mummy, it was also painful to him to suspect that she was also the improper and tempting Mummy. He was afraid that the powerful Daddy–God–would punish Mummy too; lightening which struck the Nazi aeroplane punished the treacherous and disloyal Mummy as well as Mrs K. . . . (255)

We are very close to the foolish heart, the language of anxiety, the puppet world of theory. When we hear things we do not want to hear, it feels as if we are being both persecuted and tempted by these ideas. This splitting is the basis of moralism, itself a defense against understanding the complexity of emotional life. Here is Mrs K. She is willing to speak this nonsense and so convey these worries back to Richard so that he can think again. Richard is not a leaf in the wind; nor is he the lightening that downed the plane in his drawing. He need not become his phantasy.

At the end of four months of work, Klein also noted a hopefulness in Richard:

> Another sign of the increasing predominance of the life instinct, and with it of the capacity for love, was that he no longer felt impelled to turn away from destroyed objects but could experience compassion for them. I have referred to the fact that Richard, who so strongly hated the enemies threatening Britain's existence at that time, became capable of feeling sympathy for the destroyed enemy. (466)

Our enemies should only have to be destroyed once so that there can be an afterward. The trajectory Klein describes for learning is as follows: anxiety, interpretation, resistance, splitting, cooperation, reparation. This describes as well the ways her theory progresses.

Over the course of this narrative, there are two levels of discourse, parallel realities. First, Mrs. Klein interprets the unconscious anxiety of Richard's free association. His associations have three sources: movements and actions in the playroom, his drawings and play with toys, and his running commentary as he plays or draws. The second level of discourse is more illustrative and it is to show Richard, through interpretations and responses, that his activities also say something about his anxieties and emotional states, that he is always communicating something, and that even if this something is hostile, Mrs. Klein will survive his phantasies because they are only that: phantasies, or commentaries on anxiety and defenses against it. This is a world where the child is capable of metaphorical meaning and so of destroying and constructing knowledge. Through narrative, thinking about thinking, one can elaborate psychological knowledge. But the analyst must be willing to serve as a magnet for both love and hate, the analyst must be ready to become the poor old radiator.

Some commentaries on this case study point to the problem that Mrs Klein is not paying enough attention to Richard's external conditions— the war, his separation from his father and brother, his family's safety, his worries about the U.K. and Mrs. Klein, and so on. Adam Phillip's (2000) complex essay, "Bombs Away," urges analysts to remember that history indeed is taken personally by the child and that actual bombs are not just universal symbols for internal hostility. The tension is between Klein's theoretical preoccupations and Richard's actual history, between trauma as an internal and external catastrophe and how these catastrophes, wherever they are, becomes transformed. The narrative of Richard's analysis may hint at this conundrum, making history can also mean inquiring into the nature of the relation between external and internal danger. This is a different sense of taking history personally, where one can see what is significant about the personal, where one can also have doubts to make up one's own mind.

There is also incredulity toward the induction of symbolization, of what it can mean to call forth the internal world and so encounter psychical representatives in the form of, say, a Hitler penis. This world is terribly literal and Mrs. K.'s interpretations suggest that if that x stands for y, if the toy ship can stand for the father's penis, then symbolizing this trajectory of the affect can diminish its persecutory nature. When language is encountered through its associative and metaphoric links, thoughts may become uninhibited, indeed the difference between thoughts and events, memory and perception, can be allowed, provided that the unconscious can be witnessed. Literalness, the wish for and fear that reality can be one thing only, is precisely where both omnipotence and inhibition reside. It is also a condition for war and destruction. If Klein tried to say which comes first, psychological knowledge or knowledge of the world, Richard offered a glimpse of what it is to experience both dilemmas.

Perhaps it hardly needs saying, but where else than in the analytic setting would a child and adult have such a conversation about life and learn why meaning is so fragile, so subject to splitting, so difficult to maintain? Where else would a child be encouraged to explore his doubts, to speak his mind, to change his mind? What one notices in the world, what counts as an event, how one notices the eventfulness of the event, all these processes suggest something about the qualities and conflicts of one's internal world. This is why there must be a parallel or shadow dialogue in the analytic setting, why interpretation is interpretation of what is not yet thought but nonetheless enacted, why language must be eroticized. While education is sure of what moves the child forward, Klein's curiosity is otherwise, with what holds the child back, with what holds theory back, with what the child thinks of that. Over the course of her long career, she will try various answers; perhaps her longest one is found in the narrative of analysis with Richard.

Melanie Klein was well aware that she was making a narrative about children and about the nature of child psychoanalysis, not as a prescription, and not as Kristeva (2001, 104) argued, as "a system of knowledge," but as an occasion for thinking with children and with theory. By sending education away from the analytic setting, by entering a psychoanalytic world, Klein refused the position of role model, a moralist of the child's drama, or a detective of pathology. She was able to step away from these pedagogical habits because she was most interested in the ways the child represented fantasy, not reality. She was foolhardy enough to think it was important for theory to represent these dilemmas as well and she may locate these attempts as where psychic freedom can reside. It was in these representations that one could glimpse the painful defense of inhibition and normalization, a hyper agency that she would see as the superego, whose properties of judgment and persecution depend upon splitting and idealization, and upon symbolic equation. In this puppet world, hating a parent feels as if the affect did murder the parent. But Klein also insisted that it was only through exploring the forbidden that knowledge of reality could even be made because however wrong-headed, aggressive, and foolhardy, phantasy is the beginning of interpretation. This made all the difference in her work with children; they, too, were the interpreters of her theory. If child analysis begins with the supposition that children can receive and understand the psychoanalytic utterance, it concludes with the view that it is not just the idea that children can be understood. To leave knowledge there is still to stay in the realm of inhibition. The idea is that children, too, are very capable of self-understanding, of thinking about thinking, of understanding why we have understanding at all. The idea is that theory can hold these conundrums, even if it cannot solve them.

REFERENCES

Adorno, T. (2001). In r. Tiedemann (Ed.), *Kant's critique of pure reason.* Translated by Rodney Livingstone. Stanford: Stanford University Press.

Bass, A. (1998). Sigmund Freud: The question of *Weltanschauung* and of defense. In P. Marcus & A. Rosenberg (Eds.), *Psychoanalytic versions of the human condition: Philosophies of life and their impact on practice.* pp. 412–446. New York: New York University.

Britzman, D.P. 2003. *After-education: Anna Freud, Melanie Klein and psychoanalytic histories of learning.* Albany: State University of New York Press.

Grosskurth, P. (1986). *Melanie Klein: Her world and her work.* Cambridge, MA: Harvard Press.

Klein, M. (1975). *Narrative of a child analysis: The conduct of the psycho-analysis of children as seen in the treatment of a ten-year-old boy.* London: Delacorte Press/Seymour Lawrence

——. 1930. The importance of symbol-formation in the development of the ego. In *Love, guilt, and reparation and other works, 1921–1945.* pp. 219–232. London: Delacorte Press/Semour Lawrence, 1975.

Kohon, G. (1999). *No lost certainties to be recovered.* London: Karnac Books.

Kristeva, J. (2002). *Intimate revolt: The powers and limits of psychoanalysis* (Vol. 2). Translated by Jeanine Herman. New York: Columbia University Press.

——. .2001. *Melanie Klein.* Trans. Ross Guberman. New York: Columbia University Press.

——. (1995). *New maladies of the soul.* Trans. Ross Guberman. New York: Columbia Press.

Likierman, M. (2001). *Melanie Klein: Her work in context.* New York: Continuum Books.

Petot, J. *Melanie Klein: First discoveries and first system 1919–1932* (Vol. I). Trans. Christine Trollop. Madison, WI: International Universities Press.

Phillips, A. (2000). Bombs away. In *Promises, promises: Essays on literature and psychoanalysis.* pp. 35–58. London: Farber Press.

——. (2002). *Equals.* New York: Basic Books.

Phillips, J. (1998). The fissure of authority: Violence and the acquisition of knowledge. In L. Stonebridge & J. Phillips (Eds.), *Reading Melanie Klein,* pp. 160–78. London: Routledge.

Pontalis, J.B. (1981). *Frontiers in psychoanalysis: Between the dream and psychic pain.* Trans. Catherine Cullen & Philip Cullen. New York: International Universities Press.

Rose, J. (1993). *Why war? Psychoanalysis, politics, and the return to Melanie Klein.* London: Blackwell Press.

Roudinesco, E. (2001). *Why psychoanalysis?* Translated by Rachel Bowlby. New York: Columbia University Press.

Chapter 7

PROFESSIONAL PRACTICE AND THE CHALLENGE OF CHILDREN'S RIGHTS

JEREMY ROCHE

In this chapter I explore the issues raised for professional practice by the modern children's rights movement. In order to "set the scene" and locate this movement within its proper context, I review the problematising discourses surrounding children today, in particular the way in which public discourse positions children as either victims or threats. I then identify the key features of the modern children's rights movement, the law's positioning of children, and the rise of human rights. Finally, I consider some of the practical dilemmas facing professionals working with children and young people in a context within which much greater emphasis is placed on their rights and participation.

Victims or Threats

Over the past 150 years children have been seen as either a threat to society and the well-being of its citizenry or as vulnerable and in need of protection from adults and the forces of urbanization and industrialization. One of the consequences of this positioning of children has been a neglect of children's social agency (Mayall, 2002); another related consequence has been a very particular vision of child concern. Either way, children needed to be subject to new disciplinary regimes in order to be saved from the immanent chaos of their lives,[1] and the

---

1. For these read cruel and neglectful parents.

177

depredations of the city and the factory (Behlmer, 1982). At the start of the twenty-first century it is perhaps only the "details" that have changed. Today, while there are new threats to "our children" e.g., pedophilia and child pornography, these are not quite so new as some would have us believe. For example, William Stead's campaign in the Pall Mall Gazette around the prostitution of young girls in London, which eventually led to the Sexual Offences Amendment Act 1885, drew on images of the innocent child and the debauched male client to fuel demands for reform of the law. The campaign was couched in very moralistic language at the same time as presenting a lurid and titillating account of prostitution (Mort, 1987:103–5).

Contemporary practices and rhetoric of child protection still seem inextricably interwoven with parent-blaming and anxiety about an underclass. Yet today, children are the "beneficiaries" of a new array of institutions and professionals dedicated to the promotion of their welfare and protection. This includes schools, social services departments, and a national health service and associated professionals.[2] While for many children in the U.K., the condition of being a child has been transformed materially, the social imagination concerning what it is to be a child appears, at first sight, to be traditional. It is traditional in the sense that children are still seen as objects of concern (Butler-Sloss,1988), they are in need of rescue or control and they are fundamentally incomplete. By this, I mean that they are seen to lack the rationality and competence to be treated as social actors—in a deeply disturbing sense, they are denied any authority over the meaning of their own lives and situations.

The Welfare of Children

While, as noted above, the child is at the center of a modern complex of professional concerns and practices, all of which are directed to promoting the welfare of the child, it does not necessarily follow that the child always benefits from this situation. This is not to argue that

---

2. These professionals now have to comply with agreed national occupational standards in their day-to-day practice and work within codes of practice and codes of ethics. For example, in 2002, a new Code of Practice for social workers was adopted by the General Social Care Council for England and in April 2002, the British Association of Social Workers (BASW) launched 'The Code of Ethics for Social Work' which is binding on all members of BASW.

professional practice is in some sinister sense disabling (Illich, 1979), but to point out that too often the good intentions of adult professionals have produced harmful outcomes for children. Sometimes this re-evaluation comes about as the result of a radical change in our understanding of the developmental and emotional needs of children (Robertson & Robertson, 1989) and others, the result of a direct challenge to a prevailing orthodoxy regarding how children should be cared for and looked after. In the latter part of the twentieth century, there are two examples of such challenges and shifts in the U.K. context.

First it is only in the last decade that the corporal punishment of children at school has been prohibited. In the 1960s, most teachers' organizations opposed any attempt to restrict the right of teachers to impose corporal punishment on children. It was only in 1969 that STOPP (Society of Teachers Opposed to Physical Punishment) was set up; and while the Inner London Education Authority abolished the use of the cane in primary schools in 1973, in 1978, the Handicapped and Deprived Children (Corporal Punishment) Bill, which would have abolished corporal punishment for "handicapped and deprived children" made no headway in Parliament (Newell, 1989).

It was the European Convention on Human Rights (ECHR) which provided the platform from which challenges to this practice were made. In the case of *Campbell and Cosans v United Kingdom* (1982), before the European Court of Human Rights, the applicants were the parents of children at state schools in Scotland. Mrs. Campbell asked for an assurance that her son would not be physically punished: this was refused. Mrs Cosans' son was asked to report for corporal punishment for breaking the school rules; he refused and was suspended. His parents were informed that he could only return to school if he submitted to the school's disciplinary requirements; they refused and were threatened with prosecution for failing to ensure their son's attendance at school. Both applicants claimed that corporal punishment used in their sons' schools was contrary to Article 3 and that the refusal to respect their objection to such punishment contravened Article 2 of the First Protocol which provides that:

> No person shall be denied the right to education...the State shall respect the right of parents to ensure such education and teaching in conformity with their own religious and philosophical convictions.

Here the ECHR did not find a violation of Article 3 but did decide there had been a breach of the ECHR because the government did not respect the parents' objections to corporal punishment. The court's conclusion that there had been no breach of Article 3 was based on the argument that while the threat of corporal punishment could amount to "inhuman treatment," in this instance this was not the case.[3]

It was not until the decision of the European Commission of Human Rights in the case of Karen Warwick, in 1987, that it was held that a school caning breached Article 3, i.e., breached the child's right not to be exposed to inhuman and degrading treatment and punishment, as opposed to the rights of parents to have their religious and philosophical convictions respected (*ChildRight,* December 1987). However, in order for punishment to come within the wording of Article 3, the "humiliation and debasement involved must attain a particular level of severity over and above the usual element of humiliation involved in any kind of punishment."[4]

As a result of the ECHR cases and political campaigning corporal punishment in state schools was abolished by the Education Act 1986. It was not until 1999 with the coming into force of the School Standards and Framework Act 1998 that corporal punishment was brought to an end in private schools.[5]

Second, the situation many children with special educational needs found themselves in was one in which they would end up having to go to a special school and thus were excluded from mainstream education. Now, as a result of campaigning by disabled children, their carers, and disability organizations, under the Special Educational Needs and Dis-

---

3. In a partly dissenting opinion, Sir Vincent Evans, while agreeing that there had been no violation of Article 3, also argued that there had been no violation of Article 2 of the First Protocol. He said that it was clear from the explanations, provided at the time that Article 2 was drafted, that its purpose was to "protect the rights of parents against the use of educational institutions by the State for the ideological indoctrination of children." Thus according to his interpretation of the ECHR, the views of parents on such matters as the use of corporal punishment in schools was outside the scope of the provision.

4. Thus in *Y v UK* (1992) where the headmaster's caning of the 15-year-old applicant had left weals across the boys buttocks, the ECHR did decide there had been a breach of the child's rights under Article 3.

5 . However these developments are not uncontested. In December 2002, the Court of Appeal heard an appeal from the High Court in which the applicants (all teachers or parents of children at private schools) claimed that the prohibition of corporal punishment in schools breached the parents' human rights under Article 9 (freedom of conscience) of the ECHR. The Court of Appeal dismissed the appeal.

ability Act 2001, local authorities can only refuse mainstream education for a child whose parents request it where such educational provision would be "incompatible with the provision of efficient education for other children." Many other examples could be provided and the trend seems to be one in which the traditional assumptions about children and the authority and legitimacy of adult action towards children are now open to question in new ways.[6] Children with disabilities are no longer to be hidden away in institutions nor treated as if they were not possessed of certain fundamental rights.

So in recent years, we can see quite significant shifts in ideas about children, their particular needs, and their rights and responsibilities. The important issue here is that whether we are talking about child abuse and maltreatment, children and family life, education or crime and delinquency, the public discourses surrounding children are paradoxically stable and fluid. The welfare of children is still quite properly a matter of public concern; yet how their welfare might be advanced and who has authority to speak on the issue is more openly contested. It can no longer be easily assumed that adults always know best. It is clear that there are signs of significant change taking place in the U.K. context.

Recent research into the family lives of children reveals some interesting developments. For instance, that there has been a move towards an authoritative (as opposed to an authoritarian) model of parenting which is geared towards encouraging and enabling the participation of children, fostering the development of their autonomy at the same time as promoting responsible behavior on their part by, for example, the setting of clear and reasonable boundaries (Brannen et al., 1994). An interesting recognition of this shift, at a legislative level, is contained in the Children (Scotland) Act 1995. Section 6 of the Act imposes a duty on parents to consult with their child on any major decision. The Scottish Law Commission had consulted on this matter. It stated (1992:paras.2.62-64):

> The question as we saw it was whether a parent or other person exercising parental rights should be under a similar obligation to ascertain and have regard to the child's wishes and feelings as a local authority was in relation to a child in its care. . . . There are great attractions in such an approach. It emphasises

---

6. The U.K. practice of "emigrating" children to the "colonies" for their own good and in the process separating them from their families and all that was familiar.

that the child is a person in his or her own right and that his or her views are entitled to respect and consideration. . . . Many respondents clearly regarded such a provision as an important declaration of principle.[7]

The Revisioning of Childhood

The new sociology of childhood provides further illustration of the shifts in thinking regarding adult-child relations at both a theoretical and empirical level (see also Qvotrup et al., 1994). At the theoretical level, Mayall (2002), who argues that children's agency has been ignored by mainstream social science, is concerned to explore the position of children in the social division of labor, children as agents in the "intermediate domain" and the idea of a child standpoint. These are the key building blocks of her sociology of childhood, a sociology which will of necessity advance children's rights. Thus, for Mayall, the sociology of childhood must take account of how children themselves experience and understand their lives and social relationships and recognize that children's experiential knowledge "is a vital ingredient in any effort towards the recognition of children's rights."

At the empirical level there is a growing body of research that reveals and explores the complexity of children's lives, which catches the many ways in which children, of necessity, negotiate the relationships and dangers of the environments in which they live (e.g., Neale, 2002). What emerges from these studies is an image of a competent and rational child (Alderson & Montgomery, 1996), a child with clear preferences and a voice–if only adults and adult society could hear (see also Hutchby & Moran-Ellis,1998).[8]

One has to be careful not to overstate the case here. What I am arguing is that there is significant change taking place and this is not to say that this is an even or uncontested development. These changes feed into and are fed by the new children's rights movement and they are part of the changing backdrop of professional practice; this can present serious challenges for professionals working with children. The caring professions, operating out of an explicit welfare discourse, now have to

---

7. The Act provides that children aged 12 or over are presumed to be capable of forming a view.
8. Much research is now geared to finding out what children think, how they see the world, how they view issues ranging from planning, transport policy to the politics of peace in Northern Ireland (Percy-Smith, 1998; Davis and Jones, 1996; Democratic Dialogue, 1996).

deal with the legitimacy of images of the participating and competent child who might not comply with adult requests or who might have a quite different set of priorities from those of the professionals involved (see Roche & Tucker 2003).

The Modern Children's Rights Movement

The messages from the new sociology of childhood connects in many ways with the key features of the modern children's rights movement. Before considering this movement, I need to distinguish between welfare and liberty rights (Archard, 1993) for the simple reason that this distinction can be seen as one aspect of the modern children's rights movement. As noted earlier, many of the "welfare rights" of children, with the benefit of hindsight, and from a more critical vantage point, appear to have undermined the welfare of the children involved. By welfare rights, I am referring to the child's right to basic provisions such as shelter, food, and clothing as well as his or her care and protection. Children's welfare rights provide the rationale for much professional practice and much of the contemporary debate on children is concerned with how best to safeguard and promote their welfare. However, there is no clear-cut consensus on how best to bring up children, how children should be supported through particular episodes, e.g., relationship breakdown, or how society should respond to crime and delinquency. Nevertheless, acting to promote the welfare of children is a powerful and traditional "slogan."

Liberty rights on the other hand are much more disruptive of traditional ways of viewing children and adult-child relations. By "liberty rights" I am referring to those rights associated with the child's autonomy interest, e.g., the right to make his or her own decisions on matters that concern him or her. The idea that children should have decision-making autonomy threatens the very idea of childhood; childhood, after all, is a condition of vulnerability and dependency. Liberty rights of children thus conjure up in our imagination not only the "end of childhood,"[9] but a deeply unknowable future. One consequence of the modern children's rights movement is the idea that the traditional adult-child boundaries are now uncertain.

---

9. See Cox, 1996.

Wyness (2000) views the emerging challenges to the restricting subordinate and protected roles of children as a positive development. Children may be "less subsumed within an adult world of discipline and control because we are more likely now to recognize them as able, willing and reliable contributors' within their environments." Wyness refuses to conflate children's rights with the crisis in childhood in part because the idea of children's rights embraces both their "welfare rights to care" and their "rights to self-determination"; the former confirming adult authority the latter being potentially disruptive of such authority. In other words "welfare rights" while important, are not the only concern of the modern children's rights movement–such rights do not in any way challenge "adultist"[10] assumptions about what children are like.[11] The tension between the imagery of the cared for child and the autonomous child is neatly captured in the Gillick decision.

Children and the Law

In the mid 1980s, the House of Lords gave their famous decision in the Gillick case.[12] This case was concerned with whether the DHSS could lawfully issue a notice to the effect that while it was desirable to consult the parents of a person under 16 years of age who sought contraceptive advice and treatment, in some circumstances the doctor, exercising his or her clinical judgment, retained the right to provide such advice and treatment without informing the parents. Mrs Gillick sought a declaration from the High Court that this notice was unlawful. In essence, her objection was that the law should support her in her role as a parent, not undermine her by holding out to her 15-year-old daughter the prospect of access to a fully confidential relationship with a doctor for the purpose of receiving contraceptive advice and treatment.[13] The case reached the House of Lords and in his oft-quoted judgment, Lord Scarman held that:

> The underlying principle of the law . . . is that parental right yields to the child's right to make his own decision when he reaches a sufficient understanding and

10. See Dalrymple & Burke, 1995.
11. See, for example, Kohm and Lawrence 1997–98 who see articles 12 and 14 of the UNCRC as blurring the line between adulthood and childhood (at p. 369).
12. *Gillick v West Norfolk and Wisbech Area Health Authority* [1986] A.C. 112, [1985] 3 WLR 830.
13. See the Times Editorial "Gillick's Law," 18th October 1985.

intelligence to be capable of making his own mind up on the matter in question.[14]

Thus in Lord Scarman's judgment in Gillick, it could be said that the common law was recognizing the decision-making autonomy of children. Yet it is not that clear-cut and in any event, the "mature minor," test that Lord Scarman deployed in his judgment was very onerous.

In what ways can contemporary child law be seen to respect and promote children's rights?[15] In England and Wales, the Children Act 1989 can be said to have advanced the "welfare rights" of children through its endorsement of the paramountcy principle,[16] the provision of the "welfare checklist" and the no order principle.[17] The threshold criteria[18] can be seen as an attempt to limit state intervention into family life by requiring a minimum threshold of harm to be established before any compulsory powers over a family can be acquired by the local authority. Lord Mackay argued:

> It is not proper to intervene on any level of harm. The fundamental point is that State intervention in families in the shape of the local authority should not be justified unless there is some level–'significant' is a good word for it – at which significant harm is suffered or is likely to be suffered. (cited in Allen 1992 at p. 125)

Such a "threshold" could be argued to promote the welfare rights of children by limiting the discretion of the local authority to intervene in the name of the welfare of the child.

---

14. One concrete consequence of the House of Lords judgment was that those who worked in family planning settings were now reassured that they would not be acting unlawfully in providing such advice and treatment–this was of practical significance for many young women–see "Victory for Mrs Gillick is a tragedy for thousands of young people," Guardian 30th January 1985.

15. Lord Mackay on the subject of the Children Bill said in Committee: "This Bill does nothing to change the underlying Gillick principle, which has to be taken into account by all who exercise parental responsibility over a child mature and intelligent enough to take decisions for himself" (Hansard, House of Lords Vol. 502, Col. 1351).

16. Though the welfare principle has been subject to substantial criticism within socio-legal scholarship–see for example Reece, 1996.

17. The checklist enumerates those matters the court is required to have regard to when considering making a range of orders and the no order principle states that the court must not make an order unless 'doing so would be better for the child than making no order at all'–s.1(5) of the Children Act 1989.

18. Section 31(2) of the Act provides that a court may only make a care or supervision order if "it is satisfied–(a) that the child concerned is suffering, or likely to suffer, significant harm; and (b) that the harm, or likelihood of harm, is attributable to–(I) the care given to the child, or likely to be given to him if the order were not made, not being what it would be reasonable to expect a parent to give to him; or (ii) the child's being beyond parental control."

There are, however, aspects of the legislation that can be seen supportive of children's liberty rights. First, Section 10 of the Children Act 1989 specifically provides for the eventuality in which a child can apply to the court for permission to make an application for a Section 8 order.[19] The court can only grant the child leave to apply if "it is satisfied that he has sufficient understanding to make the proposed application."[20] Nonetheless the Act in its contemplation of the possibility of the child becoming a litigant can be seen as advancing and extending the child's autonomy.

Second is the departure from the settled rule that a child could not bring or defend an action except via a guardian ad litem or "next friend," i.e., via an adult intermediary. Rule 9.2A of the Family Proceedings Rules 1991 provided that a child could prosecute or defend proceedings without a "next friend" in two situations. Where the proceedings are not "specified proceedings," and the child has the leave of the court, and where a solicitor has accepted instructions from the child having considered in the light of the child's age that the child is able to give instructions.[21] These provisions opened up the possibility for the first time of the child having unmediated access to legal services and the courts.

Third, a number of provisions of the Act gave the child, if he or she was of sufficient understanding to make an informed decision, the right to refuse to submit to a medical or psychiatric examination or assessment. Thus, Section 44 (7) provides that even where a court has directed that the child undergo a medical or psychiatric examination or other assessment, the "child may, if he is of sufficient understanding to make an informed decision, refuse to submit to the examination or other assessment."[22]

---

19. There are four Section 8 orders regulating where the child lives (residence order), who has access to the child (contact order), prohibiting a named course of action in relation to the child (a prohibited steps order), and requiring that specified steps be taken in respect of the child (A specific issue order).

20. Slightly reminiscent of the language of the Gillick decision.

21. The solicitor is under a duty to take instructions directly from the child where the child is in conflict with the GAL. In Re H (A Minor) (Care Proceedings: Child's Wishes) [1993] 1 FLR 440, the court referred to the solicitor's failure to take instructions exclusively from the child when there was clearly a conflict between the child and the GAL as constituting "a fundamental forfeiture of the child's right."

22. Though this provision has been interpreted very cautiously by the courts–see Roche 1996.

Fourth, under Section 26 of the Act, the child was given the right to complain about the local authority's discharge of their functions under Part III of the Act. This applied to children in need as well as children who were being "looked after." Prior to the Act, there had been no legal requirement on local authorities to set up complaints procedures. Local authorities were now required to set up such procedures and they had to have an independent element.

Finally, the ECHR continues to impact on the legal standing of children and with the passing of the Human Rights Act 1998, the discourse of human rights is assuming a greater prominence in local debates surrounding children and childhood.

The Rise of Human Rights

The Human Rights Act (HRA) 1998, which came into force on October 2, 2000, incorporates most of the provisions of the ECHR into U.K. domestic law. Article 1 of the ECHR states that the parties to the ECHR must "secure to everyone within their jurisdiction the rights and freedoms" contained in the Convention and Article 14 provides that the enjoyment of these rights and freedoms must be secured "without discrimination on any ground such as sex, race, colour, language, religion, political or other opinion, national or social origin, association with a national minority, property, birth or other status."[23] It is clear from the jurisprudence of the ECHR that states are under a positive obligation, i.e., are required to take active steps, to secure Convention rights and freedoms. As a result, U.K. courts and tribunals are required now to interpret and give effect to the law in a way which is compatible with the Convention rights (Section 3 HRA 1998). The HRA also provides that it is unlawful for a public authority to act in a way that is incompatible with a Convention right (Section 6 HRA 1998). The purpose of the HRA 1998 is to ensure that public authorities' policies and decision-making practices respect human rights and where they fail to do so, to make it much easier to raise directly claims that one's human

---

23. It is arguable that this includes discrimination on the basis of age. This, of course, does not mean that the ECHR views the four-year-old child in the same way as the forty-year-old adult. Indeed, the provisions of the ECHR make explicit reference to the special position of children, e.g., in addition to which the ECHR has interpreted the phrases "for the protection of health or morals" and "for the protection of the rights and freedoms of others" (e.g., Articles 8 and 9) to permit special treatment of children.

rights have been breached. So it appears that as a matter of public policy, legal doctrine, and procedure, all of us, including children, come within the protections of the ECHR. Earlier, I referred to the ECHR case law which fed into the campaign to end the corporal punishment of children; there have been a number of other decisions which have had a direct impact on professional practice. One key judgment might have very long-term consequences. In the case of *Z and others v UK* [2001] 2 FLR 612, the European Court of Human Rights decided that the House of Lords decision in *X (Minors) v Bedfordshire County Council* (1995) 2 Appeal Cases 633 breached the ECHR. In this child protection case, no action was taken for three years after the first referral to the local authority social services department (in 1987) even though there were very serious grounds for concern. Furthermore, what support was provided was limited and the children were only placed in emergency foster care in June, 1992, when their mother threatened to "batter" them—the local authority subsequently applied for care orders in relation to all four children.[24] The Official Solicitor took action against the local authority claiming, on behalf of the children, damages for negligence and/or breach of statutory duty—the House of Lords rejected the children's appeal.

The ECHR unanimously decided that there had been a breach of Article 3 of the ECHR in that the welfare system set up to protect children from serious harm had failed to protect them from the inhuman and degrading treatment or punishment prohibited by Article 3. The ECHR held (by a majority of 15 to 2) that there had been a violation of Article 13, the right to an effective remedy, in that the children, as a result of the House of Lord's decision, could not sue the local authority in negligence for compensation, however foreseeable and severe the harm suffered, and however unreasonable the conduct of the local authority. Many welcomed this decision in that while they were sympathetic to the position of the local authority and were alive to the complexity of the child protection task, including interagency working, they considered that the effective blanket immunity, on public policy grounds, conferred on the local authority by the decision of the House of Lords was inappropriate.

---

24. The child psychiatrist reported that the emotional abuse and neglect was the worst she had seen in her career.

Professional Practice

Within the past decades, no professional group or social welfare institution involved with children has escaped public censure. New questions have been asked of professional practice–doctors, social workers, lawyers, and therapists. The caring professions have been attacked as pursuing their own agendas, as being controlling rather than simply caring and as denying to those they care for cognitive authority over their own situation. One scandal in particular captures this in a deeply disturbing way. In Pindown, children in some children's homes in Staffordshire were subject to a regime of rewards and punishment which entailed amongst other things forcing the young person to "face up to his or her difficulties," periods of confinement, denial of contact visits, and denial of access to education. This regime continued for almost six years. In their report Levy and Kahan observe (1991:127):

> Pindown, in our view . . . involved elements of isolation, humiliation and confrontation to varying degrees. . . . We have no doubt that children were humiliated in many ways. . . . In addition during confrontational 'meetings' numerous children were harangued and referred to in grossly abusive terms. . . . Pindown . . . was intrinsically unethical, unprofessional and unacceptable.

It is important to remind ourselves that this practice was put into operation by a member of the social work profession, a profession which is dedicated to the welfare of the client.[25] Perhaps this episode more than the other publicized failures of social work catches the need for a more explicit engagement with issues around rights and professional power.[26]

The professional commitment to care provides the discretionary space and zone of uncertainty within which the professional's vision of the "good" predominates.[27] So what are the implications for professionals who work with children of this recognition of children's agency, rationality, and competence and the new emphasis on the child's voice

---

25. Perhaps the failure to properly address questions of children's rights is part of the explanation.
26. As Banks (1995) observes, most decisions in social work involve a complex interaction of ethical, political, technical, and legal issues which are all interconnected.
27. It is perhaps no coincidence that alongside the modern critique of professional practice is a parallel critique of the "welfare principle."

in a range of professional settings including the courtroom. I think there are some awkward issues.

An emphasis on the participation of the child presupposes clarity that the child is the client. The enquiry into the death of Jasmine Beckford found, amongst other things, that the social workers involved treated the parents as the client rather than the child (London Borough of Brent, 1985:294). The media response to this event was one of condemnation of the social workers involved for their failure to take timely action to protect the child. In contrast, the Butler Sloss report into the Cleveland scandal criticized a range of professionals. Pediatricians, police, and social workers were all criticized for their overzealous approach to protecting the children they believed to be at risk of sexual abuse: again the children were allegedly lost sight of. Worse still, the report noted that for some children, the child protection process itself was experienced as abusive–as Butler-Sloss observed "the voices of the children were not heard." Now, however, alongside an insistence that the child is the client is an emphasis on consulting with and taking into account the wishes and feelings of the child.[28]

Yet, there are still problems. For example, research carried out into the lives of young carers shows that very often the "young carer" is rendered invisible and silent by professional assumptions and practices–social workers appear to find it easier to communicate with involved adults (Tatum & Tucker, 1998; Roche & Tucker, 2003).

Assuming that the professional succeeds in keeping focus on the child as the client, how can he or she effectively promote and support the child's participation? Professionals working with children and young people experience difficulty not only because of the complexity of the situation they encounter, but also because they do not always take children and young people seriously enough. In relation to the latter point there have been numerous enquiries that have revealed the myriad way in which the voices of children, even when they spoke, were not heard. From Pindown (Levy & Kahan, 1991) to abuse in children's homes in Gwynedd and Clwyd (Department of Health/Welsh Office, 2000), repeatedly children were not listened to or believed when making complaints about their treatment or making allegations

---

28. For example, Section 1 of the Children Act 1989 requires the courts in arriving at a range of decisions to take into account as appropriate the wishes and feelings of the child.

of abuse. Much research on children tells the same story: the failure of adult professionals to take children seriously, to listen to what they have to say or to advocate on their behalf. Dearden and Becker (2001) point out that research highlights how health care professionals disregard children's needs in discussions about parental mental health needs; this can lead to inappropriate social work interventions when viewed from the child's perspective. Yet, it is important to acknowledge that often it is committed adult professionals who are responsible for innovative ways of working with children and young people[29] and challenging current assumptions and accepted practices. The crucial features of such projects is that they are involved with and work with children and young people over a period of time, they are committed to treating them and their concerns with respect, and they are open about their decision-making practices. For many children, having some control over both agendas and outcomes is what matters–hence the appeal of Childline whose success is based upon offering a confidential service. Research carried out by Childline confirms that it is this confidentiality that is so important to children who phone about all kinds of issues. It is of note that children who make use of their service often just want a totally safe place to talk about a matter that concerns them and often children are able after such confidential conversation to decide for themselves what they will do.[30]

Furthermore, while an individual professional may be committed to the modern children's rights project, including a concern to promote the autonomy rights of young people, it must be acknowledged that professionals who work with children and young people are not free agents. They will have a sense of their professional responsibility and accountability to management as well as their ideas about children, their competencies, and responsibilities. The issue of confidentiality is illustrative here.

Research carried out by the British Medical Association in 1994 found that almost 75 percent of patients under 16 and 50 percent of patients between 16 and 19 feared that their doctor would not or could not preserve confidentiality in relation to requests for contraceptive

---

29. E.g., the Dundee Corner Project, Derry Nucleus Project–see generally The Open University (1997).
30. See Roche and Briggs, 1990, for a discussion of the importance of confidentiality for children.

services. The BMA urged the importance of educating young people about the confidentiality they can expect from their doctor. It stressed that the duty of confidentiality owed to a person under 16 is as great as that owed to any other person. Regardless of whether or not the requested treatment is given, the confidentiality of the consultation should still be respected, unless there are convincing reasons to the contrary (BMA, 1994). However, while general practitioners have a strong commitment to confidentiality and know that under 16's have the same right to confidentiality as adults, it is fairly common for results of tests to be given to parents, without the consent of the young person being sought.[31] Some staff said that it was hard to explain to parents why they might not be entitled to know their child's results (Baillie, 2003).

Sawyer (1995), in her research into the way solicitors assessed the competence of children to participate in family proceedings, found that they would go beyond what was demanded of them in their legal role when it came to assessing the competence of the child; welfare considerations regularly intruded, especially in private law cases (pp. 95–96).[32] In considering the question of the separate representation of children in family proceedings she notes that two concerns were raised. First "there is the question of whether having a right to state 'wrong' opinion is so good in itself that it necessarily outweighs the risks inherent in the advocation of a view of the child's welfare which may be incorrect" (p. 168). There was also the issue "whether having the right to speak out and be heard . . . gives rise to any risks in the child's position outside the proceedings, including his or her own individual family relationships." According to Sawyer (1995:169):

> Few believed that even a competent child's view should always be followed; even the interviewees committed in principle to 'children's rights' appeared to proceed with considerable paternalist–or parentalist–assumptions in practice, albeit they used different formulations to justify the exercise of the function.

In Sawyer's later research (1999) into the role and work of the court welfare officer (CWO) in the context of private law disputes, she con-

---

31. It has now been acknowledged that this practice cannot continue and that procedures need to be put in place to seek consent from the young person to release results to someone else.
32. Scottish legislation provides a nice contrast. The Age of Legal Capacity (Scotland) Act 1991 as amended by the Children (Scotland) Act 1995 provides (s.2(4A) that "a person under the age of sixteen shall have legal capacity to instruct a solicitor, in connection with any civil matter, where that person has a general understanding of what it means to do so." Later it states the presumption that children aged twelve years or over have such understanding.

firmed earlier work, which depicted their role as one of promoting parental agreement wherever possible in order to avoid a formal trial of matters relating to the children (see also Piper, 1993). While they saw contact with a parent as the "child's right" and believed in principle in seeing the child, very few actually did so. Further some CWOs would only see a child in order to avoid criticism or rereferral by the court: "the idea of involving the child as an active participant was not on the everyday agenda at all" (1999:262).

Conclusion

Much social discussion about children is underpinned by a concern to protect them (from others, themselves, and their own choices) and an anxiety about them. As noted above children are either idealized or demonized in public discourse (Griffin, 1994) and there is little space in between for a more honest conversation about children and the complexity of the lives they lead. The demand for the right to be an active participant in one's own story is central and integral to the project of imagining different kinds of adult-child relations and thus different encounters between children and professionals. While the form such conversations might take is uncertain, especially in professional settings, ultimately, children's rights are about rethinking and redefining adult-child relations and are a means "with which to articulate challenge and hold to account relationships of power." As Federle argues (1994:355–6):

> . . . rights claims challenge existing hierarchies by making the community hear different voices. Community and claiming are part of a slow historical process that will invigorate the debate about children's rights and will, someday, lead to a better life for children through the articulation of ideal relationships between children and adults in the larger community.

The child's voice is not simply practically valuable (professionals will arrive at better decisions if they foster the participation of children and young people in decisions affecting them) but also symbolically valuable. The claims of children to an equality of concern and respect and claims which embrace children's definitions of their own needs and interests now appear to have a practical force and legitimacy that used not to be the case. Professionals and those who work with children and young people in a range of settings can be key allies in this project.

The spaces children and young people inhabit though varied are limited physically and ideologically. Part of this "limit" is a set of common assumptions about children, their incompetence and their incompleteness—to make a reality of their participation in a particular setting, adult professionals will not only have to acquire new skills and ways of working so that they can communicate with children, but also be aware of the impact of the power imbalance between adult (professional) and child. Children know that they are in a particular relation to adults, especially outside professionals, and will pursue strategies accordingly.[33] Too easily perhaps adults assume a consensus of definition and planned outcome, that what they are doing is for the best and that children share this view.

Even if adult professional and child use the same terms, such as needs and rights, it is not self-evident that the words have the same meaning for both "participants." Children may use the language of rights to signal a demand that they be treated fairly and with respect by adult professionals. In contrast adult professionals might make use of this language in order to identify their powers in a given situation and to explain to the child and his or her carer what the professional involved can do. If need is the primary language, this can eclipse the power of the language of rights. Professional commitment to participation will then be limited to informing the child as to how the professional sees his or her needs being met—not in being open to this question and including the child in its resolution.

Continued reliance on the language of children's rights is part of a shifting process and we should all benefit from taking children and their rights more seriously. Masson and Winn Oakley in their discussion of the position that children find themselves in the court process, suggest (1999:144) that "greater opportunities to participate, where they wished to do so, might encourage some children to engage with the proceedings." This would necessitate "changes in court practice, such as clearer use of language, shorter hearings and more attention to the needs of ordinary people"–this would also benefit parents, relatives, and carers.

---

33. See Griffiths and Kandel (2001) for an analysis of how children appearing before children's hearings in Scotland negotiate with, resist, and at times subvert the hearing and its personnel.

These shifts in thinking about children are uneven, contested and championed in different ways in different places.[34] Increasingly, children themselves are challenging and resisting adult constructions of incompetence. If we do not grapple with the negative ideas associated with children, to socially include children in public and private spaces they will remain distrustful of irregular and sporadic adult invitations to participate, on adult terms within adult agendas. The demand for children's rights today is a cultural project, which necessarily requires adult professionals and others to rethink their attitudes towards children and childhood.

REFERENCES

Alderson, P., & Montgomery, J. (1996). *Health care choices: Making decisions with children*. London: IPPR.

Allen, N. (1992). *Making sense of the children act* (2nd ed.). London: Longman.

Archard, D. (1993). *Children: Rights and childhood*. London: Routledge.

baillie, D. (2003). Confidentiality, access to information, human rights and data protection. In D. Baillie, K. Cameron, L. Cull, J. Roche, & J. West (Eds.), *Social work and the law in Scotland*. Basingstoke: Palgrave.

Banks, S. (1995). *Ethics and values in social work*. Basingstoke: MacMillan.

Behlmer, G. (1982). *Child-abuse and moral reform in England 1870–1908*. Stanford, CA: Stanford University Press.

Brannen, J., Dodd, K., Oakley, A., & Storey, P. (1994). *Young people, health and family life*. Buckingham: Open University Press.

BMA (British Medical Association). (1994). *Confidentiality and people under 16*. London: BMA.

Butler-Sloss. (1988). *Report of the enquiry into child abuse in Cleveland*, Cm. 412. London: HMSO.

Cox, R. (1996). *Shaping childhood themes of uncertainty in the history of adult-child relations*. London: Routledge.

Dalrymple, J., & Burke, I. (1995). *Anti-oppressive practice social care and the law*. Buckingham: Open University Press.

Davis, A., & Jones, L. (1996). Children in the urban environment: An issue for the new public health. *Health and Place, 22,* 103–113.

Dearden, C., & Becker, S. (2001). Young carers needs, rights and assessment. In J. Howarth (Ed.), *The child's world: Assessing children in need*. London: Jessica Kingsley.

---

34. In this sense, the "politics of childhood" and the debates surrounding "children's rights" will intensify.

Democratic Dialogue. (1997). *Politics: The next generation* (Report 6). Belfast: Democratic Dialogue.

Department of Health. (1990). *The Children Act 1989 Guidance and Regulations, Volume 2, Family support, day care and educational provision for young children.* London: HMSO.

Department of Health/Welsh Office. (2000). *Lost in care: Report of the tribunal of the inquiry into the abuse of children in care in the former county council areas of Gwynedd and Clwyd since 1974* (The Waterhouse Report). London: Stationery Office.

Department of Health, the Department for Education and Employment and Home Office. (2000). *Framework for the assessment of children in need and their families.* London: Stationery Office.

Federle, K. (1994). Rights flow downhill. *International Journal of Children's Rights, 2,* 343.

Griffin, C. (1993). *Representations of youth: The study of youth and adolescence in Britain and America.* Cambridge: Polity Press.

Griffiths, A., & Kandel, R. (2001). Working towards consensus: Children's hearings in Scotland. In P. Foley, J. Roche, & S. Tucker (Eds.), *Children in society contemporary theory, policy and practice.* Basingstoke: Palgrave.

Hoyles, M. (1989). *The politics of childhood.* London: Journeyman.

Hutchby, I., & Moran-Ellis, J. (Eds.). (1998). *Children and social competence arenas of action.* London: Falmer Press.

Illich, I. (1979). *Disabling professions.* Harmondsworth: Penguin.

Kohm, L., & Lawrence, M. (1998). Sex at six: The victimisation of innocence and other concerns over children's rights. *Journal of Family Law, 36,* 361–406.

Levy, A., & Kahan, B. (1991). *The pindown experience and the protection of children, The report of the Staffordshire Child Care Inquiry 1990.* Staffordshire County Council.

London Borough of Brent. (1985). *A child in trust: The report of the panel of enquiry into the circumstances surrounding the death of Jasmine Beckford.* Wembley, London Borough of Brent.

Masson, J., & Winn Oakley, A. (1999). *Out of hearing.* Chichester: John Wiley.

Mayall, B. (2002). *Towards a sociology for childhood: Thinking from children's lives.* Buckingham: Open University Press.

Mort, F. (1987). *Dangerous sexualities medico-moral politics in England since 1830.* London: RKP.

Neale, B. (2002). Dialogues with children: Children, divorce and citizenship. *Childhood, 9* (4) 455–475.

Newell, P. (1989). *Children are people too, The case against physical punishment.* London: Bedford Square Press.

The Open University. (1997). *K201 working with young people.* The Open University, Milton Keynes.

Percy-Smith, B. (1998). *Marginalisation of children and youth in urban neighbourhoods: Implications for citizenship* (paper presented to the Children and Social Exclusion Conference, Centre for the Social Study of Children, Hull University, March 1998).

Piper, C. (1993). *The responsible parent: A study in divorce mediation.* Hemel Hempstead: Harvester Wheatsheaf.

Qvotrup, J., Bardy, M., Sgritta, G., & Wintersberger, H. (Eds.). (1994). *Childhood matters social theory, practice and politics.* Aldershot, Avebury.

Reece, H. (1996). The Paramoutcy Principle Concensus or Construct. *Current Legal Problems, 19,* 267–304.

Robertson, J., & Robertson, J. (1989). *Separation and the very young.* London: Free Association Books.

Roche, J., & Briggs, A. (1990). Allowing children a voice: A note on confidentiality. *Journal of Social Welfare Law, 3,* 178–192.

Roche, J. (1996). Children's rights: A lawyer's view. In M. John (Ed.). *Children in our charge: The child's right to resources.* London: Jessica Kinglsey.

Roche, J., & Tucker, S. (in press). Extending the social exclusion debate—An exploration of the family lives of young carers and young people with ME. *Childhood: A Global Journal of Child Research.*

Sawyer, C. (1995). *The rise and fall of the Third Party Solicitors assessments of the competence of children to participate in family proceedings.* Oxford: Gulbenkian Foundation.

Sawyer, C. (1999). *Rules, roles and relationships: The structure and function of child representation and welfare family proceedings* (Vol. 1 & 2). Oxford: Centre for Socio-Legal Studies.

Scottish Law Commission. (1992). Report on family law (Scot Law Com. No. 135) (Edinburgh, HMSO).

Sparks, R., Girling, E., & Smith, M. (2001). Children talking about justice and punishment. *International Journal of Children's Rights.*

Tatum, C., & Tucker, S. (1998). The concealed consequences of caring. *Youth and Policy* (61), 12–27.

Timms, J. (2001). The development of advocacy services with and for children and young people. In L. Cull and J. Roche (Eds.), *The Law and Social Work.* Basingstoke: Palgrave.

Wyness, M. (2000). *Contesting childhood.* London: Falmer Press.

INDEX

A

Academy for the Study of the Psychoanalytic
    Arts, vii, 54
Academy of Medicine, 67
ADD, 48
ADHD, 34
Adolescence, 91,100
Adolescent mental health, 109
Agrarian age, 44
Anxiety, 165
Archaic anxiety, 157
Aries, 38
Attention Deficit Disorder, ADD, 34, 46
Authenticity, 136
Autism, 75, 79
Aveyron, 67

B

Ball, Thomas S., 70
Barkley, Russell, 49, 51
Barr, Martin, 69
Beck, Robert, 151
Bettelheim, Bruno, 76
Biddulph, Steve, 19, 28
Biklen, Douglas, 83
Body, 40
Boston School Committee, 44
Bousquet, J.B.D., 67
Bowlby, John, 104
Boy problem, 31
Brace, Charles Loring, 93
Brown v. Board of Education, 104

C

California Bureau of Juvenile Research, 97
Campbell and Cosans v. United Kingdom, 179

Capitalism, 103
Capitalism, 103
Cell theory, 36
Child analysis, 167
Child centered pedagogy, 85
Child guidance, 97
Child study movement, 39
Child, 10, 19, 38, 41
Childhood, 41
Children's rights movement, 177, 183
Clark, Kenneth, 104
Cohen, Erik, 136
Communication, 43
Confidentiality, 191
Construction of youth, 94
Contestations, 120
Corporal punishment, 179
Culture, 111

D

Darwin, 36, 39
Death, 161,
    knowledge, 162,
Delinquency, 105
DeLyser, Dydia, 136
Development of Adolescence, 103
Developmental theory, 35, 51
Diagnostic & Statistical Manual, 48
Disciplinary power, 6
Discipline, 11, 125
Disciplines through ritual, 140
Disciplines, 89
Disciplining minds, 131
Disciplining the self, 114
Discourse, 13, 23, 35
Discourse of contamination, 93
Discourse of the professions, 9
Discourse of youth, 91
Domination, 163

Douglas, Virginia, 48
DSM, 47, 49
Duffy, Michael, 24
Durkheim, Emile, 4, 13

E

Education, 42
Ehrenreich, Barbara, 106
Empiricism, 40
Epistemology, 166
Erikson, Erik, 103
Esquirol, Jean-Etienne-Dominique, 66
European Court of Human Rights (ECHR),
    179, 189
Euterpe, 130

F

Father, 20
Foucault, 6, 11, 22, 45, 139
Free Youth, 123
Freedom, 157
French National Institute, 65
Freud, 40
Freud, Anna, 165
Frith, Uta, 77

G

Gaynor, John F., 70
Gender politics, 31
Gillick, 185
Gineste, Thierry, 86
Gladwin, Tomas, 73
Government, 7
Guerin, 64
Gwynedd and Clwyd, 190

H

Hacking, Ian, 9, 89
Hall, G. Stanley, 96
Healy, William, 99
Helplessness, 165
Heuristics of fear, 116
History, 136
Hoff-Sommers, 20
Human rights, 177,
Hybridity, 134
Hyperactivity, 50

I

Identities, 146
Idiot, 67
Inattention, 50
Incorporation, 148
Industrial capitalism, 92
Infantile autism, 75
Inhibition, 161, 164
Internal world, 156
Ireland, William, 68
Itard, 63

J

Juvenile delinquents, 98

K

Klein, Melanie, 155
Knowledge, 158

L

Lane, Harlan, 75
Language of psychoanalysis, 164
Language of rights, 194
Language, 163
Liberty rights, 183
Liminal space, 134
Living geography, 133
Living history, 133, 136
Lord Scarman, 185

M

MacDonald, Arthur, 98
Males, Mike, 109
Mannoni, Maud, 82
McDermott, Dennis E., 80
Mead, Margaret, 91, 100, 113
Mechanistic thought, 35
Mental retardation, 85
Mme Geurin, 64
Montessori, 80
Morphology, 36

N

National Institute of Mental Health, 106
National Institutes of Health, NIH, 53

National Youth Administration, 103
"Normal" child, 64
Normalization, 163

O

Objective knowledge, 162,
Offshore treatment, 111
"other," 83

P

Paradise Cove, 90
Parks, Alexia, 122
Pedagogy, 43, 137
Pedagogy, scientific, 82
Phillip, Adam, 161
Phobia of being, 161
Pichot, Pierre, 69
Pindown, 189
Pinel, 63, 67
Play, 163
Political apparatus, 8
Positive Peer Culture (PPC), 115
Power, 3
Profession, 3
Professional class, 95
Professional Middle Class (PMC), 106
Professional practice, 177, 193
Professors, 3
Progressive Era, 4
Protecting children, 193
Psychoanalysis, 155
Psychoanalytic, 82,
Psychoanalytic Century, 159
Psychology, 4
Psychometrics, 37

R

Resistance, 160
Richard, case study, 167
Ritalin, 34
Rite of passage, 133, 149
Rose, 161

S

Sadism, 160
Samoa, 100

Sarason, Seymour B., 72
Scientific pedagogy, 81
Scottish Law Commission, 181
Seguin, 67
Seguin, Edouard, 67
Sites of surveillance, 98
Social construction of youth, 95
Social Darwinism, 96
Social reform, 93
Society of Teachers Opposed to Physical
   Punishment (STOPP), 179
Sociology of childhood, 183
Somoan teens, 101
Sovereign state, 3
Spaces, 130, 150, 194
Special Educational Needs and Disability
   Act 2001, 180
Specialty school, 90
State, 9
Steedman, C., 40
Subjectification, 9, 25
Subjectivity, male, 30

T

Technologies, 6
Theory of inhibition, 159
Therapeutic boarding school, 90
Troubled teens, 90
Truffaut, Francis, 63
Truth, 13, 55

V

Van Gennep, Arnold, 133
Victor, 63
Vitalism, 35

W

Warren, S.A., 73
Warwick, Karen, 180
Wild children, 64, 86
Wood, Dennis, 151

Y

Youth, 92, 94
Youth, construction of, 125